PENGUIN BOOKS

LET'S DANCE

Peter Buckman was educated in London, Paris, and Balliol College, Oxford University, where he took an honors degree in modern history. He has contributed to a number of magazines on both sides of the Atlantic and has written plays for stage and television. His other books include *Education without Schools, Playground* (a novel), and *Lafayette* (a biography).

SOCIAL, BALLROOM & FOLK DANCING

LET'S

Picture Research by Enid Moore

DANCE

by
PETER
BUCKMAN

PENGUIN
BOOKS

To the Tews, Little and Great,
with gratitude

Penguin Books Ltd, Harmondsworth,
Middlesex, England
Penguin Books, 625 Madison Avenue,
New York, New York 10022, U.S.A.
Penguin Books Australia Ltd, Ringwood,
Victoria, Australia
Penguin Books Canada Limited, 2801 John Street,
Markham, Ontario, Canada L3R 1B4
Penguin Books (N.Z.) Ltd, 182–190 Wairau Road,
Auckland 10, New Zealand

First published in the United States of America and
Great Britain by Paddington Press Ltd 1978
Published in Penguin Books 1979

Library of Congress Cataloging in Publication Data
Buckman, Peter.
    Let's dance.
    Reprint of the 1978 ed. published by Paddington
Press Ltd., New York.
    Bibliography: p. 280.
    Includes index.
    1. Dancing—History. I. Title.
[GV1601.B83 1979]   793.3'09   79-12970
ISBN 0 14 00.5325 5

Printed in the United States of America by
Halliday Lithograph Corporation,
West Hanover, Massachusetts
Set in Baskerville

ACKNOWLEDGMENTS
I want to thank Enid Moore for all the marvelous work
she did in finding pictures to illustrate the story of dance;
Ian Harris, of the Adderbury Morris Men, for his patient
explanations about the varying and dynamic traditions of
the English morris; Colin Lewis, for information about
Irish dancing; Janet Collins, for help with the physiological
analysis of dance; Kati Boland, for so much valuable and
unusual information about dance in America; Catherine
Carpenter, for her creative and helpful assistance; the
librarians of the London Library and the Vaughan
Williams Memorial Library at the English Folk Dance and
Song Society; Helen Burnett, for her patience and many
kindnesses while typing the manuscript; and my wife and
children, whose pleasure in the living dance is undimmed
by my lengthy excursions into its past. Those whose works
I have plundered are acknowledged in the Bibliography.
The errors, as always, are my own.

CONTENTS

CONTENTS *continued*

INTRODUCTION

"O body swayed to music, O brightening glance,
How can we know the dancer from the dance?"
W.B. Yeats, "Among School Children"
*Collected Poems of W.B. Yeats**

IT WAS THE other dancers' fixed and confident smiles I most admired as I fumbled my way around the floor with my long-suffering mother hissing ONE-two-three in my ear. Dance, I was told, was an essential social attribute, one that would not only improve my posture and self-confidence, but would enable me to meet and mingle with members of the opposite sex. I will admit that the girls were never wildly impressed with my footwork—but I worked on that smile, and though my shuffling progress would have made Arthur Murray sob, my expression gradually changed from a rictus of sheer terror to a gleam approaching pleasure. If I never became much of a waltzer (my admiration for those who can perform the ballroom dances with polish still borders on the awestruck), at least I began to understand the attraction of responding to the beat.

To dance, at its simplest, is to let the body express itself rhythmically. The steps matter, but they are not essential. My generation, after all, has seen history come full circle, at least in dance terms. The couple dances that were fashionable in the 1940s gave way to the jive or jitterbug of the 1950s, which yielded to the stroboscopic solos of the 1960s—which are going the way of the Charleston and appear to have ushered in a new era of couple dances. To touch is once again fashionable (though for some it never went out of style). But whatever the cultural or political climate, the dancing has never stopped.

People dance, as they have always danced, to celebrate good news. They dance on state occasions, to honor a guest, pay court to someone powerful, or simply to demonstrate their social standing. They dance to encourage a sporting team, and to exhibit the best and most beautiful of their community. They dance to express their individuality, and for physical contact with the opposite sex. As a spectacle, dance can be arousing, whether performed by sinuously beautiful Africans or long-legged American cheerleaders in short skirts using tribal chants and rhythms. Per-

formed alone, dance is both a physical and emotional form of release. Dance has been used in all these ways for thousands of years.

I was astonished, when I embarked on the research for this book, at how far back the traditions of dance stretch. Those cheerleaders are employing the same techniques as the earliest cultures to arouse their teams to victory. The diplomatic balls where the dance is led off by the highest-ranking couple reflect a precedent going back at least seven hundred years. The solo dances of the 1960s and 1970s were foreshadowed in the 1920s, though solo dancing was practiced among the most primitive tribes. What has altered most is the pace of change, but as I explain in Chapters 4 and 5, the chief cause of this accelerated change is the gap between the generations—and that is hardly a new phenomenon.

Although a new dance can become the property of the entire world within a few weeks, each culture has an inescapable dance tradition of its own. The folk dances of the Western world, with which this book is concerned, are as different from those of the East—musically, rhythmically, and stylistically—as are the rock dances of Western youth from the ballroom dances whose history

reaches back nearly two centuries. Dance, of course, is as much a reflection of the culture of a community as its art and literature; it is to some extent an expression of—or in opposition to—the social climate of its time. Even if, being a plastic art, its forms are less durable than sculpture or plays, enough traces remain to keep its history very much alive. Much of this history is hearsay, gleaned from books and pictures whose presentation has little of the precision and objectivity beloved of the scientist. But dance history is not a science. Those who actually dance have very different views on the matter from those who observe, and hence the dance historian is more a compiler of opinions than an authority on facts. No one can be absolutely certain why a new dance, whether it be the galliard of the seventeenth century or the twist of the twentieth, comes into being. The English dance expert A.H. Franks has pointed out that before 1910 the main attraction in dancing was the steps, whereas after 1910 it was the beat. One can say that new steps follow new rhythms; that a new dance comes in because new steps are required to fit a new sound. But a history of music—which this book is not—is no more precise about the origins of new sounds than the dance historian can be. These are matters of individual invention, and all one can do is chronicle their appearance and effect.

Dance draws a community together both physically and emotionally. The young have their discotheques and the old their dance halls and nightclubs. When the two worlds meet at weddings and bar mitzvahs, the gap that undoubtedly exists is shown to be perfectly bridgeable. Both use dance to affirm their own special sense of togetherness, their exclusivity; but there exists between them not so much a state of war as a prolonged exercise in competitive vigor. In tribal days the young would demonstrate their prowess through wild dances in which speed and athleticism were signs of virility. The old performed slower dances in which skill and style were signs of maturity. It is the same today. Dance, among so much else, is a badge of belonging. By their dances shall ye know them.

For a generation reared on ballroom dancing, the undying popularity of the waltz and the fox trot is proof that the old qualities endure. These qualities include male gallantry toward the female, physical contact that is close without being oppressive, a progress around the floor that preserves the intimacy of the couple without encroaching on others' space, a style that displays expertise without ostentation, and a convention which gives the lead to the man while offering deference to the woman. Such qualities are by no means those of a generation beleaguered by the very different attitudes of the young. On the contrary, some of them reach back over 150 years, to the advent of the closed-couple dance in the early nineteenth century, while the rest are the direct descendants of the first couple dances that began around the twelfth century. To have a long pedigree is not necessarily a sign of respectability, but that these conventions have lasted for so long is proof of resilience, if nothing else.

Sailors on H.M.S. Arethusa celebrate Prize Day, 1931, with a hornpipe, a dance going back to the fifteenth century.

For the young, dance means something entirely different. As with the older generation, it is a display of shared values and a common style that sets them apart from the rest of their world. It is currently a way of meeting the opposite sex on terms that reflect a looser morality than that to which the older generation pay lip service, and of moving the body in a manner as "primitive" as ballroom dancing may be considered "civilized." Dance is also a way of rejecting the all-pervasive passiveness of entertainment in the television age, of escaping the home and such conformity as a society still dominated by the middle-aged may be able to impose, and exchanging it for conformity to the standards of a peer group whose values may be just as restrictive, but whose colors are emphatically more strident. Dance is not so much an expression of rebellion as a means of sharing this common identity. For that reason alone it will continue popular even when the dances that now seem odd or outrageous to those aged over twenty-five have assumed the quaintness of the turkey trot.

Competitive ballroom dancing developed from the standardization of steps by dance teachers—most of them English—in the early twentieth century. Dancing skill has always been a matter for competition: the courtiers of the fifteenth century were constantly trying to outdo each other at the *basse danse*, and the celebrated French dancing master Cellarius took on his rival Coralli at the polka in 1844. But once the dance teachers had organized themselves into professional bodies, as they did in the United States from 1879 and in England from 1892, what was "correct" (as opposed to the merely acceptable) in their judgment became internationally binding. The dancing of candidates for membership of these august bodies could be examined and marks awarded, as in any other academic subject, and it was not long before the bodies themselves were involved in organizing competitions and giving prizes to amateurs. Competitive ballroom dancing rapidly became an international sport whose popularity has spread as far as Japan, where great efforts are being made to

Dancing in the streets of London to celebrate the signing of the armistice in 1918.

emulate the smooth English style. For the thousands who take part the world over, the sequins and tails, the balletic precision and sweet music, the tension and the glamor, are enough to make the sport as exciting as its roughest brethren.

The need for worldwide uniformity in standards, rules, and methods of judging brought together national dance organizations in the International Council of Ballroom Dancing, which in 1960 held the first official world championships in London. Held in Britain every alternate year, the event has also been staged in West Germany, Australia, and Japan. In 1973 it was held for the

first time in New York, when twenty-eight countries took part, including four from behind the Iron Curtain, for prizes totaling more than $10,000.

There are also national ballroom championships all over the world: the New York Harvest Moon Ball, perhaps the most celebrated amateur event in the United States, started in 1935. Canada held her first nationwide competition in 1955, and the United States national ballroom championships began in 1971 and have been held every year since. As elsewhere, there are sections for professionals and amateurs, and six divisions of dance:

OVERLEAF: *The French enjoying the anniversary of the fall of the Bastille on July 14th—a drawing from the late nineteenth century.*

American-style ballroom, theatrical, and formation dance; English-style modern, Latin, and formation. The official 1977 handbook stresses that "the judges will look for a display of conventional American-style competition dancing, which may feature exhibition type open and/or breakaway choreography in all dances. It must be noted that the English-style modern and Latin do not typify the conventional American style, and should therefore be avoided."

Dancers of American-style ballroom are liable for disqualification if they indulge in theatrical lifts, horizontal body drops, or acrobatic feats. As with other sports, the rules have become more and more tightly drawn, and competitors have to undergo rigorous coaching as well as training for fitness.

Ballroom dancing for private pleasure is at the moment enjoying one of its periodic comebacks. It is treated more nonchalantly than in the past, even by the teachers: the Arthur Murray Dance Studios relentlessly solicit customers, insisting that "everybody has rhythm," though a hundred years ago the Allen Dodworth Dancing Academy in New York City would have refused instruction to anybody who failed to conform to their exacting standards of decorum and good breeding. The "fun" element in ballroom dancing is emphasized over the discipline required to master the steps, but even in today's permissive society it appears that more and more people are signing up for instruction in the waltz and fox trot, the rumba and samba, the tango and the cha-cha. The polka is still to be seen in dance studios, alongside the Charleston and the latest (at the time of writing) hustle. In contrast to the solos of the 1960s, all these dances require contact between the partners.

But to write off the solo dances would be premature. They came in, as will be seen in Chapter 5, firstly because of the new beat of rock music, secondly because of a strong sense of separateness—morally, physically, emotionally—on the part of those who were then young. They—perhaps I should say we—felt that in contrast to the quietism of the immediate past (not to mention the disasters of the more distant past), everything was possible. Everything was going to happen Now, but it was not going to be an exchange of one type of authority for another, it was going to be a glittering kaleidoscope of individual patterns. The dances, of course, were a reflection of this. Perhaps you could say that our return to the couple dance reflects our need for security in our disappointment. But the revived interest in ballroom dancing is a rediscovery of pleasing sounds, steps, and rhythms rather than a willful or nostalgic return to the behavior patterns of the era from which they came. Each new generation picks up some of the forgotten habits of the old and treats them as if they were a revelation. Succeeding generations will have their solo dances, that much is certain. Their pedigree, after all, goes back to the beginning of community life. History will repeat itself, in dance as in most things, and each time it will add something new.

This book is not a "how-to-dance" manual—of those there are

Roseland Dance City, New York, the largest dance hall in the world.

plenty. All I have set out to do is to tell the story of social and folk dance so as to bring out its long and curiously unbroken traditions. I have been selective, and I have borrowed freely from other authorities, whom I gratefully acknowledge in the bibliography. But dancing is one of those pursuits that should not have to bear too great a weight of social analysis or portentous explanation. It is first and foremost a pleasure, and my object is to add some background to that pleasure, not to interfere with it. It is also a living tradition the world over, and the last thing I want to do is to mummify it. Not that I would succeed if I tried. Dance has continued to flourish despite denunciations that began with the first written records and have scarcely abated today. It has survived the incredible social changes of this millenium because it has always been ready to alter its form, to retain or return to the old while twisting around to find something new. Dance means simply people, people who want to express themselves no less than the spirit of their age. It is safe to assume that dance will survive for as long as people do.

BEGINNINGS

Apes dance. So do mountain chickens and stilt birds. That is, they perform a series of rhythmic movements, and repeat them again and again, with a purpose. They may be demonstrating admiration, desire, or territorial ownership. The dance may be a challenge, a display, or an act of worship. But the use, for communication purposes, of rhythmic body movements, measured steps, and gestures that we define as dance (movements, that is, which have nothing to do with the performance of work) appears to be older than speech itself.

Dancing is first and foremost a means of physical self-expression. The urge to coordinate movements of the body in response to some sort of rhythm—the beat of the heart, or the sound of the sea—is an inborn thing, almost beyond analysis. To begin probing such an instinct is to risk sounding mystical and pretentious. Let us rather describe what our bodies do when we dance, before considering the religious and recreational uses of dance adopted by our ancestors.

Rudolf Laban, the pioneer of modern educational dance, analyzed the five basic bodily movements that occur in dancing. The first is gesture, which is any movement not connected with supporting the body's weight. The second is stepping, which is transferring the weight from one support to another. The third is locomotion, which is simply getting the body from one place to another. The fourth is jumping, which is movement without a point of support. The fifth is turning, which is changing the position of the front. But dance, of course, does not consist simply of bodily movements. These movements are expressive of various emotions: as Laban put it, dance is "a language of action in which the various intentions and bodily mental efforts of man are arranged into coherent order." That is, when you make a wide, high, stretching gesture, you will be expressing a different emotion from that which you convey when you hunch your shoulders and concentrate on the ground beneath your feet. When you defy gravity with a jump, you experience a different sensation from that obtained by making imperceptible movements of the body in time to the music. Laban's five basic bodily movements are used in endless combinations to convey an infinite number of shifting emotions: joy, love, fear, adulation. The Whirling Dervishes of Egypt turn in place for half an hour at a time to achieve a sort of ecstasy. The couple who smooch while dancing imperceptibly in a

The whirling dervishes of Egypt.

dark corner of the floor, also for extended periods, are achieving a different sort of ecstasy. Both are examples of emotive dancing.

According to Curt Sachs, whose *World History of the Dance* was the first comprehensive comparative study of the subject, there is a basic cultural difference between those peoples who dance for sheer pleasure (he instances the inhabitants of the Andaman Islands) and those who do it solely to achieve a state of ecstasy (the Vedda of Ceylon). The Andamanese danced after a successful day's hunting to express their joy at their good fortune, and their dance consisted of a progression of stepping, sliding, hopping, and flexing figures, with balanced and fluid rhythmic motions. The dance of the Vedda, on the other hand, consisted of painful contortions and distortions in which the performers—incidentally men only, contrasted with the Andamanese dances for both male and female—worked themselves up to the point when they fell exhausted on the ground. To both these peoples dancing was of great importance, but the types of dance and the emotions expressed through them could not have been more different.

The Vedda performed a *convulsive* dance, which Sachs defines as one whose movements are "out of harmony with the body." This appears to be typical of the shaman or "witchdoctor" culture based on priestly magic, where an hypnotic frenzy, achieved

through the dance, is vital to induce a state of belief. The Vedda shaman, in fact, became possessed by the *Yaku*, or "spirit," as he danced faster and faster; though he did not lose consciousness, he was aware only of being "taken over," and when he stopped dancing he could not clearly remember what he had said or done.

By contrast, the Andamanese performed a *harmonious* dance, where their movements and bodies submitted to the rhythm and beat of the music. They too had their magical beliefs, but dance for them was a means of expressing pleasure at what life had given them. In their animal dances, they show themselves to be close observers of nature, and able to imitate certain beasts through the dance. The Andamanese reveled in the dance, and, through the variety of their movements, proved themselves good at it. The Vedda, on the other hand, had no animal dances and appeared to *submit* to dancing rather than simply to enjoy it. You can see these two contrasting types on any dance floor today: those who enjoy using their bodies and who have a true sense of rhythm, and those who move grudgingly, out of a sense of social duty.

Subordinating one's body movements to a rhythm and beat is one way of achieving the sort of ecstasy that releases inhibitions. You see this in football crowds and on great occasions no less than at a discotheque, where the combination of noise and rhythmic movements acts like a drug. Stamping is one of the commonest methods of release: the apes do it, so do the Americans (square dance), the English (morris), the Germans (*Schuhplattler*), and the

Maoris perform an expressive dance, tamed for a modern audience.

OPPOSITE, ABOVE: *New Guinea women dance to celebrate a trading mission.*

OPPOSITE, BELOW: *The Chimbu of New Guinea perform a dutiful dance before killing a pig.*

25

26

Spanish (bolero); in fact, it figures in countless dances, old and new. Stamping has the basic appeal of marking the beat with noise and vigorous use of the leg muscles, and its long survival in dance is scarcely surprising.

Zulus performing a stamping dance at the time of the Zulu war.

Leaping might seem to be almost as basic as stamping, but Dr. Sachs has shown that leap dances are a feature of a hunting society, while among tribes who devote their energies to tilling the soil, the dance is altogether a less energetic affair. Dr. Sachs goes further in making leap dances a sign of a masculine culture (but he also supposes women incapable of distinguishing themselves as athletes). In fact the Iroquois used leaps in their dances, and they were a gynocracy where all the authority resided in the women. They were also hunters, and their stamping and leaping dances were more a sign of their expansive natures than a reflection of their politics.

Dancing, for those who enjoy it, is firstly a pleasant exercise of the body, bringing into play both mind and muscles, directing physical energy into a rhythmic pattern. But men and women are prone to seek meaning even in their pleasures, and to endow them with a sense of purpose. In this way, dance was used not only in celebration of the successful birth, or hunt, or war, but as an offering to the gods to ensure more births, bigger catches, speedier victories. From earliest time dance was employed as a form of

OPPOSITE: *Voodoo dance in Haiti, where the shaman, in a light shirt, whirls around his client until an ecstatic state has been reached.*

African warriors combine leaping and stamping in a war dance.

American Indians perform an intricate round dance involving a considerable sense of balance.

The buffalo dance of the North American Indians.

prayer. Animal dances were not merely imitations of familiar beasts; they were intended to capture the spirit of the creatures, to absorb their guiles and power, to ensure their increase and propitiate their spirits. So, too, mimetic dances were evolved that retold a tribe's sacred myths in an act of commemoration no less than one of worship.

Ceremonial dance performed around the tribal totems, drawn by John White to illustrate the expedition of Sir Walter Raleigh to Virginia and Florida, 1584–1590.

The earliest dance form is the circle. The first dwellings were circular in shape, as were the first temples, if that is what the stone circles, such as Stonehenge, were. To dance around an object was to celebrate its power and ensure that it flowed both into and out of the celebrants. "God is a circle whose center is everywhere and whose circumference is nowhere," said the philosopher Empedocles in the fifth century B.C., and perhaps the circle represents the perfect mystery of creation. More practically, it was the simplest route to follow if you wanted to move around something and maintain a rhythmic step.

The children of Israel danced around the golden calf; the Iroquois danced around their sacrificial fire (containing the quarters of a wild beast covered and basted with grease), while offering prayers to the sun to accept the sacrifice, give them victory over their enemies, cause their wheat to grow, and grant their hunters and fishermen good catches. In the medicine dance of the shamanistic cultures, the sick person was placed in the center of a circle and danced around until the evil spirit was drawn out and conquered. The Ute Indians believed that by dancing around a

A carmagnole performed in the Champs Élysées in 1790.

sun pole they were keeping off rheumatism. In the funeral dance the world over, the bier was encircled to help the spirit on its way to its ancestors and seek its good offices in cheering the living. This tradition persisted in funeral wakes well into the twentieth century.

Many fertility dances were circular in form, around a tree, maypole, or other symbol of regeneration. In an aboriginal rain dance designed to increase the crop, the rainmaker heaped up a pile of stones, topped it with one that was especially magical, and danced around it until he was exhausted. In some Catholic communities there is still a sacred procession around the fields, led by the priest, to bless the crops. The carmagnole, whose name came, in the late eighteenth century, from a sort of short coat worn by the Italians of Carmagnola, from where workmen brought it into France, was a French circle dance around the guillotine or tree of liberty, to ensure that the revolution would be nourished by the blood being spilled. For centuries men have danced around women, or women around men, in a rite of possession. In medieval Germany the "bridal round" was the most important of wedding celebrations. The bride was surrounded by a circle of women dancers, who were themselves surrounded by a circle of dancing men. The bridegroom had to force his way through both circles to

*Round dance
performed as part of
the wedding
ceremonies in the
Sudan.*

gain his bride, in a symbolic consummation of the marriage.
Bridal couples danced three times around a fireplace in western
Germany, and three times around an oak tree in Westphalia.
Such rituals were not only celebratory; they also symbolized the
acceptance by the community of the couple's new status.

In all cultures' initiation dances, to celebrate menstruation or
circumcision, there was this same round dancing to ensure that the
strength of the older generation would pass to the younger, and
the purity of the novice would rub off on the mature. Dancing
around, or through, a fire was also important for the newly
pubescent no less than the newly wed: it gave strength and pro-
tected from evil, besides being a test of daring and skill. Such a
dance was seen in Ireland in the sixteenth century, and English
girls danced jumping over candles in the seventeenth century—a
custom that used to be followed in Palestine in biblical times
during Hanukkah, the "Feast of Lights."

Such dances are all of a type Dr. Sachs calls "imageless," which
is to say they were designed to create an atmosphere in which the
desired act might take place. They have their descendants in
social dances evolved to promote courtship, or the dance spectacles
led by cheerleaders, majorettes and drill teams at sporting events
in the hope of ensuring victory for their teams (war dances of a
sort). The other main type of dance employs an "image" to
achieve its object. Pantomime or mimetic dances, for example,
make it pretty obvious what the performers want. By reproducing
the wished-for event, they hoped to make certain it would happen.

French peasant women dance around a fire, painted by Jules Breton in 1875.

Examples are leaping dances, such as the English morris, in which a good high jump is performed to encourage the corn to grow tall. Less subtle are the dances representing intercourse. Karl Theodor Preuss observed the Australian Watchandi celebrating their "great semi-religious Caaro festival in preparation for the important duty of producing offspring. . . . On the evening of the festival the women and children withdraw from the company of the men . . . and now the latter may not look upon a woman until the close of the ceremony. . . . Those left behind dig a large hole in the earth. . . . Crying out and singing they dance around the hole and continue doing so throughout the night. . . . The hole is dug and decorated with bushes in such a way as to resemble the sex parts of a woman. In the dance they carry in front of them a spear to represent a phallus. Poking the spear into the ditch they chant, 'Not the pit, not the pit, not the pit, but the vulva!'"

It was important in primitive times for the women of New Caledonia, and in parts of Africa and India, to expose their genitalia while dancing, in order to increase their fertility. Men did not exhibit their own organs, but vastly exaggerated phalli in a hopeful boast of their potency. The Greek Bacchic dancers attached such artificial organs to themselves, while in 1910 it was reported of the Cobéua Indians of Brazil that they "have large phalli made of bast with testicles of red cones from the low hanging trees, which they hold close to their bodies with both hands. Stamping with the right foot and singing, they dance at first in double quick time, one behind another, with the upper parts of their bodies bent forwards. Suddenly they jump wildly along with violent coitus motions and loud groans. . . . They carry the fertility into every corner of the houses, to the edge of the wood, to the nearby fields; they jump among the women, young and old, who disperse shrieking and laughing; they knock the phalli one against the other. . . . "

The Iroquois were not merely content to reproduce something they had not yet had. When a war chief returned from an expedition he would relate every detail of his campaign and immediately, without rehearsal, everyone present would rise to dance and act out what he had reported. Father Joseph François Lafitau, who spent several months among them in the early eighteenth century, observed that "there is one Indian custom which we have in our dances, where the dancer, after his performance, goes and gives the bouquet to the one he has invited to dance next. Thus the dance continues from one to the other, each making a present—it may be tobacco or other gifts—to the one invited." He also watched the *yenonyahkwen*, the round dance of the medicine men. This was used as an exercise for general amusement, and notice was sent to every lodge, each of which deputed some men and women to dress up and appear at the dancing place, where a small platform was set up for the singers who had a drummer and a turtle rattle. The spectators accompanied the music by striking kettles or pieces of bark with sticks. "The dancers turn in a kind of round dance but without holding hands as is done in Europe. Each of them, as he likes, cuts different figures with his hands and feet and, although all the movements are entirely different according to the whim and caprice of imagination, still no-one loses the cadence. The ones who know best how to vary their attitude and make more motions are considered the best dancers. The dance is made up of several repeats, each one lasting until the breath is lost and, after a moment of rest, another is begun. There is nothing livelier than all these move-

Australian aboriginal fertility dance.

Dance around the may tree, with leaps to encourage the corn to grow, from the fifteenth century.

ments. In a moment the dancers are all in a sweat. To see them, one would say that they are a troupe of mad and frenzied people."* Father Lafitau would obviously have felt at home in a discotheque.

He also reported that, in the Iroquois "heaven," dancing was the "principal pleasure," and if further proof of its prime importance were needed, he noted that among the South American tribes feasting and dancing takes place on "the birth of a child; initiation ceremonies; a husband's penance after his wife's delivery of a child; the haircutting and naming of a child; the entrance of boys and girls into adolescence; the admission of a young man to the rank of warrior, and of a warrior to the rank of captain; the installation of a chief general; the ordination of a diviner; the launching of a new boat at sea; the sowing and harvesting of fruit; the determination of a time for fishing; the deliberation of an expedition of war; the solemn execution of a captive; marriages; the cure of illness; a consultation with their diviners; the evocation of spirits; the mourning for the dead. . . . " Dancing thus ranked with alcohol and tobacco as the Iroquois' principal pleasures.

* *Customs of the American Indians compared with the customs of primitive tribes*, translated by W.N. Fenton and E.L. Moore, for the Champlain Society, Toronto, 1974.

*English fertility
dance featuring
a man-woman
figure chased
by the fool.*

The Iroquois had a pleasing way of settling grudges through the
dance. The dancer would take his adversary by the hand and lead
him out of line into the middle of the assembly. "The dancer
continues chanting, but utters from time to time some satirical
comment which his adversary listens to in silence, but which is
greeted with great bursts of laughter from the audience. But no-
one gets angry and everyone has a turn." The Indians covered the
head of their rival in this dance with ashes, which Father Lafitau
compares with the ancient Cretans' custom of throwing food,
flour, and even excrement in similar satirical dances. But dancing
as a form of competitive rivalry survives in many European folk
dances, where the performer is judged by his athletic skill. This
competitive tradition is very much alive today, in the contests of
formation and ballroom dancing that are popular all over the
Western world.

It is important to note that in the earliest cultures the dancers
scarcely touched one another. This did not in the least inhibit their
sexual drive, any more than the "solo" dances such as the twist,
which were popular in the 1960s, marked a decrease in fertility.
But the pantomime dance led to the courtship dance, out of which
developed the couple dances that have never since died out. They
will be the subject of most of the rest of this book; let us first consider some of the other dances that have contributed to their very
mixed ancestry.

The primitive courtship dance began with a pantomime of
wooing rather than of intercourse. In northern Melanesia, near
New Guinea, the men, all masked, danced toward, then away
from, a masked woman whose favors they were seeking. Each man

Courtship dance performed by Guajira Indians.

rivaled the others in the dance, while the woman showed her feelings by pushing one man away, ignoring another, and so on. When she finally made her choice, the others withdrew. There are parallels in the courtship dances of Spain and Mexico, Eastern Europe and Germany, where the woman feigns indifference to the men, who then make every attempt to kindle her passion.

The mask used by the Melanesians in their wooing was an important part of dances in which the performer wished to achieve a magical effect. You cannot convince people you represent a god if they recognize you as merely one of themselves. A disguise is necessary, and the more elaborate the better. A disguise also releases the dancer from inhibitions: he or she becomes someone else and is free to behave accordingly. It links with the miming or representation of something the performer wishes for—an example being the man dressed up as woman who appears in so many fertility dances. The mask is part of that tradition—still, of course, extant—of decorating the face and body for the dance. Formal vestiges of the use of disguise to release inhibition can be seen in the South American carnival dances, and in the blacking of the face in certain morris dances. Informal traces are to be found in the careful choice of clothes for dancing made by our own contemporaries.

Weapon dances are now only an exercise in skillful handling and nimble footwork, yet they too once performed the dual

function of enacting victory in the hope that such would be the outcome, and celebrating it if it actually came off. They were also useful in military training, quite apart from getting warriors in an ecstatically victorious state of mind. The Spartans used weapon dances to inculcate their children with military skills and discipline, a practice of which Plato strongly approved. Today the folk-dancing troupes of, for example, Russia and China, delight audiences with their extraordinary athleticism. It is surely no coincidence that such weapon dances are kept alive among powers who take such pride in their military preparedness.

In the Fiji Islands, at least until World War II, up to six hundred dancers would undergo months of training in order to present a weapon dance that included a mock battle with an invisible enemy. More often one finds such battles taking place between dancers representing giants and dwarfs, Moors and Christians, "us" and "them." As in the sacred dances of the early cultures, these are the old legends kept alive in the dance. They also required a special skill in performance that set the dancers apart. Only warriors performed the weapon dances, in contrast to the celebrations in which the entire community joined. The weapon dance was a forerunner of all those specialist dances which flowered most spectacularly in medieval Germany, when each craft guild would have its own unique dance, whose mysteries were only vouchsafed to its members. Certainly the dance was

Masked dancers at a carnival in Trinidad.

37

performed in public, but the tricks and skills required special training that was the prerogative of the guild concerned. This is the dance as a celebration of apartness, the complete opposite of that celebration of oneness that united the early cultures.

The history of civilization is the history of specialization. From everyone struggling to be a warrior, there gradually evolved a warrior class, which turned into the professional army. Likewise, from everyone joining in the dance, there gradually grew up troupes of professional dancers, possessed of special skills which gained them the respect of their peers. Of course, in the shaman cultures there were dances reserved exclusively for the priest, witch doctor, or medicine man and his acolytes. But as religion, too, became an art for specialists—as magic was replaced by dogma, whose interpretation lay exclusively in the hands of professional priests—so sacred dance became a spectator sport, performed by the few for the edification, and perhaps even the entertainment, of the many. By that stage, dance was no longer the single most important form of celebration and release that it had been among the early cultures. Yet it still retained, and retains, the power to transport the dancer beyond herself or himself, into a state approaching ecstasy. This was the aim of the most primitive dancers of all.

Once the steps of a dance had proved themselves effective in bringing about whatever was desired, they became fixed. There were tribesmen who killed on the spot any dancer who put a foot wrong in a sacred dance, and there are dancing teachers who occasionally entertain similar ambitions. But mankind has always hankered after novelty, and this showed itself in the evolution of new dance patterns and figures to vary the venerable circle dances that had been performed from the very beginning.

Eskimo children receiving instruction in the dance.

Tanz von Tonga-Jnsulanerinnen vor der Königin Tiné

Nach Labillardière „Atlas pour servir à la relation du voyage à la recherche de La Pérouse" Paris, Jahr VIII. der Republik

The earliest of the "new" forms was the line. There is perhaps a connection between the line dance and the development of the rectangular house, which was an improvement on the round house, because its shape made it easier to build frames for the door and, later, windows. Dancing was primarily an outdoor activity, but at certain feasts and celebrations it took place inside, often in specially built dance houses. Where these were rectangular in shape, the dance gradually conformed to the demands of the space—just as the invention of the chimney opened the way for couple dances to replace the endless circles around the fire, and the longways dances of the eighteenth century reflected the architecture of the period. Of course men and women did not need a builder to tell them how to dance, but at a time when they were more in harmony with their surroundings than we are today, it was natural that the shapes of their houses should reflect the form of their dances, and vice versa.

The two great themes of mimetic dances, love and war, demanded the line rather than the circle, which made it difficult to face someone and pretend to fight or woo them. The line was also practical for an hierarchical society, first to enable the dancers to face the top personage, later in allowing the top couple to lead the

Dance of the women of Tonga for their queen, Tiné, in 1800.

Funeral procession of a Chinese nobleman.

line into the dance. The status-conscious Chinese, in the days of feudalism, allotted an exact number of lines of dancers where homage was to be performed: eight rows for the emperor, six for the top princes, and four for mandarins. As an advanced civilization, they codified the dance and reduced it (or raised it) from a spontaneous activity to an art based on precisely regulated movements and gestures.

The line dance—usually with the performers singing, later to a musical accompaniment—is of fundamental importance in the development of social dance. The couple dance owes its origin to the line, in its form of mimetic wooing dance. The evolution of dance figures—that is, performers moving about the floor in patterns—sprang directly from the line, as shown in the dances of the Greeks and the medieval farandole, from which so many basic dance figures evolved. The line also gave birth to serpentine dances, which followed labyrinthine patterns thought to represent anything from a fertility dance (the snake being a phallic symbol) to the journey undertaken by the dead. Certainly they were

capable of giving ecstatic pleasure to the participants through their sinuous movements and continuous hold. The conga is the best-known living example.

A chain dance imagined by Rubens in his Danza di Contadini.

Also claiming descent from the line are all those dances in which the performers change position while executing a variety of set figures. The most enduring of these are the country dances, where men and women in two files exchange partners through formations that often appear complex. The contemporary custodian of this form is the square dance, though the quadrilles and cotillions that were so popular in the nineteenth century are also examples. Dr. Sachs proves that this form was not limited to Europe. The Naga of Burma had a dance which featured two men and two women in the center of a circle, with the women changing places constantly; and in Sumatra there was a dance in which four girls formed a square, as in the quadrille.

The arch and bridge dances that remain in children's dance games, such as "London Bridge Is Falling Down," were line dances too, and their pantomime "executions" doubtless sprang from the

A dance to celebrate the cutting of the hay, 1855.

same roots as the death-and-resurrection themes common to much of folk dance. Dancers change position by passing through an arch made by the first couple; sometimes the arch or bridge was extended by the bottom couple beginning again at the top. As a figure in court dance, the arch virtually disappeared in the fifteenth century, because the high and pointed headdresses then fashionable made it impracticable. But the folk dances of Europe, in which the most ancient traditions are faithfully preserved, still maintain it as a feature.

The chain figure that can be seen in square dances as well as in most folk dances, for example in the Swiss Allewander, is another line dance, though probably not as early as the other examples quoted. In a chain, the man turns to the left, takes the right hand of the nearest woman, moves to the left of the woman next in line, giving her his left hand, then passes her in order to offer his right hand to a third woman. In a complex way this is possibly an attempt to transmit energy and power through a line of dancers, something the circle dance achieved without the pleasure of changing positions. It is closely linked to the weaving dances, where the participants weave complex patterns around each other, with or without connecting ropes, ribbons, or handkerchiefs. Everything to do with primitive culture can be linked to reproduction, regeneration, or resurrection, and the weaving motif is no exception. The "braiding" may represent the union of man and woman, or the combining of the forces of nature to produce the thread of life itself. It appears among agricultural peoples and, of course, is connected with the weaving of wool practiced by the earliest pastoral civilizations. Doubtless that is why it is rarely found among those who did not rely on woven materials to clothe themselves.

The couple dance as we know it, with a pair of dancers actually touching each other, did not arrive until around the fifteenth century, and even then it was a decorous affair. Among the early cultures even the crudest sexual pantomime rarely involved a touch more intimate than a grasp of the hands. Most dances were sexually exclusive—for men or for women only. Some tribes insisted on the opposite sex absenting themselves from the dance area for certain dances, though these were always of a sacred nature. But even at celebrations, or in mimetic wooing dances, men and women danced in groups *at* each other, not *with* each other. This sort of exclusivity enjoyed a very long life: "mixt dancing" was frowned upon by many Puritans in the seventeenth century, by orthodox Jews, and also by strict Muslims. Thus, not for the first time, the later religions adopted pagan beliefs and endowed them with the taboos of their own holy writ.

Leaping from prehistory to the written records of our European civilization, we find Homer describing a round choral dance in Book 18 of his *Iliad*. Socrates approved of dancing for the grace it imparted, as well as its use in keeping the weight down; Aeschylus and Aristophanes are reported to have danced in performances of their own plays. The Greeks divided their dances into the same broad types as the primitives: sacred, military, and celebratory. The difference was that dancing had become an art taught by professionals, the property of experts, part of the education process, rather than a spontaneous event. Certainly the Greeks

OVERLEAF: *A Greek chain dance.*

Greek women dancers.

brought to it the same aesthetic principles that distinguished the rest of their art: an insistence on proportion and balance, a flowing line, and a lack of unnecessary ornamentation. As a spectacle, the dance was artistically magnificent as well as popular. It was, of course, the most readily available form of bodily self-expression, and still capable of arousing ecstasy, as the Bacchic dances testified. Yet there was about it a certain formality that remained even in the twentieth-century revival pioneered by Isadora Duncan. It was a formality inescapable in an organized society, where order was expressed in everything from politics to art. The Greeks permitted little sign of that creative anarchy that distinguished the earlier cultures, save for the "divine madness" of the frenzied dances. In fact, their dances added little to the stock provided by their ancestors.

The formality of the Greeks showed in the strict divisions of the sacred dance. The *emmeleia* were round dances in honor of the gods, performed in a solemn manner, chiefly by women. They consisted of choral processions to the shrine and circle dances around the altar. They are preserved on the friezes of the Parthenon, where what are presumed to be virgins dance hand in hand. The *hyporchemata* were mimetic choral dances dedicated to Apollo

Apollo dancing with the Muses, painted by Romano.

The classical dance, as seen by Matisse.

A neo-classical interpretation of the pyrrhic dance, 1794.

in his capacity as patron of poetry and music. They reproduced the Greek myths of creation in gesture and rhythm. Also dedicated to Apollo, as god of medicine, were the *paians*, which were originally dances to ward off sickness; and in his capacity as a warlike god the *gymnopaidiai*, in which naked boys performed a wrestling dance, were addressed to him. The rules of these dances were said to have been dictated by Apollo himself to his priestesses, just as the old shamans claimed to have been divinely inspired.

The classical cult of the body, of physical beauty as well as fitness, was a sign of a civilization relying on professionals to do the necessary hunting and fighting. To worship and cultivate beauty is an immemorial thing, but when it is formalized, as it was by the Spartans and Greeks, that suggests that they could not rely, as the earlier tribes did, on the voluntary defense of their values. The Pyrrhic dances are an example of this. Said to have been invented by Pyrrhus, son of Achilles, they were used for military training by the Spartans, though they later became mere pantomime dances, performed by skilled professionals for the sake of entertainment.

The Bacchic dances were dedicated to the god of wine, first known as Dionysus, whom the Italians identified with the vegetation god Liber and preferred to call Bacchus. In them we see a combination of the sacred frenzy of the ecstatic dance in honor of the gods—as practiced by the maenads, "raving women" who danced in the spring to awaken the earth—and the dances around a tree totem, which was decorated with ivy, vine leaves and honeycombs. The tree is a universal symbol of regeneration, celebrated in the spring and mourned in the autumn. The Greeks divided their Dionysia into four, all of them great public holidays. The Country Dionysia were celebrated in December and featured processions and dramatic performances which, of course, included dancing. The *Lenaea* were city festivals held in January, and the *Anthesteria* lasted three days and included a feast to the dead, whose shades were thought to walk the earth during the celebrations. The Great Dionysia was a festival of music and drama, during which the statue of the god was taken from the temple and paraded. Men disguised as satyrs and equipped with beards, tails and phalli, became ecstatic with wine and danced around the maenads, who themselves had received instruction in the dance in preparation for the festival. The orgies associated with the Dionysian rites, and the Roman Bacchanalia, grew out of this sacred frenzy and became occasions to commit excesses much needed in a highly organized society. Periodically suppressed, their spirit lives on in the carnivals of many Catholic countries, from Latin America to Germany.

Dr. Sachs ascribed to the influence of the Orient the habit of using dance purely as an after-dinner entertainment. When the food had been cleared away and everyone's cup was filled, jugglers, singers, mimes, and, above all, women dancers, appeared to delight and tantalize the guests. From the ancient Greeks to Florenz Ziegfeld, our civilization has worshiped the female

The Dionysian dance that preceded the orgy.

A round dance performed by three Greek nymphs.

dancing figure. Over more than two thousand years, such dancing has lost its religious origins—but then as now, the primary objective was simply to arouse the spectators.

The dances of the Greeks became mere entertainment for the Romans and were performed by paid professionals and slaves. Nevertheless, dancing was a desirable social accomplishment: most patrician families had a dance teacher on their payroll, and Roman youth was taught dancing for deportment as well as exercise. The couple dance had not yet arrived, so there was no question of learning how to move across the floor with a partner. But dancing gracefully in public was still a useful means of attracting the attention of the opposite sex, whether in sacred performances or in the rounds and line dances that were practiced both by Greeks and Romans, with men and women keeping to their exclusive sex groups. It is likely that there were also dance games for small prizes, such as were popular in nineteenth-century

England and the United States, especially where religious fanatacism forbade dancing in any other form.

That there was a loyal public for professional dancing is demonstrated by the fact that under the Emperor Augustus the number of foreign women dancers in Rome was estimated at three thousand. These were kept on even when cuts in public expenditure put scores of teachers and philosophers out of work. The authorities dared not risk antagonizing the public by banishing their pleasures—and they were dealing with a fanaticism akin to that of football supporters. There were two rival dancers, Bathyllus and Pylades, whose followers used to fight in the streets around the Coliseum. Bathyllus excelled in the mime, Pylades in the fluidity of his dancing: their supporters endlessly discussed their merits to the exclusion of politics and matters of state. This situation was echoed in the nineteenth century, when the polka craze swept France, and there was talk of nothing but whether Cellarius was the reigning maestro, or his rival Coralli.

Once you have professionals, you have critics, often unable to perform that which they are criticizing. St. Augustine, who lived from A.D. 354 to 430, was an exception here. His condemnations of profane dancing, particularly as practiced in church, may be said to spring from personal experience gained in his youth. But Cicero's remark that "no sober man dances" is that of someone who prefers to find release in mental rather than bodily agility, and from Roman times to our own day we find an unceasing stream of condemnation of the dance, based on its profanity, lasciviousness, or sheer novelty. The Dionysia were abolished by order of the Senate in 168 B.C., an early beginning to a long campaign against "excesses" invariably founded on the gap between the generations.

Possibly because the professionals concentrated on the lascivious aspects of their dancing in order to preserve and increase their audiences, it became bad form for Roman gentlefolk to dance too well. Dance was associated with the public spectacles that became increasingly horrific as the empire waned. It was included in the general condemnation of such barbarism by the fathers of the Christian church. In A.D. 300 the church decided to withhold baptism from anyone connected with circus or mime, a stigma that lasted, in England at least, until Victorian times, during which actors were classed with vagabonds and could not be presented at court. This exclusion of course applied to dancers. That dance survived, however little we know of it in detail, we may assume from the denunciations frequently hurled at it by the authorities, especially the ecclesiastical ones. The unbroken traditions of the pagan rituals were also maintained in folk custom. In the sixth century, Bishop Caesarius of Arles was disgusted by the fact that at the New Year women, even baptized ones, preserved the vestiges of an animal dance by covering themselves with animal heads and skins.

The Church Fathers often preached sermons on the text of Matthew xi.16, where Jesus asks, "but whereunto shall I liken this

OVERLEAF:
Brueghel's view of the dancing mania of the fourteenth century.

aefvoongen hebben dan fin fu genefen vor een heel Jaer van finf Jans fieckte   brűegel m.cccc.lxiiij.

generation? It is like unto children sitting in the markets, and calling unto their fellows, And saying, We have piped unto you, and ye have not danced; we have mourned unto you, and ye have not lamented." Augustine used this to justify dance only if it was as harmonious in spirit as the dancers were harmonious in the movements of their limbs. The fourth-century St. John Chrysostom, the inventor of processional hymn singing (which he used to counter the influence of the Arians, who stood singing their hymns outside public buildings in Constantinople), was eloquent in his denunciations of the licentiousness of the imperial court, especially its "devilish dances," whose performers he compared unfavorably with camels. But even he was all in favor of "spiritual dances" that were pleasing, modest, and in the form of a circle, such as the angels were supposed to perform. Any dance the church found particularly objectionable was said to be inspired by the devil—a conviction that lasted well beyond the Age of Reason, an example being Satan's supposed partiality to, and personal appearance in, the Scotch reel. But then skill beyond the ordinary has always been credited to the supernatural: pious women in an audience used to cross themselves before Paganini started to play.

There was a curious combination of the devilish and the ecstatic in the "dancing mania" that broke out all over Europe after the Black Death in the middle of the fourteenth century. At funerals and church services, according to contemporary accounts, men and women suddenly began to dance and sing as if acting from some inner compulsion. They could not or would not obey the priest's order to stop, and continued to dance until they were exhausted. There grew from such happenings the legends of people being cursed with a dancing fever from which only death or exorcism could release them. Their movements were convulsive but rhythmic, as in all ecstatic dancing, and the cause of the mania has never been satisfactorily established. Possibly their bread was made with "spurred rye," or ergot, a kind of fungus that is a constituent of LSD. Ergot has been known to cause paroxysms, hallucinations, and visions, all of which were evident in the victims of "dance madness," and the connection with holy places such as churchyards may simply be explained by the need to dispel the terror of an unknown sickness with the totems of belief, such as tombstones carved with a cross. The water of the shrine of Saint Vitus was also supposed to be efficacious against the disease, hence the name "Saint Vitus's dance."

Dr. Sachs is convinced that such dances were a "piece of ecstatic inner life, which since the Stone Age has been disguised and concealed through innumerable racial influxes but never extinguished, and which must break through all restraints at the favorable moment." I cannot agree that they were a sort of *danse macabre*, in which the performers communed with the dead: the dancing mania appeared to contemporaries to be a battle with primeval forces, in which Christianity was an essential weapon for victory. The victims formed huge processions and danced along the routes of pilgrimage to various shrines in search of relief. Certainly they seemed to find release in the twitching of their limbs to the accompaniment of music. That they gathered in crowds means that they were also prey to crowd fever, where observers find themselves becoming participants. A crowd needs some physical way of releasing its tensions. Sometimes this takes the form of violence—to themselves, to each other, or to some external object; sometimes relief is found in music and ecstatic movement, as can be seen today in revivalist churches. Both violence and musical movement were features of the dance mania, outbreaks of which have been reported as recently as the 1920s. In medieval Italy the phenomenon was known as tarantism and connected with the bite of the tarantula spider. To get rid of its poison the tarantella came into being, a convulsive dance which has since been tamed into an impressive folk dance.

The ecstatic dancing madness, whose performers were transported out of themselves to who-knows-what limbo between death and life, led to the dance of death, known to the most primitive peoples, and popular in Europe in the Middle Ages. It featured a performer impersonating a skeleton; and the rattle of dancing bones as a reminder of mortality figures in poetry and legend from the fifteenth-century poet Sebastian Brandt (in his satire *Ship of Fools*) to Goethe and beyond. For a people who had suffered war, invasion and plague, death was no stranger. But the dance was perhaps a way of encompassing its terrors, in the same manner as the earliest cultures mimed their myths in order to contain them.

Dance as release, dance as celebration, dance to portray life, and dance to solemnize death: these themes come down to us from the very beginnings of our society, and are still present, however diluted, in the social dances of our own time.

French vineyard laborers from Médoc dance to celebrate the gathering of the vintage, 1871.

COURT AND COUNTRY

European Dance from 1200 to 1700

The Historical Background

THE EARLIEST EXISTING manuscript containing written dance steps is *Le Livre des Basse-Danses*, a Burgundian work, probably of the fourteenth century. There are, of course, a large number of references to dance in the time between the end of the Roman Empire and that period we know as the Middle Ages, when centuries of invasions and wars culminated in the consolidation of feudal kingdoms. Christianity imposed a certain uniformity on Europe, much as the Roman Empire had done, and the church played a vital part in the development of music by encouraging composers to provide an accompaniment to the liturgy. But it did not root out entirely the ancient pagan ways. Even in Anglo-Saxon England during Easter week, a Christian priest presided over a dance performed by little girls in which a phallic symbol was paraded, a fertility rite similar to those that survive in many contemporary folk dances.

The old traditions were also kept alive in medieval Europe by the traveling entertainers, poets, musicians, jugglers and dancers, known collectively as *Spielmänner* in Germany, as jongleurs in France, and as gleemen in England. These professional itinerants provided an important source of news and gossip, entertaining their audience by athletic dancing, leaping, jumping, and hopping, as well as inventing songs for special occasions and celebrating the epic deeds of their forefathers. They also performed tricks and jokes of the most basic kind, and were often accompanied by animals, such as bears, monkeys, horses and dogs, which they had taught to imitate them in tumbling and dancing. Social dance itself consisted largely of moving in a circle or line while singing a song: the carol, a direct descendant of the earliest dances known to us, and the forerunner of all court dances.

The Roman Empire had been divided into an eastern and a western half since the death of Theodosius in A.D. 395; and the Christian church split into a western and an eastern half in A.D. 484. But by the tenth century, the most important division in Europe was that between the two main language groups: those who spoke Latin in its various forms—the Romance languages—and those, descendants and subjects of the barbarian invaders, who spoke the Germanic dialects. This division showed in the cultural no less than the political field. The new schools of learning and the embryo universities were created by the French-speaking world—a world to which England belonged from the time of the Norman Conquest in 1066. And the first Crusade in 1096, while bringing about a fruitful cultural encounter between East and West in a modern sense, emphasized the differences between the French-speaking and the German-speaking halves of European Christendom. The Crusade's appeal was extraordinarily wide—people landed in France from no one knew where, speaking no known language, but signifying their intentions simply by making with their fingers the sign of the cross. But the Germans were notable absentees, locked as they were in a war between the Holy Roman Emperor and Pope Urban II, who had blessed the Crusade in the first place. For long afterward, the French-speaking world regarded the Germans with something more than suspicion, and this pattern of distinct and separate development showed itself even in dance.

Differences also grew up *within* the two main language groups of the west. Specifically there is the distinction between the *langue d'oc* (from the Latin *hoc*, a barbarized way of saying "yes") and the *langue d'oïl* (from which we get the modern French *oui* for "yes"). The *langue d'oc* was spoken by the French who lived between the Italian frontier and a line drawn from the south of the Gironde to the mountains of Jura. Its ecclesiastical writers used it with an archaic roll and heaviness that contrasted with the spirited ease of northern churchmen, but artistic laymen, particularly those patronized by the secular rulers of old Provence, exploited the *langue d'oc* to achieve a literary flowering that was second to none in style and influence. This cultural renaissance in the *langue d'oc* region spilled over into the field of dance, where elegant new forms were invented in place of the primitive dances that were prehistoric in origin.

A cultural style must to some extent be related to the political organization within which it flourishes. Thus in the northern kingdoms that became Norway, Sweden and Denmark, whose inhabitants were late converts to Christianity and who lived by piracy and a far-ranging sea trade, the literature consisted of epics telling of the mighty feats of wandering heroes, epics which kept alive their pagan past and ideals. Certainly their court dances were very different from those of the rest of Europe: in one wooing dance, the courtier took his partner not just by the hand or a handkerchief, but enwrapped her in his fur and withdrew with her into a corner. Because of what happened next, noble ladies usually kept away from such dances, leaving their men to partner the serving girls.

In contrast to the roving traditions of the far north, the Christian rulers to the south were attempting to base the economies of their territories on agriculture, through the exploitation of the land they controlled. For them the old sagas were no longer appropriate. The Crusades, of course, provided a rich store of source

A series of troubadours, showing how their occupations varied from knight to simple minstrel.

material for writers, but there was a significant difference in purpose, as well as in style, between the new romantic epics and the older sagas. For one thing, the Christian hero wandered in search of spiritual salvation, overcoming evil for the enrichment of his soul rather than his purse. For another, there was, by the twelfth century, a "community of knightly ideals which identified the aristocracy from one end of Latin Europe to the other." (R.W. Southern, *The Making of the Middle Ages*). The growth of Mediterranean trade did much to forge this community—and provided the costly spices that disguised the odors of people hostile to bathing, a special comfort to dancers. But the aristocracy was, above all, united in its Christian faith, its hostility to unbelievers, its adherence to a code of honor (that was only applied to themselves, of course), and, perhaps most important, to a style of living that governed not only the relationship between ruler and ruled, but also between the men and women of the ruling class. The writer of the eleventh-century *Song of Roland*, which was used to cheer up William of Normandy's troops before the Battle of Hastings, extolled the virtues of men who thought more of their lands than their women. But by the late twelfth century an entirely different attitude appears. This can be seen in the works of Chrétien de Troyes, for whom love was an inward thing, a lonely thing united to its unique object. Chrétien's knights sought solitude for the exercise of their virtues. Though part of King Arthur's court, where what mattered most was loyalty to lord and companions, these romantic knights possessed an even higher loyalty, to the object of their love. Such dedication was, of course, only expected in gentlemen: this is the era of courtly love, which was to introduce, among so much else, the couple dance in place of the group dances of earlier times.

By the twelfth century, France could claim to be the most cultured country in Christendom—cultured in the sense that she gave a lead which others followed. But her position as a united kingdom was not very secure. Her king was constantly threatened by the great feudal lords who, though officially swearing loyalty and homage, were constantly on the lookout for ways to expand their territory. The most troublesome of these were the dukes of Normandy, who were also the kings of England. In 1152 Louis VII of France added to his problems by divorcing his wife, Eleanor of Aquitaine, who promptly—in fact, within six weeks—married Henry II of England. By this marriage Henry extended his already considerable empire: running from the Cheviots to the Pyrenees, it included Anjou, Normandy, Maine, Gascony, Poitou, Touraine, and of course England and Aquitaine. The centuries of war between France and England had immense political repercussions, but they also involved a cross-fertilization of cultures that proved immensely fruitful in literature, music, and dance.

One of the most independently minded, and also one of the richest, of the French fiefdoms was Provence, whose boundaries, though constantly changing, were considerably more extensive in

the twelfth century than they are now. United with Catalonia by Raymund-Bérenger in the early part of the century, this confluence of two cultures sharing the same language—the *langue d'oc* —may have been primarily responsible for the cultural movement that was born there. (That and the prosperity of the region, for artists are attracted to wealth like other workmen.)

The poets, composers, and singers of Provence were known as troubadours, and they were the successors of those traveling musical entertainers, the jongleurs. (They were also influenced by the itinerant Latin scholars called goliards—after an imaginary bishop Golias—who earned money by extemporizing satirical rhymes and songs, and spent it on revelry and buffoonery.) But the troubadours proclaimed, in ballads with the most intricate rhyme schemes, the virtues of courtly love, which emphasized purity and self-sacrifice in the search for the perfect woman—or in the case of the woman troubadours, such as Beatrice de Die, the perfect man. The importance of these songs is that they were originally meant to accompany the dance: the French word *ballade* and the Italian *ballata* share the derivation of the English "ball." As popular musicians, the troubadours affected existing dance forms and created a demand for new ones.

The troubadour's influence spread north and east, giving rise to the trouvères in that part of France which spoke the *langue d'oïl*, and the Minnesingers in the Rhineland and Bavaria. The trouvères composed songs that were somewhat more muscular

Three dancing girls perform a carol, accompanied by a singer with tambourine.

Minnesingers, the German equivalent of troubadours, from a manuscript of the fourteenth century.

than the Provençal love poems, in the tradition of the martial chansons de geste which told of great deeds rather than great loves. Nevertheless, the lyrical element was strong, and the troubadour tradition dominated secular music until the fourteenth century. In Provence itself, however, the *langue d'oc* was strictly banned by the ecclesiastical authorities following their Crusade in 1209 against the Albigensian heretics who were numerous in the region. Thousands of people, among them the entire population of the town of Béziers, which was taken by the celebrated Simon de Montfort, were slaughtered in the name of Christian orthodoxy. Those who were able fled, and these included many troubadours, who found refuge in England where a Provençal song could, with few modifications, be readily understood.

The German troubadours, or Minnesingers (love singers), also provided songs for dancing, but they were less successful in introducing the couple dance than the troubadours in the rest of Europe were. By the thirteenth century, Germany had split into some 270 virtually independent states, but her people continued to cling to a separate national tradition that in other countries had scarcely had time to form, because of bewildering changes in rulers and territorial boundaries. Not that Germany was internally calm in comparison to the ructions shaking the rest of Europe. There were perennial struggles over who should be elected German emperor, struggles which were not stilled till the fifteenth century when the Hapsburgs established themselves as hereditary successors to the title. There were the upheavals caused by Martin

Luther's attack on papal doctrine, which in 1529 led to the gathering of princes and German city leaders who protested (hence the name Protestants) against the intolerance of the emperor, the champion of the Catholic cause. Germany was far from being isolated from her neighbors, for she was preeminent as a trading nation until the sixteenth century. Yet her cultural traditions remained distinct. Doubtless the dances that were fashionable in the rest of Europe were tried out in the courts of the more adventurous German princelings, but they cannot have held the same sway as they did, say, in France or England. We know of no German dance manuals or teachers by whose dictates the rest of the dancing world was ruled.

Among the Christian nations, nowhere but in Germany did all classes share such a delight in folk dance. Using elaborations of those ancient forms, the carol and the farandole (a line dance), the Germans danced a *Reigen* or chain dance to celebrate springtime and harvest, New Year and Pentecost, marriages and deaths, tournaments and feasts. At the time of the Black Death, in the middle of the fourteenth century, medieval Germans who had not fallen victim to the dance frenzy known as Saint Vitus's dance (since water from the shrine of Saint Vitus was supposed to cure the disease, although Germans preferred the shrine of Saint John), indulged in miming death itself, in dances of death that were terrifying in their realism. And as was common elsewhere, the pagan rituals (such as the May dances and the sword dance, which the ancient German tribesmen used to perform adorned with bells) continued long after the nation was Christianized. Modern survivors include wooing dances and the *Siebensprung*, an Easter dance in which the man has to make seven different movements, two with his feet, two with his knees, two with the elbows, and one with his head, with which he has to touch the floor.

The Germans preferred their old group dances to the newer couple dances that were becoming popular elsewhere from the fifteenth century. German guilds—the medieval forerunners of today's unions, which even included the Meistersingers who had assumed the Minnesingers' traditions—all had their own dances. Again these were for groups and not couples, though many had a strong competitive element. The tailors held their dance at Pentecost, the carpenters of Nuremberg on Ash Wednesday. Here the dance started in the street, moved to the town hall, and later ended up in the special dance halls of which most German towns boasted. The coopers (barrel makers) of Munich performed a dance every seven years which ended with filled wineglasses being swung on halved barrel hoops without a drop being spilled. Village dancing was also an all-absorbing pastime. It is said that the medieval inhabitants of Langenberg were so busy cavorting around their lime tree that they ignored the demand of their ruler for a change of horses. As a result, he ordered them to dance every year under penalty of a fine. And thus the Pentecost *Frohntanz* (meaning "compulsory dance") was performed, regardless of weather, until a beer barrel placed under the tree was exhausted.

OVERLEAF: *Village dancing, as seen by Brueghel.*

German peasants take their partners for a couple dance.

But couple dances were not unknown in Germany. On the contrary, the energy with which the wooing dances known as *Ländler* were performed excited considerable comment and disapproval. But these wooing dances, which are still performed today, were a far cry from the formal, courtly dances known to the rest of Europe—dances that remained as strange to the Germans as their own dances proved to visiting foreigners.

The courts of Renaissance Italy can be seen as the natural heirs to the cultural tradition of France in the Middle Ages. In the palaces of the great nobles like the Medici, the Sforza, and the Borgias, through the wealth of the mighty cities of Tuscany, Lombardy and the Republic of Venice, there evolved a new secular culture that rivaled, and was finally victorious over, that other omnipotent patron, the Church of Rome. Northern Italy also boasted the first professional dancing teachers to enjoy a respected position. They evolved a technique different from that of France, although dances traveled easily across national boundaries, to be adopted and modified as they went. In Italy the feet were more carefully controlled during the dance, through a rising and falling from the instep. This was made possible by the existence of polished marble floors that ornamented the homes of the rich. Italy also pioneered the division between stage dancing by professionals and the dancing of the courtiers, which in turn was separated from the dances of the people by the growth of an increasingly rigid class system based on wealth and ownership. Folk and court dancing were not to come together again for more than two centuries.

In northern Italy the dancing teacher was the companion and even the confidant of princes. At Venetian weddings, where it was the custom to present the bride in a silent dance, the dance master might even appear in place of the father. The guru of Italian teachers was Domenico de Piacenza, who in 1416 produced a manuscript which went into great detail about the theory as well

as the practice of dance. Domenico took on those who criticized
the art as being "lascivious and wanton . . . all things are liable to
corruption and degeneration if they are employed indiscreetly:
that is, with exaggeration. It is moderation that conserves."
(Translated by Mabel Dolmetsch in her *Dances of Spain and Italy*.)
He also maintained that it was no good going in for dancing if you
lacked suppleness or were in any way deformed. Beauty and
physical aptitude were of great importance, he brutally insisted.
But beauty alone would not do, as it was equally important to have
an intellectual grasp of the scientific principles of dance. What you
needed most of all, he said, was a sense of rhythm and space, a good
memory, and agility and grace—and, as for this last, you should be
able to move as smoothly as a gondola.

Guglielmo Ebreo (William the Jew) and Antonio Cornazano
were two notable teachers who claimed Domenico as their master,
and, while plagiarizing his ideas, produced dance treatises of their
own. Francesco Sforza, duke of Milan, thought enough of

*Medieval Italians
dance to music,
though the men seem
to be enjoying
themselves more than
the solitary woman.*

A masked ball of 1393 which ended in tragedy when the costumes of the "wild men," which were made of pitch and cotton, caught fire.

Guglielmo's technique to commission a copy of his manuscript: perhaps one of the things that appealed to the duke was Gugliel- mo's view of the class system. He told his readers that if they studied his words carefully, they would "be able to dance in any festive surroundings with ease and security and much praise, and to exercise this virtuous art with confidence; which, to all en- amoured and generous hearts and gentle minds, led by divine inclination rather than through fortuitous talent, is most lovely and suitable; but is entirely alien and mortally inimical to de- praved and mechanical plebeians, who at most times, with corrupted and perverse minds, make of a liberal art and virtuous science one that is impure and servile." (Translated by Mabel Dolmetsch.)

One of the things the Italian dancing masters did was to differentiate between the ordinary couple dances (*danzi*) and the pantomimic dances (*balli*). Anyone of quality could take part in the *danza*, but the *ballo* was reserved for the most noble personages. They acted out, through dance alone, that etiquette of courtliness —advance, retreat, encirclement—which ruled their lives. By an apt choice of partner, steps, and rhythm, all sorts of intrigues and *affaires* could be alluded to. Leonardo da Vinci was com- missioned to design a spectacle—he produced a working model of the heavens—for a ball given in honor of the duchess of Milan in

1490. Here the *ballo*, led off by the duchess herself, was followed by mimic dances performed by professionals, groups of dancers of various nationalities, masquers, and then a *danza* in which everyone joined. In time (actually in the court of the French king Louis XIV) the *balli* were taken over by professionals and led to the development of ballet as an art separate from social dancing.

Though the rulers of England and France were perpetually at war—a state of affairs that persisted until the nineteenth century—their courtiers could, and often did, move easily between London and Paris. The dynastic and territorial links between the two nations ensured that they shared a cultural tradition, and even when Calais (the last remnant of the English possessions in France that had once stretched as far east as the Saône and as far south as the Garonne) was lost in 1558, people of fashion on both sides of the Channel continued to rival one another, especially when it came to new dances.

Polydore Vergil, the Italian cleric and historian who became a naturalized Englishman, wrote that as early as the reign of Henry II (who ruled the Angevin empire from 1154 to 1189), it was the custom of the nobles to celebrate Christmas with dancing, plays, masques, and disguisings, all of which remained popular until the seventeenth century. Chaucer writes of the dancing that took place after dinner—and also of the dancing girls, an oriental import for which the crusaders were responsible. Even the Arthurian knights danced out their courtly love, according to the romances of the period. In Thomas Chestre's poem *Launfal*, four of them performed before an appreciative audience consisting of the queen and more than sixty ladies.

Dancing usually took place in the hall or gallery of a noble house, and since chimneys were only introduced in the thirteenth century, the dancers were probably reduced to performing carols around the fire. But when the fireplace was moved to the side of the room, as became common from the fifteenth century onward, more varied and vigorous figures were possible. The *basse danse* came into vogue at this time and had a long run of popularity: it was the first social dance to be described in detail in England, in a treatise called *The Manner of Dauncynge the Bace Daunces after the use of Fraunce*. This was a translation made from the French by Robert Coplande, who in 1521 had it printed as an appendix to a book on French grammar. This in turn was probably first compiled for the use of young courtiers invited to attend the glittering summit meeting between Henry VIII of England and Francis I of France, at the Field of the Cloth of Gold.

In 1588 Jehan Tabourot, a sixty-nine-year-old monk of Langres in eastern France, published under the pseudonym Thoinot Arbeau (an anagram) the first-known comprehensive book on contemporary dance. Called *Orchésographie*, the work is full of valuable advice, including the following: "Dancing is practised in order to see whether lovers are healthy and suitable to wed one another; at the end of the dance, the gentlemen are permitted to kiss their mistresses, in order that they may ascertain if they have agreeable breath. In this matter, besides many other good results which follow from dancing, it becomes necessary for the good governing of society." Couched in the form of a dialogue between the author and an imaginary questioner, Capriol, the book dealt with all the fashionable dances of the period, as well as some that had fallen out of fashion.

The publication, and immense influence, of *Orchésographie* was a sign of the growing formality of dance technique, which affected all of western Europe, with the qualified exception of Germany. The tyranny of written records presided over by bureaucrats, who codified everything from circus regulations to fashions, extended to the dance. Court etiquette became similar, regardless of which capital you were in. Even in Spain, where seven centuries of Moorish occupation left an indelible impression on the native culture, an observant courtier from Italy, France, or England could pick up Madrid's court dances without too many problems. Each country maintained certain traditions that were peculiar to it—such as church dancing in Spain and the mime that became the commedia dell'arte in Italy—but a novel fashionable dance could cross national boundaries as quickly as the rest of the news. England boasted two dancing monarchs, Henry VIII and Elizabeth I, who did much to encourage vigorous court dancing and the country dances of the people. But when it came to setting the fashion, the lead in the seventeenth and eighteenth centuries was undoubtedly taken by France.

Louis XIV ascended the French throne in 1643 at the age of five, and ruled as absolute monarch for seventy-two years. The personality of the Sun King—an apt title, since everyone and everything revolved around him—went a long way toward explaining France's domination of the political and cultural arenas. His claim to rule by divine right was accepted by his subjects at a time when such a concept was under attack everywhere else. In 1649, for example, Charles I of England lost his head over it.

The galliard illustrated in Arbeau's influential work Orchésographie.

But the French were so convinced of the rightness of their institutions, and their king so magnificently indulged his vanity—who else would commission an entire Hall of Mirrors?—that their national self-confidence was enough to awe the rest of Europe. For a country to set a style it must be rich, confident to the point of arrogance, and glamorously led. France in the seventeenth century was all of these. The invention and initiative that characterized the Sun King's youth gave way in time to an obsessive reliance on protocol, explained partly by the monarch's aging, and partly by the miserable state of the economy at the end of his reign. New glories were no longer possible, so it was necessary to keep alive the memory of the old. Yet French fashions continued to dominate the world. A nation that has once tasted this supremacy can never quite forget it.

Style itself is decided by economic and political considerations no less than by purely social ones. The seventeenth century saw a great increase in population, but the countryside was not crowded, so this had little effect on the living conditions of ordinary people. But it did mean a larger pool of labor for the rich to draw on, at the same time that increasing wealth—partly amassed through the plunder of wars, partly through more intensive exploitation of the land—meant they could indulge their fancies in building and in leisure. Since there were more people to do the work, and more money to pay them with, this meant the rich had more time on their hands. Louis XIV knew and used this. He made of Versailles the most magnificent honeypot to attract all the noble bees, and once they were there—in the glittering center from which all royal favors were dispensed—he kept them there in expensive idleness. Partly this was to neutralize any disaffected elements by ensuring they were under his own eye, and partly to milk them of their money (he created an astonishing number of nobles, strictly for cash) to pay for his own extravagance. To keep them amused, there were entertainments of all kinds—musicians and dancers were drawn to the honey no less than other artists—and, as palates got jaded, these amusements became more and more spectacular. In dancing they became so complicated they were given to professionals to perform: the renaissance man of the preceding two centuries, the man who could turn his hand to anything, was being forced out by the specialist in the arts, no less than in politics.

Professional dancers came to prominence partly because the king himself stopped appearing in the masques or musical dramas that employed the best court artists available. Louis himself always played the gods in these allegorical amusements, but once he reached his thirties he got bored with such roles (some say he grew too fat to do them justice), and they were taken by other dancers. Naturally, no courtier would presume to step into the king's shoes, so the parts had to be given to people outside the court hierarchy— to professional dancers whose social position was negligible. The king continued to lead off the couple dances that constituted the program of the great balls held at Versailles, which Louis employed to enhance his own prestige and maintain, if not increase,

70

the distance he kept between himself and his subjects. The dances therefore were of great stateliness and formality. Dancing for amusement, to express exuberance, or for the pleasure of physical contact became a spectator sport in which the courtiers watched paid performers.

For any person of fashion it was still important to dance well, but it was equally important to avoid doing it too well, and thus being confused with a professional. If the king kept his distance, how much more vital it was for the French aristocracy to separate themselves from the common herd, in manners, speech (which became incredibly artificial, the instruments used to accompany the dance being known as "the spirits of the feet"), deportment, and, above all, costume. High heels for men came into vogue, perhaps to emphasize the calf which was encased in stockings, perhaps to give a man additional height at a time when women started piling up their hair. Certainly such heels set a gentleman apart from working people, since no strenuous labor could be performed by someone forced by his footwear to trip on tiptoe between puddles. And obviously such a fashion affected the dance: wild abandon on the floor would entail the risk of serious injury.

In deportment, as the dance expert Belinda Quirey points out, this was the time when the upper classes started to walk with their toes turned out. There were some dances—the *branle* was a prime example—in which movement sideways was made much easier when the feet were kept at an angle instead of being parallel to one another. There was also a fashion for wide-topped "Cavalier" boots in which such an artificial walk—which persisted among the upper classes until World War I—grew from the passion for setting themselves apart that the aristocracy began to develop from the seventeenth century. Every age has a set of mannerisms which differentiates one class from another: it may be how you

A seventeenth-century French ball, in which the gossip is as important as the dance.

OPPOSITE: *French Court ballet, performed by professionals at Fontainebleau.*

crook your little finger when drinking tea, how you cut and eat your meat, whether you wear or carry gloves when visiting. When deportment really mattered, a walk designed to call attention to the walker—for anyone anxious simply to get from A to B would employ the most natural movement and keep the feet parallel— was one more sign of the difference between those who worked and those who did not have to. In court dancing such a turned-out walk became *de rigeur*. It also became the basis of the ballet step, because ballet as an art form was formalized at the time when turned-out feet were in vogue.

The Académie Française was founded in 1635 to safeguard and purify the use of the French language, and this was followed by the creation of sister academies to protect the interests of those who wished to dictate policy in painting and sculpture, music, science, and architecture. It was Louis's minister Jean Baptiste Colbert who encouraged the foundation of such institutions, through which the arts could be directed—by men who owed their jobs and influence to royal favor—to the greater good of the monarchy. What it meant was that "official taste" became the monopoly of those in charge of the academies—and the men who taught the king and his courtiers to dance saw no reason why they should be left out. They wanted official control over the forms and styles of all court dance, and they also wished to be free of the musicians, whose own organization and power, especially over dance, appeared to them to be increasing. In 1661, therefore, Charles Beauchamps, one of the king's dancing masters, became the first director of the Royal Academy of Dance, thus cementing that dictatorship of style by the professionals which lasted until the French Revolution. Anybody who wished to teach dance to the people who mattered had to be a member of the Academy and subscribe to its rules—and anyone who was anyone could not be taught by anybody else.

What started simply as an entertainment forming part of the general diversions with which the court amused itself came to be one of the most spectacular, artificial, and yet inventive forms of dance known to the "civilized" world. The ballets, fêtes, and masques whose purpose was to glorify the Sun King often had words by Molière, scenic designs by Charles Lebrun (who became director of the Academy of Painting and virtual dictator of the visual arts), and music by Jean Baptiste Lully, a boyhood friend of the monarch who frequently partnered him in ballets, and who was rewarded with the directorship of the Academy of Music. Such a galaxy of talent was not to be wasted when the king ceased his personal appearances. On the contrary, the use of hired dancers gave even more control to those who conceived the spectacle. Foremost among these was Charles Beauchamps who, apart from inventing a method of writing down the steps of the dance, is also credited with enumerating the five basic positions in ballet that countless little girls are taught today. The turned-out step, of course, is foremost among these. Though we are not concerned with the history of ballet, its intimate connection with social dance in the seventeenth century can scarcely be ignored. Many of the dances performed by the courtiers provided the basis of the fantastic elaborations performed by the professionals, while the former were quite prepared to watch dancers executing steps they themselves could never follow. Russia, perhaps the country which has given most to the form, was first introduced to court ballet by Peter the Great, who also took French dance teachers and court dances back to St. Petersburg from his European travels.

Whether or not Louis XIV actually appreciated music, he was certainly surrounded by it. Music was provided to eat to, dance to, doze to, and as a background for conversation. His musicians were fully occupied and his music masters, notably Lully, saw that they played only pieces which had the official seal of approval. This did not mean that the king liked what he heard, merely that it was provided by those to whom he had given the authority to do so.

Of course the royal favor could be withdrawn, which meant that compositions had to fall softly on the royal ear, if not actually delight it. As the king, at least in youth, enjoyed the dance, it was natural for the royal composers to assume that dance rhythms and tunes would continue to appeal. Thus the names we know as dances came to be compositions simply for listening to, related to the originals purely through the rhythms they employed. Of course the music could also be used for dancing, but just as today's radio pumps out dance tunes purely as background music, so the baroque instrumental suite became something for the ears alone.

James I, who ruled England from 1603 to 1625, enjoyed watching his favorites dance, especially if the dancers showed off their legs; his successor, Charles I, who married Louis XIV's aunt, ensured that the French style of dancing gained the chief place at court. During the Commonwealth (1649–60), public and theatrical dancing were discouraged, but dance nevertheless continued to be popular. Lord Protector Cromwell himself gave a mighty ball at Whitehall to celebrate his daughter's wedding, at which he and his guests danced until dawn to an accompaniment provided by fifty trumpeters and forty-eight violinists. John Playford's *The English Dancing Master* was first published under the Commonwealth, but the dance did not flourish publicly until the Restoration of Charles II in 1660, who had spent several years of exile in France and was influenced accordingly.

But the social climate of England was very different from that of France: the divine right of kings had been cut off with Charles I. That questioning of accepted belief that had begun in the age of Francis Bacon was given a tremendous boost by the toppling and restoration of the throne, and, though dissenters were given short shrift (many of them emigrating to the United States), there was a political and literary freedom unknown elsewhere. Thus, where Louis XIV's mistresses found themselves entombed in magnificent residences that somehow made them respectable, Charles II's affairs were merely part of a general atmosphere of boastful bawdry. In dance, the king, like his predecessors, encouraged the acceptance at court of the lively country dances of the people.

The Dancing Master :

Or, plain and easie Rules for the Dancing of Country Dances, with the Tune to each Dance,

to be playd on the Treble Violin.

The second Edition, Enlarged and Corrected from many grosse Errors which were in the former Edition.

London, Printed for *John Playford* at his shop in the Inner Temple near the Church Door. 1652.

Cover engraving for the second edition of Playford's The Dancing Master, *the manual that was as influential in America as it was in England.*

These were exported to France, and then reimported as contredanses, the basis of the contras that were, and remain, so popular in New England.

The eighteenth century saw the slow decline, not only of French influence in fashionable matters, but also of the position of the courts of Europe as supreme arbiters in every sphere of life. Of course French fashions are still highly regarded, while the activities of the world's surviving monarchs remain a source of fascination to the most republican spirits. But a power unrivaled for five centuries was gradually ousted by the hesitant growth of democracy. The split between the dances of the people and those of the court—a split begun by the troubadours in the age of courtly love—was slowly healed as society was reorganized, not on a vertical level, but on a horizontal one. Fashion was no longer the exclusive preserve of courtiers, traversing the boundaries of a nation with more ease than the boundaries of a class. The tone still came from above, but the people were unafraid of adopting

the ways of their social superiors. This in turn led to an accelerating pace of change, for the men and women of fashion were quicker to adopt new styles in order to keep themselves ahead. The nineteenth century saw almost as many new dances introduced as had the preceding five. But the important thing was that these dances were universal. Only a courtier would bother to learn the stately figures of the *basse danse* or the courante. But the waltz was a dance for all classes, just as the carol had once been.

Fifteenth-century courtiers perform a decorous carol.

THE DANCES

The Carol

Dancers were originally accompanied by a rhythmic song or chant, until musicians took over around the thirteenth century, when there are manuscripts containing dance steps with music but no words to go with it. The carol (its original spelling, carole, is still used in Europe to distinguish it from the song) was a choral dance (the words are very similar) whose origins are prehistoric. It could be danced in a round—one surviving example is "Ring-around-a-rosy"—or in a line. The form, that of dancing around or toward something while singing, was common in the earliest cultures, and survived intact into the Middle Ages, when it provided the basis for all courtly dances. It appears in many folk dances, too. In Anglo-Saxon times the carol was accompanied by a wind instrument, which had greater carrying power than a voice; many illustrations from the Middle Ages show the dance being performed in decorous circles, with a tambourine to reinforce the singing and, later, shawms and other wind instruments. But the dancers were not always decorous: young maidens had to be warned "to be bashful, to pay proper attention to dress, but not to be too eager in dancing." And a certain Monsieur de Montaiglon,

Sixteenth-century carol performed in Augsburg.

a medieval adviser on etiquette, insisted that, unless they kept the rhythm, girls would be taken for mad by those who watched them. On the other hand, the angels themselves were imagined by Renaissance painters to perform circular carols—a fine example of pagan practices gaining the highest possible acceptance.

Twentieth-century farandole still to be seen in Provence and the Basque country.

The Farandole

If it was not danced in the form of a circle, the carol became a line or chain dance under the name farandole. Such a dance is described in Homer's *Iliad*, and it retains its popularity in southern France even today. There is a French romance of the late thirteenth century which describes a farandole over half a mile long. Always with a leader (who in the nineteenth century had to be young and unmarried), the dancers linked up by hand, ribbon, or handkerchief and set off weaving their way around the hall or even the town. From this dance many of the steps of later dances are derived. Sometimes the leader would make an arch by extending one arm to the next dancer and the rest of the line would have

to pass under it. The arch of the children's game "London Bridge is Falling Down" is a descendant of this form of farandole. But such figures fell out of favor in the Middle Ages because of the difficulties of passing under someone's arm wearing the tall headdresses that were then fashionable. Another more complicated farandole was the snail-shell pattern formed by the leader winding the line around himself without anyone breaking their hold. These dances gradually acquired an instrumental accompaniment, often a pipe and a tabor (a small drum), whose sounds would carry far better than a singer's if the farandole was being performed outside.

The Branle

A society that considers itself sophisticated soon insists on the division of labor, chiefly in order to distinguish "us" from "them." So with the dance. The carol that could be danced by anyone with everybody singing to keep the rhythm going gave way to the *branle* (pronounced "brawl" by the English), which required proper instrumentalists as a separate form of accompaniment. Country people continued to dance carols, while *branles* became the dance of the courtiers, only to be taken up in time by the country folk, who invented an astonishing variety of local variations. The *branle* became the basis of French folk dance; the dance name probably comes from the old French *branler*, meaning "to sway," and this has been interpreted as a swaying of the whole chain of dancers to the left and then to the right. But its lasting importance lies in the fact that it was the first formal dance to

contain alternating rhythms—the "quick" and "slow" that has been drummed into the ears of countless dance pupils ever since.

Country branle *of the sixteenth century accompanied by bagpipes.*

In societies as strictly hierarchical as those of the Middle Ages—and with formal orders of precedence as binding as those of Imperial China—dancing as an entertainment and exercise for ladies and gentlemen was an organized affair. In the competitive atmosphere of the courts you could not just call for musicians, seize a girl, and show off your paces—not, that is, if you wanted your reputation to survive. Dance, like everything else, became subject to regulation. Not only did the most distinguished couple lead off the dances, but the order in which *branles* were danced rapidly became fixed. A suite consisted of the *branle double, branle simple, branle gai,* and then whatever may have been the local favorite.

According to the historical dance expert Belinda Quirey, the *branle double* was responsible for the introduction of the eight-bar musical phrase, which is also the basic phrase of the ballads that were first composed for dancing. In the *branle double,* the leading gentleman held his lady by her right hand or sleeve and took three steps to the left, pausing on the fourth beat. This was then repeated, stepping to the right (the repetition explains the "double" of the title). It was a stately dance, suitable for the elderly, as was the *branle simple,* in which the three steps and pause made to the left were followed by a "simple" or "single" of one step and pause made to the right. During the pause the feet were brought together.

The *branle gai* was an altogether jollier affair presumably danced by younger couples. Instead of walking there was leaping: with six beats to the musical bar the dancers shot from one foot to the other for the first four counts and then paused for counts five and six. These movements were made toward the left, but apparently after the pause they continued leftward, not "swaying" to the right at all. The *branle gai*'s rhythm and leaps were the basis of several later dances, which became especially popular in England.

Of the many regional variations, some were miming dances. For example, the movements of washerwomen were imitated in the *branle des lavandières*. Of this type of dance a late survival is the round dance to the tune "*Sur* (or, more properly, *sous*) *le Pont d'Avignon*." One local favorite, the *branle de Bourgogne*, was also for the young and athletic, since it consisted of a mixture of walking and leaping, to the eight beats of the *branle double*. Dancers performed three steps and a hop, turning to the left and to the right, and ending with a high kick to knee height. When this was over, everyone often joined up to do a circle dance. We know little of the speed at which they moved, but one can imagine an after-dinner *branle* becoming a real brawl, given the right amount of high spirits.

The Estampie

Life at court was very competitive, as it always is around the seat of power. The more cultivated rulers competed with their courtiers to see who was the best versifier, although few great nobles committed their compositions to paper, as did the professional troubadours. And in dance, while the young men showed off their paces, their legs (encased in skintight hose), and their courtship, to perform well was a matter of competitive pride for the great personage too, especially as he and his lady would usually lead off the dance.

But *branles* and farandoles scarcely gave much opportunity for the dancing courtier (as opposed to the professional but lowly tumbler) to exhibit his skill. To do that, and at the same time show reverence to the opposite sex—a necessary part of courtly love—a new dance form was required: a dance in which a man might partner a woman, and the pair of them might shine without the encumbrance of a whole line of other dancers. Perhaps that is how the first couple dance, the estampie, came into being in the twelfth century. Naturally, since the orders of precedence had to be observed, the highest-ranking couple would take the floor first and set an example for the others to follow. Those who danced after, pair by pair with the rest as onlookers, addressed themselves to the ruling couple, showing their reverence by facing them whenever possible, much as the primitive dancers had faced their altars or totems. The estampie thus allowed for competitiveness, courtliness and reverence.

If the actual word may originally have come from the Frankish *stampon*, a stamping dance, by the time the estampie came into vogue it was extremely sedate, a gliding dance suited to the costumes and customs of the court. Country people ignored it al-

together. We do not know much about how it was danced—probably a few figures executed to the four-four rhythms of the *branle*—but we do know something about the musical accompaniment. This was slow, because it was contrasted with the saltarello, which is a lively leaping dance, and pictures and manuscripts show that the estampie was danced to the strains of the bow fiddle, the hurdy-gurdy, the bagpipes, the tambourine, the hautboy, the cornett, or the flageolet. Voices too were still used as backing, sometimes with a solo alternating with a chorus. Such scanty information should not be allowed to obscure the dance's significance. It began a new style, that of dancing in pairs, which has often come under assault but has not died out yet.

A bal champêtre, or outside entertainment, from the sixteenth century. The dance is probably an estampie.

The Basse Danse

The invention of printing in the middle of the fifteenth century made it possible for dancing masters to impose their will on the public by citing the authority of a text. One of the earliest such texts was *Le Manuscrit des Basses Danses de la Bibliothèque de Bourgogne*, written in the first half of the fifteenth century. The first printed manual on how to dance was *L'Art et Instruction de Bien Danser*,

published by one Michel Thoulouze around 1490. It consists of five
pages of music and the steps of forty-nine *basses danses*, which are
almost identical to those cited in the Bourgogne manuscript. The
steps of the *basse danse* had obviously been around for some time
before this book was published, but the attempt to prescribe the
"proper" way of doing them did not prevent the better dancers
from inventing new steps in a display of individual skill. These too
gained acceptance, as shown by the number of variations which
found their way into print.

The *basse danse* was so called because the dancer's feet were kept
low on the ground, as opposed to the *haute danse*, which meant those
dances which included leaps, high kicks, and so on. The *basse danse*
was directly derived from the estampie, and was a slow couple
dance that took the form of a parade around the floor. The movements, each of which took four measures to perform, were five in
number: the double (three steps and bringing the feet together);
two singles (a step and bringing the feet together); the *branle*,
whose steps have been described; the reprise, described by Cecil

Sharp as "a curious shaking step on alternate feet, executed four times"; and the reverence, which was a deep bow or curtsy. It was often performed as part of a suite which included other types of dance before the performers came back to the *basse danse* and ornamented the steps with small hops. (Dance variations frequently take a form outside its original limitations, in this case that of keeping the feet low.) There was usually a final section, the *tordion*, or *tourdion*, which consisted of an elaborately stately dance in three-two time, requiring restrained forward kicks. This was also processional in form, with the partners ending up facing the noblest in the audience.

But the *basse danse* was certainly not so stately as to be downright boring. In his rhyming treatise on *basses danses* and *branles* published in 1536, the Provençal poet Antonius de Arena describes the reprise as being "performed advancing, but sideways; for it is ornamented in the intricate manner, and gliding always towards the right, agitating the legs and moving the feet." He goes on to say, "in joining shoulders with the lady, take care not to bump against her in your rapid approach, for if you should jostle her too much, you might cause the maiden to stagger backwards. Because of such small occurrences a woman always scolds a lover." (Translated by Mabel Dolmetsch in her *Dances of England and France*.)

The *basse danse* was known in Italy as the *bassa danza*, which the dancing teacher Antonio Cornazano regarded as "the queen of measures." As in France, it was a slow dance with small, gliding steps, embellished by rising on the toes. As well as dancing it in couples, hand in hand, the Italians also danced it *alla fila*, "in a line," as the farandole was performed. Up to eight people could take part in such a lineup, though the masters favored but two or three. The rhythm was "quick, quick, slow," and the agility and control that Cornazano's master Domenico de Piacenza had called for was concentrated in the feet. Domenico also warned against musicians who speeded up the time during a dance, blaming their ignorance and lack of understanding. All in all, it was obvious that dance was becoming a specialized art form, whose practitioners felt themselves superior to the musicians, on whose compositions they nevertheless had still to rely.

The Quadernaria

In Italy the *bassa danza* was part of a suite of dances, of which the *quadernaria* came next. It was slightly quicker than the dance that preceded it (hence Domenico's warning about taking the music too fast) and it was in four-four time (from which it got its name). The chief difference between the two dances was that the *bassa danza* began with a rising movement of the foot on the first, or down, beat, while for the *quadernaria* you had to begin by placing your foot, rising only on the second, or up, beat. The steps apparently consisted of two singles (one step and a pause during which the right foot is brought up to the left), followed by a backward movement of the right foot. Doubtless there was flourishing footwork in the execution of these steps. Fashionable men were wearing short tunics and had soft leather shoes that would have given them every opportunity to show off.

The Saltarello

The third of the *bassa danza* suite was the saltarello, known in France as the *pas de Brabant* (a duchy that was part of Burgundy in the fifteenth century, before being transferred to the Austrian Empire, then to the Spanish Crown in the sixteenth century). Though the name saltarello is connected with the Latin for leaping or jumping, Cornazano insisted that only the best dancers were permitted to leave the ground, and then only rarely. The dance was, after all, part of a suite in which the feet were not supposed to rise high. Nevertheless, the saltarello was a jolly affair, faster than the *quadernaria*. After the procession around the floor, it appears that the man often performed a solo in front of his lady, and included a series of hops during which one leg would be thrust forward, as well as a special step in which the left leg was struck against the right and then shot backward. When the man had finished, the lady had her turn, though her steps were altogether more restrained. The man's "striking" movement was also performed in the *quadernaria*. In time the various forms of the *bassa danza* suite became mingled (despite the teachers' attempts to distinguish them), and only the different speeds, or tempi, at which the music was played remained.

Contemporary choir-boys practice for los seises, *held in Seville Cathedral.*

The Piva

The last of the *bassa danza* suite was the *piva*, which was in four-four time and played twice as fast as the *bassa danza*. Domenico was rather rude about it, partly because of its speed, but chiefly because of its low origins: it was once a peasant dance to the accompaniment of a bagpipe, from which it derives its name. Of course the nobility made it dignified; but as Cornazano, writing in the middle of the fifteenth century, put it, "at the present time, having been minced up by the ingenious ones into more florid movements, it has become low and vulgar and unsuitable for magnificent persons and dancers of good standing." (Translated by Mabel Dolmetsch.)

The Bergamasca

This was a popular Italian round dance in even time, performed in couples, with each dancer making a leap and neatly crossing his feet every six or nine steps (a step known in ballet as the entrechat). It was supposed to be a native dance of the peasants of Bergamo in Italy, and perhaps was originally a rustic wooing dance. Certainly it retained its rustic overtones when it crossed to England, since Shakespeare makes Bottom perform a "bergomask" in *A Midsummer Night's Dream*. As far as we know, it did not make the climb up the social ladder to gain acceptance at court.

Church Dancing

Ever since the anathemas hurled by the medieval Church Fathers at those who got carried away dancing in the aisles, porches or churchyards, the habit of expressing piety through dance had fallen into disfavor in every Christian country except Spain. In the year 1313, a Jewish dance teacher, Rabbi Hacen Ben Salomo, of Tauste in Saragossa, was brought in to teach Christians to perform a choral dance around the altar of the church of St. Bartholomew. Cardinal Ximenes (1436–1517) who acted as regent on the death of Isabella and again when Ferdinand died—and who was so zealous in burning heretics that some 2,500 were consumed during his reign—revived in Toledo the old custom of dancing in the choir of the church during service.

Such dancing was also performed in Seville, where it persists to our own times. There the dance was called *los seises* ("the sixes"). In its original form, twelve choirboys in two groups of six would perform the dance on the Feasts of Corpus Christi and of the Immaculate Conception, as well as during the carnival. In medieval costume—red for the first feast, blue for the second—with bells sewn onto their clothes and ivory castanets in hand, the choirboys danced in lines facing each other, executing weaving, circular, and chainlike figures, together with some crosses. The dance was performed in front of the high altar, in the presence of the archbishop and the kneeling clergy. It was naturally a stately affair, but although performed in a cathedral, it has indisputable links with Muslim culture through the Mozarabic liturgy of Toledo and Seville—those rites practiced by Spaniards permitted to proclaim themselves Christians under Moorish rule. *Los seises* can still be seen, though only ten choirboys now take part.

The Moresque

A *Moresco* meant a Moor (many remained in Spain by converting to Christianity when Granada was overrun by King Ferdinand and Queen Isabella, the founders of the unified Catholic state). The *moresque*, which was a popular dance in the fifteenth century, was apparently so called because it contained an element of mime —that of the battle between Christian and blacked-up Muslim. In his book *Orchésographie*, Arbeau relates how, in certain French noble houses, a dancer blackened to look like a Moor, with a band around his forehead and bells on his legs, would perform the *moresque* up and down the hall. The dance consisted chiefly of stamping with the heels in two-four time—presumably because it was thought that was how the Moorish courtiers danced. The name came to be applied, however, to choral dances in double-file formation. If the two lines were supposed to represent warring sects, the fighting element rapidly became purely symbolic (as in the British morris dance). *Los seises*, the dance of Seville Cathedral, is a form of *moresque*, but double-file dancing goes back to primitive times, as does painting the face so that the dancer will be unrecognizable. Perhaps the Spaniards employed the dance in order to assimilate an intractable part of their culture, the fact of a Muslim occupation whose cultural influence remained strong.

The Pavane

By the mid-sixteenth century the *basse danse* was no longer in favor in Italy or France. What replaced it as the introductory dance to a suite was the pavane, which originated in Italy, the name meaning "a dance from Padua." This was a slow dance, well suited for court ceremonial, as a man could perform it struttingly, with simple steps. These consisted of two singles, to left and to right, and a double (the left foot making a step, the right foot going past it, and the left foot finally joining it), all made going forward. The pattern was then repeated going to right and to left, ending with a double going backward. Even Arbeau described the dance as easy.

Pavanes, in two-two time, were played to usher in the bride at society weddings, and the music was also used for solemn processions (though of course the backward step was not employed). The dance was a favorite of Queen Elizabeth I of England. Since she had an eye for a good leg, which the male attire of the day left exposed—albeit encased in hose—to the knee or even the buttocks, it was a good dance in which to show off fancy footwork. The meteoric rise of Sir Christopher Hatton, who was for a while the queen's most intimate companion and who ended up as lord chancellor, was supposedly due less to his political ability than to his athletic prowess as a dancer. He was said to wear green bows on his shoes and to dance the pavane with brilliance. No wonder there were some who complained that Englishmen were more

respected by their enemies when they carried proper weapons instead of "light dancing-swords . . . which they carry now more like ladies than men," as a contemporary observer put it.

A highly stylized and artificial version of the pavane.

The Canaries

Another solemn dance to come from Spain was the *canaries*, which perhaps derives its name from the Canary Islands. Originally danced around a dead body—as was the later jota in Spain—the dance changed its theme from death to love, and became elaborated into a courtship dance. After the initial promenade, the gentleman left his partner and danced away from and then toward her, using skipping and stamping movements alternately on heel and sole. The lady then performed before her partner, though the dance in this form was considered so difficult that only the most practiced dancers attempted it. As a result, it had disappeared from European court dance by the second half of the sixteenth century.

The Saraband

Some claim this dance received its name from a devil in woman's shape who appeared in Seville in the twelfth century, and who labeled it the *zarabanda*. In the sixteenth century, certainly, the dance and the song that accompanied it were considered by a Jesuit historian to be indecent in its words and disgusting in its movements. Even Cervantes described it as having "a diabolical sound." So seriously did the Spanish authorities take the threat of the *zarabanda* (which the rest of Europe, less concerned by its devilish origins, altered to saraband) that in 1583 anyone caught singing or reciting its words was to be punished with two hundred lashes, in addition to being exiled (if female) or sentenced to six years in the galleys.

For better or worse we know almost nothing of the actual dance in its original form. Apparently it was once a sexual pantomime, for in Barcelona couples twisted their bodies to the rhythm of castanets, and by the time it came to Italy the breasts of the dancers were allowed to collide and the lips to kiss. But from being erotic it became a gliding, processional dance, and it ended up as part of an instrumental suite. It was introduced to the French court around 1588, and was a favorite of Louis XIII, not to mention his minister Cardinal Richelieu. It remained popular well into the seventeenth century, since Charles II of England often called for it to be played. Perhaps it is an example of what happened to the dances of the people once they got to the court: their rude energy was canalized into something fit for the most delicate disposition—even if they became somewhat anemic on the way.

The Chaconne and the Passacaglia

Two further forms which originated in Spain as exotic dances of the people before being translated into part of the court ballet were the *chacona* (which the French changed to *chaconne*) and the passacaglia. The first was supposed to be even more unbridled than the saraband, but apart from Cervantes' description—the feet run like quicksilver, is how he put it—our only knowledge of the steps comes from the seventeenth century, when it was danced in two lines at the end of a French ball. The passacaglia, whose name is a corruption of the Spanish for "street song," was related to the chaconne with its three beats to the measure. The French took it up and slowed it down. It too ceased to be a dance and lived on only as part of an instrumental suite.

The Measure

The *basse danse* we know from France and elsewhere was known to Elizabethan England as the measure. As Beatrice put it in Shakespeare's *Much Ado about Nothing*: "Wooing, wedding and repenting, is as a Scotch jig, a measure and cinque-pace: the first suit is hot and hasty, like a Scotch jig, and full as fantastical; the wedding, mannerly and modest, as a measure, full of state and ancientry; then comes Repentance, and, with his bad legs, falls into a cinque-pace faster and faster, until he sinks into his grave." The "bad legs" referred to in the last part is an obscure joke, presuming that Shakespeare's audience was familiar with fashionable dance teaching. It is a reference to Arbeau's description of the *cinque pas*, a five-step dance that was an antecedent of the galliard, in which the performer is called upon to make four "limping hops"—hence the "bad legs." Perhaps Shakespeare himself attended one of the dancing schools for which England was famous, since he makes many expert references to the art.

Like the *basse danse*, the measure was a slow, smooth affair, beginning with a salute to the spectators and a reverence or bow made to the partner. In the "My Lord of Essex measure," this was followed by a double forward and a single back, repeated four times; two singles sideways, a double forward, and a reprise—a swaying back to the original position with the feet being slowly drawn together through four beats. For those who want to know just how stately it was, here are Mabel Dolmetsch's directions for performing the double: "On the first beat bend the knee of the right foot and step with the left flat on the ground; then rise on the toes at the close of the beat. On the second beat step with the right foot on the toes with straightened knees, sinking the heels at the close of the beat. On the third beat step once more with the left foot flat and the right knee bent, rising at the close of the beat; and on the fourth beat join up the right foot with the left (on the toes) in the first position and sink the heels at the close of the beat. As you step with the left foot, advance the left hip slightly and turn the head towards the lady." (From her *Dances of England and France*.)

The Hey

The "antic hay" referred to as a dance by the playwright Christopher Marlowe in *Edward II* (produced around 1590) was certainly very old, since it came from the farandole line dance. It took its name from the French word meaning a sort of hedge or hurdle, made from upright stakes interwoven with crossed sticks, and the dance formed part of the more energetic *branles*. It involved a rapid interweaving of one dancer between the rest; each danced in place until it was his or her turn to weave up the line. The hey continued until all the dancers were back in their original positions. It lives on in the chains and reels that are an important part of folk dancing.

The Galliard

This was the dance for which the Elizabethans became famous, and it was sufficiently energetic for the queen herself to perform half a dozen or so before breakfast, for exercise. Musically derived from the pavane, which preceded it in the English dance suite, the galliard got its six-beat rhythm from the *branle gai*, and took some of its steps from the *cinqu pas*, though ornamenting these fantastically. Known in France as the *gaillarde*, and in Italy as the *gagliarda*, it perhaps derives its name from the Celtic word for

First steps of the galliard.

strength and prowess. Certainly these two qualities were much needed for the dance: Arbeau says that the virtue of the man lies in his agility, precision, rapidity of footwork, and muscular strength. He also maintains that the dance used to be performed with discretion, whereas "those who dance the Galliard nowadays in the towns dance tumultuously, and content themselves with executing the *cinqu pas* and some few passages without any set plan, and do not trouble, provided they fall in cadence."

Though ostensibly a couple dance, the galliard came to be virtually a solo for a man, in which he showed off his leaps and jumps while his partner gyrated gently, occasionally performing a figure or two while her fellow caught his breath. After a preliminary bowing and procession up and down the floor, the steps —on which infinite variations could be made according to the skill of the dancer—included crossing the feet, high and low kicks, forward and backward kicks, and a leap in the air (the capriole) during which the dancer might make two complete aerial revolutions before landing on his toes, knees bent slightly outward. The tune of "God Save the Queen" (known in the United States as "America") is a galliard air, as is Verdi's "La donna e mobile." It was a unique dance, requiring the sort of qualities of exhibitionism and skill that Elizabeth encouraged in her courtiers. It did not long survive her.

La Volta

This dance, another favorite of the queen's, was considered highly indecent by contemporary moralists. Its name means "turning dance," and it was a form of galliard, a near relative of the Provençal dance known as *la nizzarda* (from the town of Nice). In *la volta* the couple, holding each other closely, performed two hopping and turning steps together, then leaped high into the air, the man supporting the woman with his thigh. To keep her steady, he had also to hold his left arm around her right hip, jam his left thigh against her right, and during the lift put his right hand under her busk, the front part of her corset. For all this he was rewarded with a kiss. No wonder some people were worried: what were things coming to when you might get a flash of the royal knees? Arbeau warns the woman to keep her left hand against her own thigh to hold her skirt, "lest in gathering the wind it should display her chemise or bare leg." And, he goes on, "After having turned by as many cadences as you please, restore the demoiselle to her place where she will feel (no matter what good countenance she makes) her head whirling, full of vertigo and giddiness, and perhaps you will be much the same: I leave you to judge whether it be a proper thing for a young girl to make large steps and wide movements of the legs: and whether in this Volta her honor and well-being are not risked and involved." (Translated by Mabel Dolmetsch.)

La volta *in its original sixteenth-century version.*

A mocked-up version of la volta, *for the film* The Sword and the Rose, *made in 1952.*

La volta was the only court dance in which the hold between the couples was so close. It was considered by some to be a forerunner of the waltz, but that is doubtless because both dances were once thought equally immoral.

The Courante

This dance, known in England as the coranto, was in Elizabethan times a lively skipping dance in triple time. It had the same basic steps as the pavane, although it was much faster and performed with hops and leaps. Arbeau talks of the courante being used as a miming dance of wooing and courtship between three young male dancers and three young girls. The love play ended in the courante being danced pell-mell. But, says Arbeau, dancers became careless and standards fell. It was common for a man's friends to steal his partner in a courante, or for him to pick up somebody else, if his "first one is fatigued."

In the seventeenth century, the tempo of the dance changed to six-four, and from being a carol, the courante became a stately couple dance, named the slow courante to distinguish it from its predecessor. As such it was the young Louis XIV's favorite dance, which he was claimed to perform better than anyone. The pantomime wooing the dance had previously contained was dropped; to the king dignity and distance mattered above all things. The courante had to be performed with none of the visible "effort" that the professionals put into their work. And the fact that the monarch excelled at it meant that all aspiring French courtiers had to learn it before tackling anything else.

The Allemande

Arbeau described this as "one of our most ancient dances, since we are descended from the Germans." It was the only old German dance (which is all the French name means) performed by German courtiers and not by ordinary people. In contrast to the lively German group dances, the allemande was a solemn, professional dance, performed in "open couples," facing the prince and audience. It had simple, even monotonous steps, to left and right, forward and back, though there was a more lively after-dance with which it concluded, played to a different tune. This after-dance was the same as the Italian *saltarello*—so much so that the Italians dignified it by the name of *saltarello tedesco* (or "German saltarello").

The allemande was the only German court dance to be taken up by other courts before the waltz swept all before it. In England, where spelling was by no means a precise art, it was variously labeled almain, alman, and almayne, and it concluded with a hop on the left foot and a kick with the right to knee height. According to Belinda Quirey, it opened with a series of double steps, after which each couple performed some simple figures. The procession then moved off once more into double steps. As well as being popular at the French court—where it also became part of the instrumental suite—the allemande was a favorite with English courtiers, who danced it with the actors of a court masque during the "communings," when performers and audience mingled.

The Bourrée

This was a folk dance which reached the French court only as part of the ballet, where Madame de Sévigné considered it to be "one of the most amazing dances in the world." The dance came from the Auvergne, where it was performed in clogs, but the origin of its name is obscure. As a couple dance, the bourrée involved skipping steps, which meant that the skirts of the women had to be held well off the ground. Perhaps this was responsible for its avoidance by courtiers and its adoption by ballet dancers, who were already beginning to shorten their skirts in order to show off their entre-chats. Considering their social position was no higher than that of the medieval tumblers—that is, they were social outcasts fit only for exploitation—the professional dancers had little to lose.

The bourrée was also performed in two facing lines, one of men and one of women, to the accompaniment of a hurdy-gurdy or bagpipes (which were by no means the monopoly of Scotland). As the two lines advanced and retreated, the leader changed places with the person opposite him, and one after the other all the dancers followed suit. The ballet step known as the *pas de bourrée* shares only the rhythm of the original.

The Rigaudon

Here was another of the suite of dances popular with the court ballet, which had originally been a folk dance. As performed in southeastern France, it had two parts, the first similar to the

bourrée, the second a courtship dance where the man performed various lively movements to attract the attention of his partner, who was required to appear reluctant. By the time it reached the court, however, it had become something of a virtuoso turn for a professional to perform. Nevertheless, the great liveliness of its rhythm ensured its popularity among courtiers where etiquette was not quite so restrained—for example, in the court of Charles II of England.

Charles II at a ball in the Hague, probably dancing the rigaudon.

The Gavotte

The French court, like that of Queen Elizabeth I of England, was amused by watching country people dance; and the peasants of Gap in the Dauphiné, who were known as Gavots, performed in a manner which was particularly pleasing. In the original form the dancers stood in a line or circle and after some *branles doubles*, embellished with little jumps, one couple would take the floor and perform alone, saluting one another with a kiss. After they had their turn, the man would kiss all the women in the line, and the watching men would take turns in kissing his partner. But as the seventeenth century wore on, all such exhibitionism became purely symbolic: kisses were replaced by posies, and the gavotte became a stately number totally divorced from its peasant origins. This is not to say that it was merely tedious—in due course Marie Antoinette, that ceaseless seeker after new diversions, revived it as a popular society dance. But as the Sun King grew old, the pace of his pleasures slowed, and the gavotte was one victim of this.

OPPOSITE, ABOVE:
A stately allemande of the late eighteenth century.

OPPOSITE, BELOW:
An allemande practiced before a critical audience.

A nineteenth-century impression of the medieval mummers' play, the forerunner of the masque.

The Passepied

Deriving its name from the dance step in which one foot is placed over the other, the passepied was originally a *branle* from Brittany which became an extremely popular court dance. Like the courante, it got shorn of its elements of courtship, and by changing its pace and rhythm it became fairly sedate. Nevertheless, its gliding steps, turns, and constant changes of position gave it a certain jollity which undoubtedly contributed to its popularity.

Court Masques and Theatrical Dancing

Reference has been made to the extravagant spectacles mounted to delight the court at Versailles, but "masks" and disguisings—masquerade parties that included plays and dancing—were also popular English diversions in Tudor times. The English court masque reached its peak in the seventeenth century. The Stuarts could boast of masques with words by Milton or Ben Jonson, scenery by Inigo Jones, and music by Henry Lawes, or later Purcell, talents to match anything Louis XIV could commission, although the Sun King's productions were on a far more lavish scale. When it came to entertainment the English were rarely extravagant.

As in France, the masque's most important feature was the entrance of certain of the nobility, playing the part of gods or mythic heroes, and dancing a specially composed piece. At Versailles, these parts soon came to be taken by professionals, and thus gave birth to the court ballet. In England—where masques were often performed in country houses as well as at court—the final part of the drama was followed by revels, the descendant of the old "communings" in which masquers and audience joined in dancing together. Nevertheless, professional dancers came increasingly to dominate these entertainments, and that, plus the growing interest in theatrical machinery for creating special effects, led to the development of English theatrical dancing, and its divorce from the social dances which had spawned it. Madame Marie Camargo, the first dancer to wear short skirts on the stage—and get away with it, as she was received "in the best and strictest set of Paris"—performed all of the French dances then current when she made her debut in London in the eighteenth century. Her rival, Mademoiselle Sallé, who claimed friendship with philosophers of the caliber of Locke and Voltaire, came to England in 1734 when Handel was musical director of the Queen's Theater. She was so popular that people actually fought to get in, and when she appeared she was showered with banknotes and coins. But although English theatrical dancing soon developed its own stars, it was still to France that they looked for a lead.

The Minuet

As proof of the importance of music in dictating the forms of dance, the minuet was set as part of a suite by Lully, and Louis XIV then hallowed it by dancing it in public. Depending on which authorities you believe, the name comes from *pas menu*, meaning "small step," or *branle à mener de Poitou*, *mener* meaning "to lead" in reference to the man leading the lady (Poitou was the place in which this particular *branle* was danced.) Certainly the form of the dance was an old one, but it had to become ornate and dignified before the French court would consider dancing it. (Because things were slow and stately does not mean they lacked vigor. Anyone who has seen the splendors of Versailles, and can imagine the gorgeously costumed courtiers performing a graceful, gliding dance there, will realize that you could get just as much pleasure out of a slow courtly dance as you could out of faster rhythms, which would not have been suited to baroque architecture and fashions.)

French courtiers who had mastered the courante went on to spend three months learning the minuet, of which there were several varieties, though the Academy of Dance prescribed one form for the ballroom which lasted throughout the eighteenth century. It was a couple dance in three-four time—slow, quick, quick, slow. Its four steps consisted of leading the lady into the dance; performing a Z-pattern (which had been revised by one of the royal dancing masters from an S-pattern); a turn during which the couples circled each other holding first the right hand and then the left; and finally a turn in which the man leads his partner with both hands. As Belinda Quirey says, it was more of a ritual performance than a dance, and those courtiers who could not do it properly were looked upon as failures. Nevertheless, it outlasted all its contemporaries and enjoyed a strong following for over 150

The minuet in full stately swing.

years at all important court balls. Perhaps one reason for this was the amount of time spent in learning its intricate figures, an investment which the upper classes were loath to squander. It had a revival in the nineteenth century, at a time when, with Napoleon defeated, the tastes of the upper orders turned back to the baroque. But the ornamentation they then loaded onto the dance had little to do with the original.

Country Dances

From the England of the late sixteenth century we have many references to various dances popular with country people. That we know about them at all is due to the interest of Elizabeth, herself an enthusiastic dancer, as was her father, Henry VIII. The queen was wont to travel around the country, partly in order to save money by living off her richer subjects, partly in order to show herself as mistress of the realm. Whether she encouraged country dancing for political motives—to assert the "Englishness" of a nation beset by foreign threats—or simply because she enjoyed it, we cannot be sure. But under her patronage country dance got taken

up by the court, where it later assumed the formality and restraint that marked it off clearly from its origins. Even in court, however, the boisterousness of a Sellenger's Round burst through the music.

Sellenger's Round is a carol whose name is a corruption of the St. Leger Round. We know its steps, and those of other country dances, from a collection by John Playford called *The English Dancing Master*. This was first published in 1650 and, as *The Dancing Master*, had an immense influence and popularity, especially in the United States. (It went through seven editions before its author's death, and reached seventeen by 1728.) Playford described Sellenger's Round thus: "the dancers take hands, go round twice and back again; then all set, turn, and repeat; then lead all forward and back, and repeat; two singles and back, set and turn single, and repeat; sides all and repeat; arms all and repeat; danced as often in circles as in parallel lines."

Country dances were rounds and line dances with complicated figures performed by several sets of couples, who exchanged positions. The dances had wonderful names: "Rogero," "Basilino," "Turkey Loney," "All the Flowers of the Broom," "Pepper

Seventeenth-century beaux indulge in a dance on the village green.

99

is Black," "Greensleeves," "Peggy Ramsey," and "Sir Roger de Coverley," which as the Virginia reel survives today. A country dance entertainment might conclude with Joan Sanderson, or the cushion dance (which was also popular, in more stately fashion, in court, and which was danced in the United States up to the turn of the eighteenth century). This was begun by either a man or a woman taking a cushion in his hand and dancing to the end of the room, where he or she stopped and sang, "This dance it will no further go." The musician replied, "I pray you, good Sir, why say you so?" "Because Joan Sanderson will not come to." "She must come to whether she will or not," replied the musician, and then the dancer laid the cushion before a girl; she knelt and he kissed her, singing "Welcome Joan Sanderson." Then she got up, picked up the cushion, and they both danced and sang, "Prinkum, prankum is a fine dance." She then took the cushion and repeated the man's actions.

Villagers perform a country dance in the late sixteenth century.

Kissing was an important part of English dance. The Puritan pamphleteer Philip Stubbes wrote in his *Anatomie of Abuses* (1583), "For what clipping, what culling, what kissing and bussing, what

smooching and slavering one of another, what filthie groping and uncleane handling is not practised in those dancings?'' But the country dances that have come down to us were still for a group rather than for a couple. Perhaps this was to reinforce the country people's sense of community, unlike at court, where it was every man for himself.

One exception to the country dances for groups was the jig, of whose origins we know little, except that it was an opportunity for a country dancer not only to whirl about at high speed on his own, but also with a girl. The sociologist Frances Rust found an example of this in a seventeenth-century ballad which includes the lines "Priscilla did dance a jig with Tom/ which made her buttocks quake like a Custard." Although the jig has since become associated with Scotland and Ireland, it seems it was a pretty general solo country dance in the sixteenth century, a forerunner of the galliard. Frenchified as the *gigue*, it was toned down to become part of the courtly suite, but it also became a stage dance, often used to conclude a play.

A boisterous Sir Roger de Coverley of the eighteenth century.

Under the Tudors country dancing was chiefly an outdoor

pursuit, but as the upper classes began to spend more on their houses, they adapted the style of their dances—made respectable by royal approval—to the shape of their rooms. Thus there were fewer round dances, and more squares and "longwayes" for four, eight, or "as many as will." The names of many of these dances reflect local traditions—the "London Gentlewoman," the "Stanes (or Staines) Morris"—while personalities and places of the time were also immortalized. One example was "Kemp's Jigge," named after William Kemp, a comic actor who appeared with Shakespeare and in many of his plays, but who was more celebrated for the jigs with which he concluded his performances, and for his "Nine Daies Wonder" when he danced the morris all the way from London to Norwich (it actually took him twenty-three days, of which only nine were spent dancing).

Some of the dances detailed by Playford were undoubtedly genuine survivals from previous generations, but many were obviously the inventions of his fellow dancing masters, since they commemorated events and places strictly of his own time. Their long life must largely be due to Playford printing them with easily followed instructions, rather than the complicated stenochoreographic code favored by the French masters. The popularity of country dances today surely has something to do with the mania for rustic simplicity that occasionally seizes the most hardened sophisticates. Even Charles II of England, for example, had a favorite country dance called "Cuckolds-all-a-Row."

William Kemp in the costume of a morris dancer.

The form of the country dance involved honoring your partner with a bow or curtsy, performing a figure together, then exchanging positions with another couple. Each dance provided variations

on these basic themes, and the fun was provided by the need for a large number of people to perform intricate maneuvers without missing a beat. Many of these dances, and some newer ones, are taught and performed today. Then, as now, they were full-blooded affairs requiring strenuous efforts from both sexes. This would explain their popularity in the houses of the country gentry; even when performed more decorously at court, they had a certain vigor that contrasted well with the stateliness of the fashionable French dances. They remained popular throughout the eighteenth century, their form was easily adapted to the rectangular rooms that became the special haunt of the upper classes, and no grand ball of the nineteenth or even the twentieth century was complete without at least one country dance.

The Contredanse

Toward the end of Louis XIV's reign, when there was little amusement to be had at a court where everyone was watched by royal spies, where protocol had become empty and oppressive, and where even the lotteries were rigged, some dancing teachers brought from London the English country dances, which gave French dancing a much-needed breath of fresh air. In Paris and Versailles they were called contredanses, which can be interpreted either as a transliteration from the English, or as a word used to describe the form they took—sets of couples dancing counter, or opposite, to one another, instead of facing His Majesty. The contredanses were square dances. As such they were reexported back to England, and proved enduringly popular in the United States. Even the Germans took them on as the *contredanses à l'Allemagne*. French preeminence in setting the tone of fashion by no means expired with the Sun King, but with his passing his subjects' unquestioning acceptance of the absolutism of the monarchy came under increasing strain, as was the case in other parts of western Europe and the United States.

THE BALLROOM ERA

The Historical Background
The United States and Europe

THE FIRST FAMILIES of Virginia were Cavaliers fleeing debt rather than religious persecution. Their English manners and fashions were little modified by the climate, and those who made money from their tobacco plantations sent their sons, and less often their daughters, back to England to be educated. Their society was organized on English class lines, with the bigger landowners acting the part of country squires. Since large distances separated each estate, a visit by neighbors was an occasion for a party, at which eating, drinking, and dancing were the chief pursuits. Music was provided by the girls of the family, or by servants and slaves. As dancing was considered to be a proper accomplishment for gentlemen, dancing masters were soon in demand, and by the end of the seventeenth century Virginia was well stocked with them.

The New England colonies, by contrast, were founded by Puritans seeking freedom of worship, and here dancing, if it was not employed to glorify God, was frowned upon. Dancing schools were outlawed wherever possible by the New England theocrats, and the fashionable court dances like the allemande or the minuet could only be learned surreptitiously. Since the Bible encouraged dancing on appropriate occasions, it was permitted, for example, at Connecticut ordinations. Yet despite solemn utterances against "lascivious dancing to wanton ditties with amorous gestures and wanton dalliances," the social dance would not go away. "Samuel Eaton and Goodwife Halle, of the towne of Duxburrow," were "Released with admonition" for mixed dancing by the court of New Plymouth in 1651, while in Boston in 1685 a dancing teacher named Francis Stepney not only set up a school for mixed dancing, but claimed that through it he could teach more about divinity than the local preachers—for which blasphemy he was fined one hundred pounds. He compounded the felony, and satisfied the authorities that dancing teachers were of very low character, by fleeing the colony without paying his fine. Nevertheless, by 1700 the New England "People of Quality," according to dance historian Joseph E. Marks III, began to give balls, and would not be dissuaded from the practice. Some ministers actually sanction-

ed dancing schools run by "Grave Persons" who taught "Decency of Behaviour," and Playford's *The Dancing Master* proved enduringly popular, with its simple instructions for country dances, which were not regarded as "mixed" and which taught reverence for the opposite sex.

A ball given by Martha Washington, whose husband was an enthusiastic dancer.

Although the *Boston Newsletter* objected that the new generation cried out for "Musick, Balls and Assemblies like Children for their Bells and Rattles," Dr. Alexander Hamilton noted in 1744 of Boston that "assemblies of the gayer sort are frequent here; the gentlemen and ladys meeting almost every week att consorts of musick and balls. I was present att 2 or 3 such and saw as fine a ring of ladys, as good dancing, and heard musick as elegant as I had been witness to any where. . . . I saw not one prude while I was here." In the New England countryside, dancing was often disguised as "games of romps and forfeits" in which kissing played a large part. But high society saw no need to be so devious: under the Anglican governors of Massachusetts state balls and private junkets were as popular for the snobbish elaborateness of their etiquette as they were for the actual dances, which were those of the European courts. There were even rival gatherings for those who, before the Revolution, supported the king, and those who participated in the "Liberty Assembly."

John Quincy Adams took part in marathon dance sessions at Newburyport, where he was studying law, and admitted in his diary that he had passed a whole afternoon "in rigging for the ball." George Washington was a Virginian with an insatiable appetite for dancing. He once danced for three hours nonstop with

Mrs. Nathanael Greene, a feat General Greene laconically described as "a little frisk," and on another occasion he shocked those around him by dancing with a mechanic's daughter. Thomas Jefferson planned a schedule for his daughter in which she was to spend three hours, every other morning, in dancing. Yet despite this leadership, the Continental Congress was prevailed upon by the New England delegates to adopt, on October 12, 1778, resolutions desiring the states to restrict theater, horse racing, gaming, and "such other diversions as are productive of idleness, dissipation, and a general depravity of principles and manners." That meant dancing too.

OPPOSITE: *An eighteenth-century assembly ball.*

The English court under the Hanoverians inaugurated the celebrations known as "The King's Birthnight Ball." These featured the court dances of the preceding century, including country dances and the minuet. But the royal dancing master would also compose a new dance for the occasion, which was printed in the stenochoreographic notation invented by Louis XIV's dancing masters, and offered for sale to the public. It was a wonderful thing for dancing schools, since anyone of fashion simply had to learn the new dance, which consisted of a different arrangement of steps to a familiar rhythm—though a mistake in performance could be fatal to the chances of a social aspirant.

In the United States, before the Revolution, the king's birthday was celebrated in similar manner. There was tremendous social

A birthnight ball in Virginia.

A country dance in Oregon in the early nineteenth century.

cachet in being invited to the governor's ball, from which all beneath a certain social standing—that is, those engaged in trade —were excluded. After the Revolution, Washington's birthday was also celebrated with a ball, and inauguration balls were soon a feature of the new republic.

In England, the birthnight balls came to an end when George III became too ill to attend. There arose centers of fashion apart from the English court, perhaps because the aristocracy tended to look down on their German sovereigns, who anyway made little attempt to dictate the tone of English society. The true dictator of English fashion, at least for the first half of the eighteenth century, was Richard "Beau" Nash, who assumed the direction of etiquette in the Assembly Rooms at Bath in 1704.

Gentlemen who attended his gatherings were forbidden to wear top boots or use coarse language, and they had to lay aside their swords when entering the Assembly Rooms. Balls began at 6:00 P.M. sharp, and ended equally promptly at 11:00 P.M., even if a dance was in progress. The program opened with a minuet danced by the highest-ranking couple present—snobbery was the cement that held the whole system together. After two hours of court dances, there were country dances, also opened by those with the top titles. (These dances were not performed in a square pattern, but in the longways progressive formation that suited the rectangular shape of the room. Couples faced each other in lines, and took it in turn to move to the top position.) At 9:00 there was an interlude for tea, after which country dancing occupied the rest of the evening. Perhaps so rigid a pattern was deemed necessary to impose some order on the miscellaneous collection of people who could afford to "take the waters" at Bath. To accept so severe a discipline showed that fashion, at least, was proof against the skepticism that characterized the age of reason.

OPPOSITE:
Beau Nash, whose word was law in the Bath Assembly Rooms.

The second half of the eighteenth century saw the opening of several assembly rooms in central London where fashionable people could dance and gossip. There were already two mighty palaces of public amusement, the Pleasure Gardens of Vauxhall and of Ranelagh in Chelsea, of which Dr. Johnson said, "it gave an expansion and gay sensation to my mind, such as I never experienced anywhere else." But these were not discriminating in their clientele: anyone who could afford it could wander around listening to the music, take tea or supper in the boxes around the amphitheater, or a turn around the dance floor. The new assembly rooms were a good deal more select: foremost among them was Almack's in King Street, St. James's.

When Mr. Almack first opened his three new rooms in 1765, they were in such an unfinished state that the ceilings were still dripping. Nevertheless, society flocked there, and for a ten guinea subscription (about $60) you could enjoy a ball and a supper once a week for twelve weeks. But admission was strictly limited to those approved by a council, whose most notorious head was Lady Jersey. In her day you could only get in with a voucher awarded by her personally or by one of her copatronesses. As each lady was permitted to bestow only a limited number of tickets, these became highly prized possessions. It was said that of the three hundred guards officers knocking about London only half a dozen ever

Dancing in the Assembly Rooms in Bath, 1798.

succeeded in getting into Almack's; so choosey was Lady Jersey that three-fourths of the nobility were reputedly excluded. Naturally, "sons of commerce" were never permitted entrance, and the rules of the house were so strictly enforced that the duke of Wellington himself was twice kept out, once for arriving a few minutes after midnight, and once for wearing trousers instead of knee breeches.

Despite the proclaimed egalitarianism of the American patriots, the snobbery that lay like a crust around all "civilized" societies remained firmly in force. There was a Boston Almack's run by an Italian dancing master for the benefit of some hundred families whose heads were subscribers. The City Assembly of Philadelphia existed from 1748 until the Revolution, and resumed functioning in 1781 with "the tory ladies . . . publicly excluded," but with a set of regulations as elaborate as any devised by Lady Jersey. At a subscription price of three pounds fifteen shillings (nearly $15) for a session every two weeks, the dancers were perforce select. According to Chastellux's *Travels in North-America*, in the last decade of the eighteenth century the assembly held its functions in Oeller's Hotel, which boasted a ballroom sixty feet long, wall-papered in the latest French fashion, with a music gallery at one end and the assembly's rules framed at the other. That there were American dictators of fashion to rival Beau Nash is shown by an

Jubilee ball and masquerade at Ranelagh, 1749.

Lady Jersey, the dictator of Almack's.

BELOW: *Caricature by Cruikshank of a quadrille at Almack's.*

incident at a Philadelphia assembly in 1781, quoted by Mr. Marks: "'Come, miss, have a care what you are doing,' shouted the Master of Ceremonies to a damsel who was permitting a bit of gossip to interrupt her turn in a contradance. 'Do you think you are here for your own pleasure?'"

At the end of the eighteenth century, the chief items in the assembly's program were the minuet (now diminishing in popularity), the cotillon (or cotillion, as it was more usually spelled in the United States), the allemande, and the contredanse (the fashionable folk preferred the French spelling). Country people, however, enjoyed themselves with less restraint at bees, frolics, or barn dances at which scattered homesteaders danced to the strains of the "simple negro fiddle," as the eighteenth-century observer St. John de Crevecoeur put it. Nevertheless, the dance traditions of the preceding generation held uninterrupted sway—until the rude incursion of the waltz in the nineteenth century.

The French revolution may have heralded the end of an era, but the French style in clothes and manners—without, of course, the abhorrent equality professed by the sansculottes—continued to dominate Europe and the United States. Napoleon destroyed the hopes of radicals the world over, but he gave France a national pride and reputation which she had not known since the death of the Sun King, and this in turn gave her preeminence in fashionable matters another lease of life. Napoleon's conquests in the name of "the rights of man," and the alliance of forces that combined to undo them, gave the West a new unity which drew the cultures, as well as the political attitudes, of each nation closer together. Russia was still a byword for backwardness, and the East, with the Turkish Empire undergoing its final spasms, seemed ripe only for plunder. Thus, at the very beginning of the nineteenth century, the Western world gained a cohesive identity it still possesses.

Of course the revolution, and the fighting necessary to defeat it, had an effect, at least on the young. There are few connec-

A ball at Almack's in 1815. The figure in the foreground on the left is the notorious dandy Beau Brummel.

tions between a generation's political beliefs and the dances it enjoys, but there is one fact that has been little noted. Following the conclusion of a general war, a war involving the cream of society as well as its working men, there appears a craze for speed among the young and fashionable. Perhaps this has a lot to do with the anticlimax and the depression that inevitably follow the end of hostilities. A man who has risked his life will find it hard to return to a society where his elders, who sent him out to fight in the first place, behave in their old ponderous way, as if nothing had happened. In his pleasures, therefore, such a man will look for release, for excitement, for something that will use up the adrenalin that had so recently been primed by the sound of gunfire. This, I think, is at least a partial explanation of why dancing in Europe after Waterloo was a much more frenzied occupation than it had been when the minuet had ruled supreme.

There is little sign that the radical ideals of 1789 had much direct effect on the dance, save for the carmagnole, a circle dance performed around the guillotine and the tree of liberty. It took at least two generations before the politicians of Europe became converted to the democratic ideals their predecessors claimed to have defeated. But, meanwhile, the young insisted on amusing themselves at a new pace, as shocking to their elders—and to several of their own generation—as the notions of liberty, equality, and fraternity.

Styles in dress and manners have as important an effect on dance as does music. The hooped skirts and piled-up hairstyles that made it necessary to move with such caution—which was fine for the minuet and the statelier contredanses—gave way to the softer, more clinging dresses of the French Empire style. Wigs, in both men and women, were progressively abandoned in favor of natural hair (which continued, of course, to receive all sorts of unnatural curls and colors from hairdressers). Trousers for men, worn good and roomy by the French soldiers, came gradually to replace knee breeches. Captain Gronow reported that when he attended a ball in Paris in 1816, breeches were only worn by "old fogies," but when he appeared in trousers at a London ball, the prince regent himself considered this an insult to his presence. Nevertheless, within a year the prince was sporting trousers wherever he went.

Though breeches continued to be a part of official court dress (and still appear there to this day), the new fashions certainly allowed greater freedom on the dance floor. The floor itself was becoming a lot more polished, which meant that turns and gliding steps could be performed with a great deal more show. It also meant that footwear became lighter and less precarious, to safeguard the floor surface as well as to permit greater agility. Finally, music underwent a change that ultimately made itself felt in the dance: classicism gave way to romanticism, the myths of Greece and Rome were replaced as inspirational themes by the folklore of each national tradition, and new tunes, new harmonies, and new rhythms finally cracked the mold of the old baroque style.

Dressed to kill: the dandy caricatured in 1816.

Fashionable Americans perform a country dance in the mid-nineteenth century.

This did not happen without a stiff fight being put up by the guardians of the old order. They employed that most insidious weapon, the blunderbuss of morality, and from Frankfurt to Philadelphia there poured a steady stream of denunciations of the waltz and all that it portended. A New York commentator complained in 1849 that the critics of dancing wrote of it "as if it were the only really *deadly* sin in the whole category, worse than Perjury, and scarcely equalled in its enormity by malicious Homicide." The god of profit was replacing that of the Bible as the chief totem in American life, but the nineteenth century saw several religious revivals, culminating in the Great Awakening that followed the economic crash of 1857. Dancing was in the front line of sins attacked by the preachers, because of its "late hours, extravagance of dress, and exposure of health." Although a New England dance fan complained that the art had been "banished . . . more by half-expressed doubts and misgivings as to the propriety of it, and by innuendoes and ominous shakes of the head . . . than by any positive objections that have been raised," such objections continued to be raised until the end of the century in the United States, and indeed are still applied today.

Yet dancing masters still enjoyed good business in the New World as well as the Old. The French Revolution sent a large number of dispossessed and impoverished aristocrats across the

Atlantic, and many of them found employment teaching courtly manners and dancing, being welcomed both as enemies of that old tyrant England, and as representatives of the ancient régime still admired in the republican United States. They made of Charleston, South Carolina, for instance, a social center in which the ballrooms exuded the genuine flavor of old-fashioned European elegance. Mr. Marks quotes the *American Journal of Education* for 1830 saying that though many parents complained at spending three dollars every three months for instruction in the elementary branches of education, they did not mind paying three times as much for dancing lessons. Doubtless they felt their children had need of dance-floor training. Mrs. John Farrar, author of *The Young Lady's Friend* (published in Boston in 1838), complained, "Some girls have a trick of jiggling their bodies (I am obliged to coin a word to describe it); they shake all over, as if they were hung on spiral wires, like geese in a Dutch toy shop; than which, nothing can be more ungraceful, or unmeaning. It robs a lady of all dignity, and makes her appear trifling and insignificant. Some do it only on entering a room, others do it every time they are introduced to anybody, and whenever they begin to talk to anyone. It must have originated in embarrassment, and a desire to do something without knowing exactly what; and being adopted by some popular belle, it became, at one time, a fashion in New York, and spread thence to other cities."

New York took an early lead in providing glamorous social amusements in which dancing was a principal feature. The assemblies of the eighteenth century were replaced by glittering balls: the annual Firemen's Ball had become a regular event by

Grandfather teaches the young the jig: a Thanksgiving dance, 1858.

OPPOSITE, ABOVE:
*The model yacht club
holds its annual ball
in 1859.*
OPPOSITE, BELOW:
*The ball given for the
Prince of Wales at the
Academy of Music in
Boston.*

1830, and was attended by some 2,700 of the city's beautiful
people. There were balls held by groups as diverse as the Bachelors
and the Horticultural Society, and those given to honor visits by
Charles Dickens and the Prince of Wales were lavish affairs talked
about for years afterward. By the middle of the century, a contemporary commentator, Thomas I. Nichols, could say, "If there
is anything New Yorkers are more given to than making money, it
is dancing. . . . The whole city is made up of clubs and societies,
each of which has its balls."

Books and articles enthusing about the dance and describing
the latest steps and fashions being followed in London, Paris,
Washington, and even West Point (where dance became an
official course in 1823) soon equaled the volume of antidance
literature. It became respectable, in all but the most religious
circles, to regard dancing as the best form of indoor exercise, and
one doctor pointed out to a convention of his colleagues that "ten
thousand people injure themselves by the abuse of eating, for one
who does so by that of dancing." But much of the tolerance
extended to the art evaporated when first the waltz, and then the
polka, made their sensational entries onto the social scene. These
dances were shocking because of their speed, their rhythm, and,
above all, because of the close hold between the partners as they
whirled around the floor. Even the dance teachers joined in the
criticism, since the new round dances had none of the formality of
either steps or deportment that characterized the old—and they
could be learned by watching instead of through hours of expensive instruction.

Small wonder that the dancing masters made haste to repair the
damage by doing all they could to codify the steps of the new
dances so that there would be a "right" and a "wrong" way of
performing them. Allen Dodworth, one of the most celebrated

*West Point cadets
enliven a hop in 1859.*

dancing teachers in the United States, published toward the end of his long career a book called *Dancing and Its Relation to Education and Social Life* (1885), in which, among much valuable observation and advice, he codified five basic positions for good dancing, which bear a remarkable resemblance to his Renaissance predecessors Domenico de Piacenza and Antonio Cornazano. "The upper part of the body should be slightly inclined forward, the hips backward —the forward inclination just enough to cause a tendency in the heels to rise from the floor; the head erect, legs straight, arms hanging at sides, elbows very slightly turned outward, so that the arms will present curved lines to the front." This position, he added, "was at one time exaggerated into what was known as 'the Grecian Bend'; the phrase had reference to the fact that in all Grecian statuary, where gracefulness is intended, this beautiful curved line is always present. This should be termed the normal attitude, which should be maintained at all times."

Dodworth's prestige and insistence on decorum, propriety, and good taste ensured that the newer dances were made respectable for American society, just as the ponderous etiquette of Queen Victoria's court tamed the polonaise and the lancers. The queen's widowhood had as depressing an effect on social dance as did the financial crash of 1857 in the United States, though the recovery and growth of the economy in both Europe and the United States led to a kind of top-heavy ostentation that showed itself in every aspect of fashion. The Dodworth Dancing Academy was so exclusive that three letters of introduction were required, and socially ambitious mothers formed their own exclusive dancing classes, managed by patronesses as formidable as any Almack's could have boasted. Jazz, and the new dances it spawned, filled these worthies with the same horror that the waltz had aroused in their predecessors.

The dance teachers began forming themselves into protective

LEFT: *The right way to dance, according to Allen Dodworth, contrasted with* (CENTER) *the wrong way and* (RIGHT) *the vulgar way.*

OPPOSITE: *President Grant's White House ball, 1873.*

121

The Waldorf Astoria ballroom transformed into a replica of Versailles for the Bradley Martin Ball, February 1897.

professional associations, in England and in the United States, from the 1870s on. Their great success was in establishing a ballroom style that was formal, elegant, polished, and which is still the basis of competition dancing. Their failing was that, in taking the spontaneity out of the round dances that had revolutionized their era, they were unable to appreciate the new revolution in music and dance ushered in toward the end of the century by that most spontaneous, and most American, of forms—ragtime.

THE DANCES

The Waltz

Germany was the home of the waltz. Wooing dances featuring giddy turns and a close embrace were a part of German tradition, while everywhere else people were performing the courtly dances that involved at most a light clasping of the hands. (The only European court dance that required a close embrace was *la volta*, but that was more a show of agility than a bodily response to a strong beat.) The German *Ländler* had a very powerful rhythm which incited the dancers to faster and wilder turns; the *Weller* was of a similar nature, and likewise the *Walzer*, which first crops up as a name in the middle of the eighteenth century. The word *Walzen* is derived from the Latin word *volvere*, meaning "revolving," but for a long time such turning dances were simply known as *Deutsche* ("German"). Thus Mozart, writing from Prague in 1787, noted with pleasure that the music from his *Figaro* was used for "all kinds of Contres (Contredanses) and Teutsche," though we know from Goethe that in the middle of the century such dances were better known among the country people than the smart folk of the town, who found the steps difficult.

Yet the waltz, with its three-four rhythm and terrific first beat, slowly conquered the whole of German society. It had its roots in folk dancing, which was much in its favor at a time when the importance of folklore was becoming increasingly recognized.

The waltz performed with Parisian precision.

The "lewd grasp" that Byron objected to.

More important, it had a swing that demanded a new style of dancing, a close hold (to maintain balance), and a breathless turn of speed that was itself intoxicating. Naturally, the pleasure it gave to the couples who lost themselves in each other's arms, who pressed breast against chest and who, as the music whirled on, embraced each other more and more tightly, itself attracted strong criticism. In parts of Germany and Switzerland, the waltz was banned altogether. A German book proving that "the waltz is a main source of the weakness of body and mind of our generation" proved popular as late as 1799. Dancing teachers were against it, partly because when people got carried away they tended to forget all they had been taught, and partly because the teachers belonged to a generation reared on distance and ceremony. But that did not stop the dance's progress.

Part of the loot of Napoleon's invasion of the German lands was the waltz, which returned to Paris with his soldiers. From there it crossed to London; the fact that the two countries were at war was no barrier to fashion. Captain Gronow recollected that the waltz arrived around 1814, "but there were comparatively few who at first ventured to whirl round the *salon* of Almack's; in course of time Lord Palmerston might, however, have been seen describing an infinite number of circles with Madame de Lieven. Baron de Neumann was frequently seen perpetually turning with the Princess Esterhazy; and, in course of time, the waltzing mania, having turned the heads of society generally, descended to their feet, and the waltz was practiced in the morning in certain noble mansions in London with unparalleled assiduity."

A reviewer of Byron's poem *Childe Harold's Pilgrimage* wrote, "language can hardly exaggerate the folly that prevailed in 1812, when waltzing and Lord Byron came into fashion." Byron himself displayed an extraordinary hostility to the dance. He objected to the "lewd grasp and lawless contact warm," especially between strangers; to the foreign origins of the dance and its adoption by the lower classes; and to the fact that "thin clad daughters" leaping around the floor would not "leave much mystery for the nupital night." But then he also objected to mixed bathing.

When the waltz was included in the program of a ball given in the summer of 1816 by the prince regent, *The Times*, in the magisterial style that earned it the nickname of "The Thunderer," had this to say:

> We remarked with pain that the indecent foreign dance called the "waltz" was introduced (we believe for the first time) at the English Court on Friday last. This is a circumstance which ought not to be passed over in silence. National morals depend on national habits: and it is quite sufficient to cast one's eyes on the voluptuous intertwining of the limbs, and close compressure of the bodies, in their dance, to see that it is indeed far removed from the modest reserve which has hitherto been considered distinctive of English females. So long as this obscene display was confined to prostitutes and adultresses we did not think it deserving of notice; but now that it is attempted to be forced upon the respectable classes of society by the evil example of their superiors, we feel it a duty to warn every parent against exposing his daughter to so fatal a contagion. . . . We owe a due reference to superiors in rank, but we owe a higher duty to morality. We know not how it has happened (probably by the recommendation of some worthless and ignorant French dancing master) that so indecent a dance has now for the first time been exhibited at the English Court; but the novelty is one deserving of severe reprobation, and we trust it will never again be tolerated in any moral English society.

In reply, the dancing master Thomas Wilson defended the dance as being "a promoter of vigorous health and producive of an hilarity of spirits . . . totally destitute of the complained of attitudes and movements used in warmer and lighter climates . . . *not* an enemy to true morals and endangering true virtue." Not for the first time *The Times* was mounted on the wrong high horse.

The waltz reached the United States around the turn of the century. Senator John Tyler, who as President Tyler held dances twice a month at the White House, and whose reputed "folly and dissipation" turned the presidential mansion "into a great ballroom," first saw the waltz in 1827. He told his daughter of a "dance which you have never seen, and which I do not desire to see you dance. It is rather vulgar I think." Joseph Marks also quotes *The Gentleman and Lady's Book of Politeness*, a work translated from the French that went through no less than fifteen editions between 1833 and 1872: "The waltz is a dance of quite too loose a character, and unmarried ladies should refrain from it

THE BOZ WALTZES,

As performed by
DODWORTH'S BAND,
At the grand Festival

Park Theatre.

FLEETWOOD'S   ILLUMINATED   LITHOGRAPHY.

respectfully dedicated to
CHAS. DICKENS, ESQ.
composed by

JOS. LANNER.

Pr 50 cts. nett.

in public and private; very young married ladies, however, may be allowed to waltz in private balls, if it is very seldom and with persons of their acquaintance. It is indispensable for them to acquit themselves with dignity and decency." American religious leaders refused to accept the "closed couple" position required by the waltz until the century was well advanced. Even so, Allen Dodworth wrote in 1885 of the waltz as "the culmination of modern society dancing, the dance which has for fifty years resisted every kind of attack, and is today the most popular known." He merely demanded that the gentleman wait until the dance had begun before encircling the lady's waist, and that he was never to put his bare hand on that portion of her anatomy. Should he lack gloves, the least he could do was to hold a handkerchief in his hand.

OPPOSITE: *The waltz performed in New York at a ball in honor of Charles Dickens.*

The European waltz was scarcely a lewd affair. Indeed, it was more reminiscent of a ballet than of anything indecent. The French danced it on tiptoe, in the classical mode, while the Viennese, who used more speed, danced it on the flat foot, gliding and turning around the room while throwing head and body from one side to the other. Such was the Viennese craze for speed that for a time a form of waltzing known as the *Langaus* became the rage. To quote a contemporary description, "the Mondschein-Saal made an immortal name for itself by the mortality among the younger people who visited it, and there danced nothing but the *Langaus*. At that time it was the fashion to be a dashing dancer, and the man had to waltz his partner from one end of the hall to the other with the greatest possible speed. If one round of the immense hall had been considered sufficient, one might perhaps have allowed this bacchantic dance to pass. But the circle had to be made six to eight times at a breathless speed and without pause. Each couple tried to outdo each other, and it was no rare thing for an apoplexy of the lungs to put an end to the madness. Such frightful intermezzi finally made the police forbid the *Langaus*." (From Mosco Carner's *The Waltz*.) But it was also in Vienna that the composers most associated with the waltz, Josef Lanner and the Strausses, father and son, lived and worked.

The Vienna Woods, which surrounded the city in the early nineteenth century, were famous for their taverns and inns. Each of these would have a small dance floor for the pleasure of their customers, and the benefit of their digestion. Traveling bands of three or four players—a couple of violinists, or a fiddler and a wind player or guitarist, with someone on the bass (the sort of dance combination that lasted until the age of electronic amplifiers)—would stop off the boats that plied the Danube and make music during meals and afterward. In the city itself, the demand for "table music" was sufficiently great to support several permanent dance bands, and it was in one of these, led by Michael Pamer, that Lanner was employed as a violinist and Johann Strauss the elder as a viola player. Pamer, in common with other bandleaders, composed several pieces for his players to perform. Formal training was not so important as knowing what the public wanted.

Josef Lanner was gifted in this direction, for when he was seventeen he left Pamer to form his own band, consisting of himself and two brothers who played violin and guitar. Soon Strauss joined them with his viola, and they became a quintet with the addition of a cellist. Obviously Lanner knew what he was doing, for the quintet grew into a string orchestra—which boasted of being the first to play in the open air—and then into a full-blown concert orchestra, with percussion, wind players, and all. So popular did it prove that Lanner divided it in two, with Strauss in charge of the second team. Like most bandleaders, Lanner was not always easy to work with, and Strauss naturally resented his boss pinching his tunes and issuing them as Lanner's own. In 1825, therefore, Strauss formed his own group, which rapidly became as famous as Lanner's. The new waltzes that poured forth from each orchestra excited the Viennese to the same extent as modern pop fans are excited. Each group had its fanatics, and every new composition was greeted with an enthusiasm and a seriousness that quite eclipsed the attention given to Mozart and Beethoven. Chopin complained that "their waltzes obscure everything," but Wagner was entranced by Strauss, and his admiration was later repaid by Johann the younger, who endorsed the principles of the new romanticism and had his orchestra play Wagner when the musical establishment refused to touch him.

Strauss the elder took his band on several international tours, and such was his fame that he was engaged to play at Almack's during Queen Victoria's coronation year (1838). Since supply of new waltzes could scarcely keep up with demand, he borrowed freely from other composers, a common practice at the time. Thus, as well as "waltzifying" Mozart, Meyerbeer, and Beethoven, Strauss also included "Rule Britannia" and the national anthem in his "Victoria Waltz" to honor the new queen. The practice of giving names to waltzes so that the public would remember which one to ask for started around this time.

Strauss was heavily opposed to his three sons following in his footsteps, partly because he wanted them to build a more "respectable" career on the foundations he had laid, and partly because he wanted no rivalry within his own family—of that he had enough outside. But, although Johann the younger worked in a bank for a while, and Josef studied engineering (earning some renown as an inventor), all three in the end ignored their father's wishes. The youngest, Eduard, finished by taking over his father's baton, while his brothers set out to compose waltzes of their own. Between Johann and Josef there was a certain competitiveness, but that was nothing compared to the rivalry between Johann and his father. When he was nineteen, the younger Johann conducted his first concert despite everything the elder Johann could do to stop him. The program, which included many of the younger Johann's own compositions, was extremely well received, and the son proceeded to take to new heights the waltz form his father had pioneered. The younger Johann represented a new generation of assured and sophisticated Viennese, whose stylishness contrasted

Waltzers and Waltzing

The Mall
Kensington

My dear Genty

You say that as you know I go out a good deal you would like me to give you my opinion on this subject of 'Waltzers & Waltzing'

Well:— I have "danced" with a short man who held me out at arm's length and walked with me

With a tall man who squeezed me up against his waistcoat and ambled with me

With a big man who walked over me

With a little one who walked under me

With a conversational one who trotted about laughing at his own weak witticisms

With a dignified one who strolled about with me in forbidding silence

With an energetic one who strode about knocking me against the other dancers.

With an even more energetic one who pranced all round me treading on my toes

But Jack's the only man who ever "waltzed" with me

Do you Reverse? Waltz

BY
PAUL LINCKE.

COPYRIGHT.

THE FREDERICK HARRIS COMPANY
89, Newman Street, Oxford Street

PRICE 2/- NET.
60 ¢.

Small Orchestra.... 9d 25 ¢
Full Orchestra.... 1/- 30 ¢
Brass Band.... 3/- $1.50.

strongly with the small-town attitudes of the older generation. Right up until his death in 1849, the older Johann was never completely reconciled with his son, who nevertheless so adorned the dance that he was accorded the title of "Waltz King."

OPPOSITE: *The Edwardian waltz.*

In England and North America the original *valse à trois temps* with its ONE-two-three flashing footwork, gave way in popularity to the simpler *valse à deux temps*, with a step-together-step that was a good deal less demanding on the average dancer. Those who wanted to demonstrate their skill and breeding on the dance floor continued to favor the *valse à trois temps*, which the dance teachers have maintained as the basis of the modern ballroom waltz. The simpler version was so frowned on by "real" waltzers that, in North America at least, it was given the name "Ignoramus Waltz," to be danced by those unable to perform the genuine article. Such insults did nothing to stop the popularity of the *valse à deux temps*, which had its greatest flowering in the Boston, or hesitation waltz. This featured a syncopated "hesitation" on the second and third beats, and involved the dancers in "dipping" movements that contrasted strongly with the turns of the rotary waltz. The dancers used the flat part of the foot rather than the tips of the toes, and favored the "American" hold in which they danced hip to hip. But the Boston took up a lot of space on the floor, and this killed it, much to the dance teachers' relief. The rotary *valse à trois temps* crept back into popularity, and often a few measures of waltzing were, and still are, thrown into dances of similar tempi but different floor patterns, such as the mazurka, the lancers, or the American contra dances.

The Cotillion

More usually spelled cotillon in Europe, this was originally a French contredanse which found its way back to England in the early eighteenth century. Its name derives from the French word for petticoat, a flash of which might occasionally be seen by spectators of the dance. It started out as a square dance for four couples requiring no little skill in performance, and reached the United States in the middle of the eighteenth century, to become the oldest direct ancestor of the modern square dance.

But in those places where mixed dancing was frowned upon, young people satisfied their cravings by dressing up the dance as a game. Nothing could be more innocent than a contredanse involving no hold more intimate than a joining of hands, and the cotillion was thus acceptable where the waltz was not. Such, however, was the inventiveness—or deviousness—of the young, that the "cotillion parties," held weekly in the smartest houses in the early nineteenth century, developed into elaborate games with forfeits, as popular in England as in the United States until the end of the century.

As the English expert Mrs. Lilly Grove described the cotillion in 1895, in her definitive work *Dancing*, "there are now several firms whose chief business it is to manufacture the many accessories by which hosts and hostesses of today bribe their guests to come to their balls. Forty or fifty years ago only, a Cotillion consisted of simple figures with accessories at hand, such as cushion and mirror, handkerchief and chair, etc. The leader of the Cotillion had then to be not only nimble of feet but fertile of brain. After consulting with his hostess and with his lady partner, he would arrange the most suitable figures for the evening. But the affair has become much more elaborate of late years."

Mrs. Grove described such figures as *la conversation*: "the leader introduces two dancers to a lady. Both must address her in one single sentence, and she will bestow the favor of a dance on the man who has been able to please her most"; *la trompeuse*: "a lady advances towards a man and invites him to dance, but just as he accepts the honor with much pleasure she whirls round suddenly and dances off with another partner. This figure may be reversed"; and such complicated jollities as *le parapluie*: "two partners are brought to a lady; she gives an umbrella to one and she dances with the other. He of the umbrella has to hold it open over the waltzing couple and follow them thus through the whole figure"; *la pêche à la ligne*: "a lady holds a fishing rod and line at the end of which hangs a biscuit; several men are brought up to her, they kneel before her and must try and catch the biscuit with their teeth. He who is sufficiently skillful has the honor of dancing with the fair angler"; and the heavily symbolic *postillon*: "the Cotillion leader gives to his partner a large collar ornamented with bells; he and other men dance around her and she places the collar around the neck of the man with whom she wishes to dance. This figure is lively, especially if danced to the tune of a polka."

The cotillion in the late eighteenth century.

Mrs. Grove, clearly an enlightened woman, concludes, "inventiveness and high spirits, aided by flirtation, and perhaps by a spice of malice, are the best tutors. Women like the Cotillon, and, to do them justice, not all like it for the sake of the spoil they may gather of it; for it gives them the rare chance of showing their preferences and of enabling them to pay out now and again the men who, through conceit, neglect or indolence, have displeased them. As this is an age of woman, we may expect to see the Cotillon flourish for some time yet in our ballrooms, and as its accessories give employment to many hands and comfort the dowagers for their sleepless nights, we must not grudge it its success."

The Quadrille

This was another square dance for four couples that was extremely popular in the first half of the nineteenth century. The French term is derived from the Italian *quadriglia*, a troop or company of magnificently caparisoned horsemen who formed a square when taking part in a tournament. Under that military genius Napoleon, the quadrille became a contredanse with several complicated figures. Almack's most dictatorial patroness, Lady Jersey, brought the dance to England in 1816 as part of the allied spoils, and the first quadrille to be seen at the assembly rooms was performed by herself, Lady Ryder, Lady Butler, and Miss Montgomery, partnered by Mr. Montague, Mr. Harley, Mr. Montgomery, and Count Aldegarde.

The sets of figures of a quadrille were immensely varied, to such an extent that one of Almack's masters of ceremonies published

A fancy dress quadrille at Almack's.

1. Le Pantalon.

2. L'été.

3. La Poule.

4. La Trenise.

Quadrille dancers perform an elaborate figure.

sixteen versions, printed on cards small enough to be held in the hand. But the dance always fell into five sections (later reduced to three), each of which stuck to the names inherited from France: *le pantalon*, from an old French air; *l'eté* ("summer"), a complicated dance of 1800, of which only the name remained; *la poule* ("the hen"), a contredanse involving an imitation of the fowl; *Trénis*, named after its inventor, a well-known dancing master—though this section came to be known as *la pastourelle*, dances based on village tunes; and the *finale*, whose turn of speed caused it to be called the galop. All new suites written for the quadrille adopted the labels of these five sections, which were in different rhythms. Some wits added their own titles, such as "La Saint-Simonienne" for a section in which the changes of partner were supposed to resemble the French philosopher Saint-Simon's radical views on marriage. It was, nevertheless, unusual to change partners during the original dance. Captain Gronow reported that at a masked ball in Paris, "a young man of herculean strength had intruded himself among a party of dancers in a quadrille, and laid violent hands on a young lady already engaged. The gentlemen of the party flew to the rescue, and for a few minutes all was confusion; but four or five of the secret police presently appeared on the scene and arrested the cause of the disturbance. It was surprised to observe that none of the other persons engaged in the disturbance was molested, but allowed to dance as if nothing had occurred, and on quitting the ball I determined to unravel this secret. After some trouble I found that the party was composed of the sons of Louis Philippe and some of their friends, who were completely

OPPOSITE: The five sections of the quadrille.

Le Bon Genre, N.° 19.

The exhausting fourth section of the quadrille.

metamorphosed by the aid of false wigs, etc." The exchange of partners, however, became common in the many variations to which the quadrille gave birth.

The English royal family also enjoyed the dance, as shown by the following description of a ball in Buckingham Palace. "In 1838, and until the extension of the Palace in 1853 was completed and new rooms opened, two of the State Apartments were set apart for dancing; a band was stationed in each room so that the dancers were divided; and the fine picture gallery separated the ballrooms. Weippert and Strauss, Jullien and Coote, were among those who played in the Palace. Her Majesty and her Court entered the ballroom before 10 o'clock, when, choosing a partner, the Queen opened the ball with a first Quadrille, and also joined in other dances; later in the evening a move was made to the second ballroom, where Her Majesty finished the ball by leading off a country dance, sometimes as late as 3 o'clock."

The formalities and intricate steps of the dance introduced by Lady Jersey gave way in time to a "lazy, nonchalant fashion of walking through the figures." Naturally, this upset those who were concerned about the general lowering of dancing standards as the Victorian era progressed. They thought it vulgar to blur what had once been a most carefully executed dance, but perhaps that was because the strict rules they had learned from their dancing masters were being generally flouted.

The Americans danced the quadrille more rapidly than any

other dance, and it was taken westward by the pioneers and contributed to the growth of square dances. Those on the East Coast considered these variations as rather uncouth, and certainly unsuitable for use in the reception room—a sign of the cultural gap between the West and East Coasts.

"A certain quadrille party."

The Lancers

It was the quadrille that gave rise to the lancers, which was first recorded as a set of the parent dance in 1817 and was apparently named for the regiment then stationed at Fontainebleau. Here was another example of the craving for speed among a generation learning to live with peace, although it could be performed with an elegance that would please a dowager. The steps involved military-style salutes, a progress and retreat across the floor, as in a square dance, and ended with a grand march and a waltz. If there was ever any connection between this dance and the habits of lance-carrying warriors, no such weapon was seen in the ballroom; on the contrary, contemporary writers found the dance quite boisterous enough without such additional hazards.

One English writer, the Honorable Mrs. Armytage, claimed that the lancers was invented by a fashionable dance mistress, Madame Sacré, in the middle of the nineteenth century, and that the steps and figures, which were then considered "particularly pretty and graceful," were "most carefully gone through." She lamented that by the end of the century the dance had become mere "lively friskiness." One waltz figure even became known as the "Kitchen Lancers" (perhaps because of its vulgar appeal, perhaps a corruption of "kissing"), in which the lady was actually swung off her feet by her partner. Nevertheless, the lancers proper was included in the program of Her Majesty's state balls, and was popular in the United States across the entire East Coast, spreading as far as New Orleans. One variation invented by a New Haven dancing master, the "Loomis Lancers," is still performed in Rhode Island and southern Massachusetts.

The Galop

This was one of the few dances whose name—the French for gallop—was an entirely accurate description of its form. It grew out of the fast finale of the quadrille; those dancing it careened up and down in two-four time, using gliding steps (chassés) to zigzag down the floor. It made a change from the turns of the rotary waltz, and nothing could have been simpler or more exhausting. We are told that it was "first introduced into England at H.M. Ball, St. James's Palace, on 11th June, 1829, when the Princess Esterhazy, the Earl of Clanwilliam, the Duke of Devonshire and some of the foreign ministers exerted themselves in teaching movements to the company, and was danced alternately with Quadrilles and Waltzing during the whole of the evening." Although dances at formal balls were no longer performed in strict order, as they had been in the eighteenth century, the galop proved a popular finale to an evening in England and North America, finishing the dancers no less than the musicians.

The correct version of the lancers.

DANCE MUSIC.

MUSICAL BOUQUET

THE LANCERS QUADRILLES.
The only correct edition published.
AS PERFORMED BY THE BANDS AT BUCKINGHAM PALACE, ALMACK'S, & THE NOBILITY'S BALLS.

MUSICAL BOUQUET

Préparation pour le Bal.　　A.ASHLEY　　Fatigué après le Bal.

THE CELEBRATED GALOP
IN
HEROLDS OPERA LE PRÈ AUX CLERES
ARRANGED AS A RONDO BY CHARLES CZERNEY.

Nº 61.

THE ORIGINAL

SCHOTTISCH,

COMPOSED & DEDICATED TO

MONS. E. COULON,

BY

JULLIEN.

B. 31.

ENT. STA. HALL.

LONDON, PUBᵈ BY JULLIEN & Cᵒ ROYAL MUSICAL REPOSITORY, 214, REGENT ST. & 45, KING ST.

34. (3)

The Écossaise

OPPOSITE: *The schottische, performed with balletic precision.*

That sentiment in favor of native folklore which was the core of the romantic movement made a strong showing in the dance. Scotland was a popular source of inspiration, partly because it delighted many to think of her as a subject nation under English tyranny, and partly because of the immensely influential writings of Sir Walter Scott. The French fascination with Scotland had long historical roots, and the *écossaise*, which was a French invention of the late eighteenth century (the name simply means "Scottish dance"), can be seen as another of those contredanses that the French had done so much to refine. It was often danced to the music of bagpipes, but since its rhythms bore little resemblance to the traditional Scotch reels and strathspeys, it must be assumed that the name was bestowed on it out of perversity. The dancers were in two lines, and the first couple performed a few simple figures with the second couple, skipped down and up the line, and then danced with the third couple. By the time they got to the fourth couple, the second was dancing with the third, and so it proceeded until every couple had danced with every other couple. In this form the *écossaise* proved popular even in Russia: Tolstoy in *War and Peace* has a ball in which little else is danced. When it came to England in the mid-nineteenth century, it was performed somewhat faster than across the Channel, and was sometimes given Scotch tunes, doubtless in the hope of making the dance live up to its name.

The Schottische

In order to confuse matters further, the Germans named a round dance of their own after the Scotch (the final "e" being added by the English and French). This dance had nothing to do with the *écossaise* (which was a contredanse) nor the reels of the true Scot. It was an adaptation of a traditional round dance to the music of the polka, and it was in this form that it came to England and the United States when polka dancing was the rage of society. What it had in common with the *écossaise* (whose popularity did not last long) was its waltzlike turns, which alternated with walking, hopping or gliding. It started as a closed-position dance, with the partners clasping each other, but toward the end of the nineteenth century it became an open-position dance, except for the performance of the turns.

Scotch Reels and Strathspeys

The popularity of things Scottish cannot entirely be credited to Sir Walter Scott. After all, Boswell and Burns had been there before him, not to mention the fame attached to David Hume and Adam Smith. As far as dance is concerned, the fact is that Scotch reels were the only British dance to rank in venerability with the morris—and they appeared a lot easier to perform. They perfectly combined an appetite for old country things with a mania for fast and energetic dancing. Sir Walter's chief contribution in this field was to make something romantic out of the "skirl of the pipes." At

The Scotch reel on its own ground.

an open air fete given by the prince regent in 1813, his daughter Princess Charlotte, making her first appearance in public, "entered so much into the spirit of the fete as to ask for the then fashionable Scotch dances." As to the manner of their performance, the dancing teacher Monsieur Louis d'Egville described them as follows: "Scotch dances are picturesque to look at, amusing to dance, and afford excellent practice. Vigor and sharpness must be freely employed in forming the various steps, while the general Scotch characteristics of their performance should never be lost sight of. There are two *tempi* chiefly used in Scotch dancing —viz., the quick or reel *tempo* and the slow or strathspey *tempo*. To the former, short, sharp, sliding movements are danced; to the latter, hopping, lifting, pointing, and turning movements such as those of the 'Highland Fling' and 'Sword Dance' are executed. . . . Those who essay Scotch dancing should be able to dance at least four slow and four quick steps, otherwise their performance will be monotonous."

However popular they were with Queen Victoria, English society did not embrace the reels for long, and they soon returned to their native soil, where they continue to be danced in the manner they deserve.

The Polka

The polka came from Bohemia and was made fashionable by the French. There is a romantic story of its origins, whereby a Czech servant girl, a certain Anna Chadimova, was moved one Sunday

to dance in a way not seen before. The steps and the tune were noted down by musical observers who just happened to be on the scene, and thus a new dance supposedly was born. From there it came to Prague, the Bohemian capital, and then it was taken to Paris and danced on the stage of the Odéon Theater by a Czech ballet master. Its rhythms and steps took a firm hold on the audience, and Paris ballrooms promptly went polka-mad, to which fever England soon succumbed.

It is likely that Anna Chadimova did not so much invent new steps as put together in a new way traditional steps well known to her circle. One such step was the schottische, which was based on a traditional round dance. (In Paris there was one version of the polka called the *schottische Bohème*.) The name polka itself is linked to the Czech *pŭlka*, meaning "half," because a half-step is much used in the dance. Some authorities think that the Czechs named the dance in honor of the Poles, to commemorate their revolt against the Russians in 1830. This, however, appears to be taking nationalistic sentiment to excessive lengths; the reason the dance proved so popular was not the radical yearnings of those dancing it, but the vigorous and unforgettable rhythm—the fast da-da-dum, da-da-dum in two-four time—that would make anyone want to take to the floor. The folk origins of the dance would certainly commend it to many, but the rhythm was what really got under the skin, plus the appeal of a floor movement that somehow combined the turns of the waltz with the lines of the galop.

The Times's correspondent in Paris reported in March 1844 that

LEFT: *Music cover for a polka composed by Allen Dodworth, showing his Dancing Academy on Broadway.*

RIGHT: *West Point polka, 1852.*

OPPOSITE: *The polka performed in Buckingham Palace, 1848.*

"politics are for the moment suspended in public regard by the new and all-absorbing pursuit—the Polka—the dance recently imported from Bohemia, and which embraces in its qualities the intimacy of the Waltz, with the vivacity of the Irish Jig." Such was the dancing public's belief in experts that dance teachers were besieged by demands to learn the new dance. Cellarius, the most fashionable of these (the inventor of the slow Cellarius waltz), actually employed members of the *corps de ballet* to partner his pupils and teach them the steps. Naturally the use of professional partners, who were accustomed to display their limbs in public, led to all sorts of accusations of impropriety. In New York and other large U.S. cities, the demand to learn the polka similarly outstripped supply. Allen Dodworth wrote disapprovingly that "small rooms were generally used . . . with surroundings not conducive to delicacy, to say the least. Many young men became very expert . . . but in gaining skill they lost the modesty and innocence that should accompany the pleasure." Nevertheless, he composed many polkas himself, one in honor of his wife, and one a souvenir to his pupils.

As a round dance involving a close hold, the polka aroused even more hostility than the waltz. It was first danced at the National Theater in New York on May 10, 1844, and was introduced into fashionable society the same year by Gabriel De Korponay and

Mlle. Pauline Desjardins. The outcry it caused—George Templeton Strong wrote, "Wish I had the man here that invented the polka—I'd scrape him to death with oyster shells"—did not prevent James K. Polk exploiting the dance in his successful presidential campaign of 1844.

In Paris at the height of the craze there was a famous match between Cellarius and one of his rivals, Coralli, to see who was the best polka dancer. Each master was accompanied by a handful of his most skilled pupils, and Cellarius was the first to take the floor. He was to polka to a brand-new tune, but as it turned out he was unable to dance to it. More than somewhat humiliated, he stopped the musicians and insisted they play a more familiar tune. To this he and his pupils managed a lively polka, but when Coralli's turn came he totally eclipsed Cellarius, who retired vowing vengeance. The defeat did not appear seriously to dent his reputation, however, as he remained in business for many years afterward.

When it arrived in England, also in 1844, the polka gained immediate popularity, although the "Polish" costumes adopted by certain dancers at a fancy dress ball caused something of a stir: "Short skirts of scarlet cloth edged with white fur were worn by the ladies under Polish jackets, and showed high scarlet boots with clattering heels, while coquettish little caps completed their dress, the whole eliciting much comment at the time." The *Illustrated London News*, a journal that constantly aspired to be the arbitrator of fashion, declared in April 1844 that the Parisians had "never imported anything more ridiculous or ungraceful than this polka. It is a hybrid confusion of Scotch Lilt, Irish Jig and Bohemian Waltz, and needs only to be seen once to be avoided for ever."

Within a month, however, they had completely changed their tune, and were "much gratified in being enabled to lay before their readers an accurate description of the veritable, or Drawing-room Polka, as danced at Almack's and at balls of the nobility and gentry in this country." In true bandwagoning spirit, they boasted of obtaining the details from "Monsieur Coralli Fils, the instructor of the young noblesse and gentry in Paris," and they described the first steps as follows: "At the one, hop on the right leg, lifting or doubling up your left leg at the same moment; at the two, put your left leg boldly forward on the ground; at the three, bring your right toe up to your left heel; at the four, advance your left foot a short step forward; now at the one in the next measure or bar of the tune, hop on the left leg, doubling or lifting up your right leg, and so on—proceeding in this step with your arm circling your partner's waist round the room. . . . " Despite such complicated instructions, the dance triumphed over all objections and, like the waltz, its steps were incorporated into other round dances which called for the close hold that no amount of sermonizing could loosen.

The Redowa

This was another Bohemian folk dance, taken from the *rejdovak*,

which had much in common with the waltz, both as to origin and style. It became popular at the same time as the polka, and one of its features was an advance down the room in which one of the partners was forced to go backward. Perhaps because of the risks this entailed, it never became popular in England. It fared better in the United States, although the complicated steps were gradually simplified and subdued until they closely resembled the modern ballroom waltz.

The young Queen Victoria being amused.

The Polonaise

Here was a genuine Polish dance that enjoyed a brief period of popularity soon after the polka was introduced. The history of the polonaise is very old: its name is French for "Polish," and in the seventeenth century it was a stately court dance "marked by poetic feeling under the national character, the outstanding trait of which is a ceremonial dignity." It was popular, too, as part of the musical suite: Bach wrote several, as did Handel, Mozart, and Beethoven, but it was not until Chopin's time that the distinctive rhythm of the "modern" polonaise was given full musical expression.

In England it was often danced at costume balls. Here is a journalist's description of a royal occasion in 1846:

Her Majesty gave one of the most magnificent Balls even seen at the Palace. This was a "Historical Costume Ball" at which the guests wore dress of the 1740–1750 period—that is of one one hundred years earlier. The Queen did not impersonate any particular person but wore the dress of a Queen of England of that time. Prince Albert wore an elaborate embroidered costume of a civilian of the same period.

The Ball was opened with a Polonaise led by the Queen and Prince Albert through all the rooms, the various Bands playing, of course, the same tune which had been specially composed by Musard for the occasion. The assembled guests then passed in procession before Her Majesty and the Royal Party. For this Ball, the Minuet was revived and both the Menuet de la Court and the Menuet d'Exaudet were danced, presumably by those who had been specially coached for the occasion. Special music for a set of Quadrilles was composed by Musard called "Quadrille de 1845 de la Court d'Angleterre, ou Souvenirs de 1740." Musard, Weippert and Collinet led the dance bands, and the Ball concluded with Sir Roger de Coverley danced in the Picture Gallery.*

A more marked contrast between the polonaise and the polka could not be imagined. The polonaise, despite its lively rhythm, was almost purely processional, with each couple bowing or bending the knee to mark the beat. This promenade around or through the hall concluded with a waltz. Sympathy for the oppressed Poles was not the reason for the dance's adoption by society: such a notion would hardly have cut much ice in St. Petersburg, capital of the Poles' oppressors, where the polonaise was also popular. One could say that the dance reflected the more sedate mood of the middle years of the nineteenth century, years in

A very proper Victorian dance-game called "Pop Goes the Weasel," 1847.

* Quoted by P.J.S. Richardson, *The Social Dances of the Nineteenth Century*, Herbert Jenkins, 1960.

which revolt gave way to acquiescence. (As G.M. Young described those years, "there is an answer to every question, and
usually the answer is no.") Perhaps the new generation showed
their acquiescence on the dance floor. The polonaise was ideal for
those who wanted to preserve the social pecking order that was
being progressively eroded by pressure from below. Just as in the
court dances of the past, it was led off by the highest-ranking
couple, and precedence determined who should follow them.

The Mazurka

This was a Polish round dance, of the people rather than the court,
which found favor in the rest of Europe in theatrical dance rather
than the social variety. Nevertheless, it was to be seen in ballrooms, where it was probably introduced by that doyen of
Almack's, the duke of Devonshire, on his return from a special
mission to Russia in 1826. It was performed by four or eight
couples, and a certain "latitude for improvisation" was allowed
for in the steps. The speed was not great, but the rhythm, with its
stress on the second beat often marked by a tap of the heel, must
have brought a certain wildness to ballrooms where making noises
with the feet, like uttering cries, was usually reserved for foreign
barbarians and Scotchmen.

The polka-mazurka was, as a matter of fact, neither a polka nor
a mazurka since it was in three-four time rather than the two-four
of the polka, and it stressed the third beat, rather than the second
of the mazurka. It was fashionable in Vienna and Budapest,
though not in England. The reason might be found in Monsieur
d'Egville's description of the steps: "the feet should never entirely
leave the floor, and great use should be made of the knees, which

149

should bend and straighten continuously during the movements. Galop steps and Waltz *à deux temps* may be interpolated occasionally by way of variation; but this must be done with judgment and skill, or the effect may prove uncomfortable for the dancers, though, no doubt, amusing to the onlookers."

The Varsovienne

The name—also spelled *varsouvienne* and *varsouvianna*—simply meant "Warsaw dance," and it came to western Europe from Poland in the 1850s. Its European reputation was short-lived (around twenty years) compared to its longevity in the United States, where it is still being danced. In its earliest form it was a mixture of the polka and the mazurka; it is certainly an enduring example of the beauty and grace of the latter. But as the round dances gained popularity in the United States, the *varsouvianna* step—characterized as sweep-glide-close—alternated with waltzing during a dance, and it is still a favorite with modern square and round dancers.

The Barn Dance

A local hop at one of the newly opened dance halls.

All the dances hitherto discussed in this section were performed in the highest reaches of European society. Some, as we have seen, took a little time to be accepted at the top—the waltz was a prime example. But once they had arrived, their style and fashionableness were decided from on high. In the last third of the nineteenth century, however, society began to amuse itself more in private

Music cover for the barn dance.

than public. The self-assurance of the upper orders was shaken by the series of assaults made on them by those below. The extension of the franchise meant that democracy was rearing its head, and rather than embrace it society retreated to the security of its own mansions and country houses. This meant that they abandoned the role of setting the public style, which was eagerly taken over by people with money instead of pedigree. In dance terms, it meant that society balls were no longer held in exclusive assembly rooms but in the houses of the hostesses. Fashion was not spread solely from above but, on the contrary, began to percolate upward. Dance itself was democratized, and dance halls opened to cater to a far wider public than the assemblies and ballrooms had ever done. The barn dance was one of the first examples of this trend, as it was a popular dance that spread upward through the ranks of society, only to stop short of reaching the very top.

Known also as the *pas de quatre* (which was very misleading, as it was a dance for two people), and the military schottische, the barn dance consisted of three sliding steps and a hop, performed four times while advancing hand in hand and side by side with your partner, at which point the gentleman took the lady by the waist, as if to waltz, and did the schottische step of walking, hopping, and turning, eight times. The galop step was sometimes used instead of the hops, and a fair amount of foot stamping was employed, which scandalized the older generation who had never accepted the mazurka. The name barn dance apparently originated in the United States, where the form was very popular: dancing to celebrate the completion of a new barn had a long history. Although the steps were European, being based on the schottische and the galop, and although it was a music hall tune that first popularized the dance in England, the American influence evident in the barn dance was a major portent of the coming wave.

The Two-step

In 1891 John Philip Sousa, the American composer and bandmaster, who felt that "the march should make a man with a wooden leg step out," published the "Washington Post March." It was full of patriotism and military pride, bursting with self-confidence; as such it caught on in the Old World that was beginning to feel these qualities slip away. The chief reason for its popularity as a dance was, of course, its rhythm, but its importance as the spearhead of the American cultural invasion can hardly be exaggerated.

I have a theory that the morality of a nation prevailing at the time of its greatest influence long outlasts its national decline. Europe was by no means on the point of collapse, but the pace of change was accelerating at a time when the national temper was stuck in the grooves laid down in earlier, more certain years. The United States reflected that temper through its own glass: a national assertiveness that was often crude; rapidly expanding industrial wealth that masked the miseries of exploitation; a boundless faith in its own destiny and the inestimable benefits this would bring to the rest of the world. Those were qualities Europe recognized as her own, but experience had proved she could no longer be certain of possessing them. She regarded the United States, therefore, with a sort of patronizing indulgence. Also, the long years of peace in the nineteenth century had brought a certain dullness, a desire for challenge, novelty, and change. This was what American culture offered, and the offer was grabbed by Europe with both hands.

The "Washington Post March" gave birth to the two-step in six-eight tempo which, as the following instructions will testify, could be an extremely lively dance.

The gentleman stands behind the lady with his right shoulder level with her right shoulder, both hands joined above the lady's shoulders, right hand to right, left hand to left. Both start with the right foot.

First part (four bars): first step—spring up from both feet to land on the toes of the left foot with the right foot pointed in

the second position. Second step—spring up from the left foot and simultaneously bring the right behind the left (one bar). Again spring on the left foot and point the right in the second position, then with another small spring on the left pass the right foot in front of the left (one bar). Repeat the four steps commencing with the left foot (two bars).

Second part (four bars): take four long Galop slides obliquely forward with the right foot (two bars). Repeat with the left foot (two bars).*

Not all two-steps required such energy, and in the early years of the twentieth century the extreme simplicity of two-step dancing —a quick marching step with skips—led to it being adopted for every type of music and floor pattern. This simplicity ended by boring many dancers rigid. Nevertheless, one could not imagine the "Washington Post" being danced by that generation of Victorians grown old with a queen who for so many years had cloistered herself as a widow. The young Victoria who had danced quadrilles until three in the morning was an age away from the old spider who imposed her mourning on the nation. The new century was awaited by the young with all the excitement of those who know their time must be coming. In dance, at least, they were not to be disappointed.

OVERLEAF: *Knocking 'em cold in Paris at the end of the nineteenth century.*

* Description by William Lamb, quoted in P.J.S. Richardson, *The Social Dances of the Nineteenth Century*, Herbert Jenkins, 1960.

THE DANCE BAND YEARS

Ragtime

THE COMING OF ragtime revolutionized the dance but, like most revolutions, ragtime's roots were firmly in the past. By the last quarter of the nineteenth century, the United States had developed a self-confidence, about her past no less than her future, which released an energy and inventiveness that led her to dominate the popular musical scene. Within that scene it was the music of the blacks that dominated that of the whites. Of course it was the white musical establishment that took over and exploited black forms, but to understand why black culture took such a hold on the white majority requires some sort of probing of the national psyche. Was it to compensate for all the indignities heaped on blacks over the years? Was it because fashion-conscious whites found an echo of their own idealism in the first stirrings of black consciousness, stirrings later stimulated by the contribution of black soldiers to World War I? Or was it simply that black musical

culture outlasted the burlesque that whites made of it in the middle of the nineteenth century and came to be recognized as an art form to be admired rather than parodied?

Minstrel shows, with blacked-up white actors, were a popular form of entertainment as early as the 1820s. The success of a song called "Jump Jim Crow," as performed by one Tom Rice, with accompanying dance movements supposedly based on the antics of a crippled black who called himself Jim Crow, inaugurated a craze for minstrel shows that spread all over the United States, and from there to England. The rest of Europe was less enraptured, possibly because they had not exploited the blacks on quite such a colossal scale, and therefore had less contact with them. The most famous name among such groups was the Christy Minstrels, whose leader, Edwin P. Christy, gained such wide renown for the songs of Stephen Foster (such as "Swanee River" and "My Old Kentucky Home") that he published some of them under his own name.

The shows—which became especially popular at British seaside resorts at the end of the Victorian era—consisted of imitations, usually crude, of Negro talk and manners, some "Negro" jokes, and songs to the accompaniment of the instrument chiefly associ-

OPPOSITE:
*"Ethiopian
serenaders" of the
nineteenth century.*

157

ated with black music, the banjo. Rhythmically these minstrel songs owed most to the country dances and jigs with which white society amused itself but, when the blacks adapted these songs for themselves, they overlaid them with the African rhythms they had inherited from slavery. One distinctive result of this "marriage" was syncopation, where the beat or emphasis in a musical line is displaced and does not fall where you would expect it to. This idea is natural enough to be common to the folk music of all races, and it was (and remains) especially popular in black Africa, where singing in groups to elaborate rhythms was very common. The catchy tunes and marches of white America gained immeasurably from such syncopation.

Ragtime itself was music to move to—dances and marches arranged for the piano, which was the most popular and accessible form of household entertainment. Ragtime's harmonies were based on those of contemporary popular music, and the right hand played the tune while the left kept up a regular vamping beat. (This, incidentally, is one difference between jazz and ragtime: in the latter the beat is consistent, and the syncopation is a matter of melody, whereas in jazz the rhythms of right and left hand are, as it were, set against each other. Also, ragtime is written music, whereas jazz relies heavily on improvisation.) As for the origins of the name "ragtime," opinions naturally vary. Rudi Blesch has a story that when the prostitutes were having a party just for themselves, they hung out a white flag, known as the white rag. Since the new music was largely played in brothels, where black piano players could earn a casual living, their music came to be named after the rag. Another, more plausible, etymology (from Peter Gammond, Scott Joplin's biographer) is that the music was known as "ragged" because of its syncopation; originally called "jig time" music—doubtless because of its catchy rhythm—"rag" was a simple substitution for "jig."

The career of Scott Joplin is perhaps the best illustration of the rise of the new music. He was not the first to publish a composition called a "rag." According to Tony Palmer, that honor belongs to William H. Krell, whose "Mississippi Rag" appeared in 1897. But ragtime music had been around for a generation, ever since printed sheet music for piano and/or banjo had been widely and cheaply available. Joplin, who was born on the border between Texas and Arkansas in November 1868, would have been exposed to the compositions of Louis M. Gottschalk (1829–1869), a pianist of sufficient virtuosity to have attracted, at the age of fifteen, the praise of Chopin. Gottschalk wrote pieces that made use of syncopation, as well as employing the sounds of instruments common to black and Latin American culture. Joplin would also have heard the "pop" songs of the day, which had titles like "Oh! Dem Golden Slippers" and "Always Take Mother's Advice." More important, what were known as the "minstrel" songs of the southern white Stephen Foster (1826–1864) were as much favorites in Joplin's youth as they are today. The marches of John Philip Sousa (1854–1932) must also have been a strong influence, and it is worth stressing that the popular dances of the 1880s, when Joplin came to maturity, were the waltzes and square dances (such as the quadrille) that had originated in his grandfather's day.

Joplin's father was a railroad worker who had been born and raised a slave, becoming legally free a mere five years before Scott was born. Music was something of a family pastime, as it was everywhere. Scott's mother and two of his younger brothers all sang and played banjo, guitar, or violin. Scott learned the guitar, and also the bugle, which he played for the local band, but when he discovered the piano his precocious talent was such that his father was persuaded to buy him one secondhand. By the age of eleven, Scott had a reputation as a proficient player and improviser, and so impressed a neighboring German music teacher that he gave Scott lessons free. Scott's father understandably wanted him to take a steady job, but the young Joplin wanted nothing but a musical career. At the age of fourteen, with his mother dead, Scott had a final quarrel with his father and left home.

Wandering musicians were as common in the United States in the last quarter of the nineteenth century as troubadours were in medieval France and England. They played on steamboats and in cafés, brothels and bars; they "rode the rods" underneath the railroad cars, and were admired for their apparent freedom by those whose conditions had scarcely improved since the abolition of slavery. The staple fare offered by these "ticklers" (from "tickling the ivories," or playing the piano) were the tunes of the day played in the syncopated, banjo-based style that was the basis of all ragtime minstrelry, whether performed by blacks or whites. It was music to sing to, eat to, dance to, and it was an intimate part of the foreplay encouraged by the best brothels. It was above all popular music, rooted in the tunes used for dances such as cotillions and the lancers, tunes which the blacks had taken from the whites. The dances that prove enduringly popular combine a catchy rhythm with folk roots that somehow make the dance familiar. That which made ragtime widely popular was no exception.

THE DANCES

The Cakewalk

A popular finale to the minstrel shows was a sort of strutting walk or promenade in pairs, with a prize awarded to the couple who produced the most inventive steps. At first these prizes consisted of candies or ice cream, but a tradition developed whereby a cake was awarded to the winning couple (originating the expression "that takes the cake"). Apparently this competition originated in the South in the 1880s, where the blacks were supposed to have got it from the Seminole Indians. Alternatively, the cakewalk can be seen as a black parody of white "society" manners, which seems altogether more likely. Performed to syncopated music, the dance alternated wild jumps and solemn processional steps. In the United States it was at first a dance performed by blacks, who took lessons in it and dressed themselves ever more elaborately for the competitions, while in Europe it was enthusiastically adopted by young and fashionable whites, who took instruction and dressed elaborately for their pleasures anyway.

Dancing to the syncopated rhythms of the cakewalk led to a craze for "ragged" music that publishers were quick to fasten on. Krell's "Mississippi Rag" may not have been the first ever ragtime two-step, but it was the first composition to carry the name "rag," and once christened, there was no holding the form. Scott Joplin, who for some fifteen years had been developing his piano style anywhere from St. Louis to Sedalia, Missouri, wrote his "Maple Leaf Rag" in 1897; it was turned down by one Sedalia

The cakewalk.

publishing firm on the grounds that they had already done well with a piece entitled "Maple Leaf Waltz." Joplin refused to alter his title, being a proud man who wanted his compositions to enjoy the same status as "serious" music. A Kansas City publisher proved equally unobliging, though accepting a compilation called "Original Rags" which Joplin had put together with Charles N. Daniels. In one of those scenes beloved of Hollywood bio-pics, Sedalia's music publisher, John Stark, happened to be in the Maple Leaf Club on Sedalia's Main Street when he heard Joplin playing his rejected rag. He asked Joplin to go to his house on the following day, and heard "Maple Leaf Rag" played through in a more sober atmosphere. A deal was concluded that was to make the white publisher rich and the black composer famous. Joplin forthwith started work on a ragtime ballet, based on the folk music of the time. His ambition—which in the end proved fatal to him— was to elevate ragtime above mere "pop" status. Meanwhile, "Maple Leaf Rag" made enough money for Stark to move to St. Louis—and the piece did not take many years to sell one million copies.

Joplin also moved to St. Louis, and in 1900 published a cake-walk called "Swipesey." This was followed by "Peacherine Rag,"

*The cakewalk in the
United States and
Europe.*

"Sunflower Drag," and "The Augustan Club Waltzes." The
craze for cakewalks continued. Debussy made his contribution in
1908, when he published "Golliwogg's Cakewalk" as part of his
suite *Children's Corner*. One thing the dance did was to break up the
turns and glides common to almost all its predecessors. It thus set a
fashion for "novelty" dances that next engaged the attention of the
young, who felt that appreciation of the "new" music was what set
them apart from their elders.

"Animal" Dances

At the beginning of the century, according to F. Scott Fitzgerald,
"daring young women were already gliding along Fifth Avenue in
electric 'mobiles.'" Ever since the Industrial Revolution in the
eighteenth century, each new generation had been criticized by its
predecessors for inaugurating a dangerous new age of speed, but in

OPPOSITE: *A
prize-winning
cakewalk couple.*

Cake-Walk

A development of the cakewalk: the Yankee tangle.

the 1900s there was some justification for this view. Henry Ford, who had discovered the limitations of the electric car while employed by the Edison Company, set up the Detroit Automobile Company (from which he resigned in 1902, disagreeing with his codirectors' policy of restricting production to the number of cars ordered). Under his own name he produced the "T" model in 1909. It was not simply that the mass production pioneered by Ford enabled so many to be mobile. It was that young people were beginning to be recognized as a specialized market by commercial entrepreneurs.

Before, there had been the male market, the female market, and the family market. The art of commercial specialization, which Henry Ford perfected in industrial terms, was a child of the twentieth century. New markets were needed, invented, exploited. The installment plan, that venerable device for persuading people to mortgage their futures, enmeshed ever-growing numbers of hard-working families. Factory work ended the need for long years of apprenticeship; the young vied with the old for jobs, competed in output, and earned money of their own to spend before they themselves were encumbered with family responsibilities. Perhaps more than anything else, this helped to create the generation gap. Who could say that father knows best when he had no more, and probably less, to jingle in his pockets than his son? The family that spends together stays together, but that spending pattern was being broken up. There was a new freedom, at least for the young who were in work, and once the financial barriers crumbled, the other barriers—notably those surrounding morality—were sure to follow.

Ragtime, the new beat, was a young person's thing. To a great extent it was classless. Gilded youth had haunts of its own wherein the wealth it had inherited could be transferred to the deserving entertainer, but ragtime was also heard in bars, brothels, and dives across two continents. Dancing was still very much a family affair, and the waltz, like the poor, was ever with us. But the young, in their new commercial militancy, demanded dances of their own, dances that would make the old look ridiculous. And what they demanded, they got. Nothing is more faddish than dancing, and the new science of sales promotion, coupled with cheaper printing processes, made a fad easier to exploit. What was happening was a new sense of division in society, a division that had always existed, but which was now commercially exploitable. This division, between old and young, gave the latter a new sense of their own power—which perhaps explains the extraordinary acceleration in the pace of social change. Patience has never been youth's strong suit.

"Animal" dances were *the* ragtime dances. In them the supposed gait and manner of various animals was imitated. The last time this had been done in social dance was in tribal days, when it was thought that the power of the animal would flow into the dancers, or that the dance would make such an animal easier to kill. Neither of these reasons explains the sudden arrival of dances like

The monkey dance, complete with original monkey.

the crab, the kangaroo dip, or the horse trot. There are two other possible explanations. First, the jerky rhythms of ragtime demanded jerky steps, which many of the chosen animals practiced. Second, behaving like animals was a declaration of independence from the more decorous habits of the older generation. It is worth noting that the new dances had to be performed properly. They were not improvised, but usually taught by a new generation of dance teachers, as ragtime itself was taught in academies run by Axel Christiansen (who between 1903 and 1923 had more than two hundred thousand pupils enrolled across the United States). The young may have claimed a certain independence, but they still depended heavily on experts. Of course there was not the strict insistence on accuracy that had lain on social dance for so many centuries, but there was a right way and a wrong way, and those who espoused the latter were consigned to a social outer darkness. After all, if anyone could do it, who could tell a bright young thing from a grizzled old fogy?

Inevitably there was a certain reaction in the ranks of the establishment. The Dancing Teachers Association of America refused to teach syncopated dancing. The bunny hug, with all that its name implied (and perhaps bearing in mind the breeding habits of rabbits), was considered indecent enough to be banned

The Texas rag, as performed in 1914.

from many American dance halls. The new commercialism stepped in to save the day, and girls appeared wearing "bumpers" in order to fend off too enthusiastic an embrace. The grizzly bear was lucky to escape such censure, involving as it did a swooping, swaying walk that culminated in the hug for which the grizzly was famous. But perhaps the best-known animal dance (apart from the fox trot, of which more later) was the turkey trot, or one-step, which conquered Europe more thoroughly than any of its stable-mates. (His Holiness Pope Pius X so disapproved of the turkey trot that he suggested that the faithful dance the ancient furlana as an alternative. This was a surprising choice, as even Casanova considered the dance a violent one. The Dodworth Dancing Academy, among others, tried to teach it, but it never caught on.)

The ubiquitous two-step, as danced to one of Sousa's tunes, involved two steps to the bar (a rare instance of a dance living up to its name). With corresponding simplicity, the one-step required only a single step per beat, performed in a smooth and rhythmic walk, the man going forward and the woman backward, with the eccentric wing movements of the turkey (a syncopated fowl if ever there was one) thrown in for good measure. The ease with which this dance could be fitted to ragtime ensured its popularity. In England the one-step was known simply as the "rag," and it completely ousted the Boston as the fashionable dance of the time.

American blacks, to whom ragtime properly belonged, performed animal dances that were even less restrained than those censured by white society. Most of these, such as the fish tail, the eagle rock, and the buzzard lope, involved a grinding of the hips, which in dances whose names were more straightforward descriptions of their movements—the fanny bump, the funky butt, the squat, the itch, the grind, the mooche—became emphatically erotic. One favorite was the slow drag, in which couples would hold onto each other and grind to and fro in one spot all night. A generation reared on speed needed at least one dance which gave the new sexuality time to ripen.

In 1911 the first popular song to achieve the status of instantaneous world best-seller was published. It was "Alexander's Ragtime Band," by Irving Berlin. In that year, too, the most celebrated dance teachers of the era made their appearance: Vernon and Irene Castle, an Englishman married to an American who caused a sensation by going around uncorseted, with her hair cut short and simple, wearing soft and simple dresses. Shock and horror were caused by such outrageous self-expression, but in due course New York society, in the shape of such formidable champions as Mrs. Rockefeller and Mrs. Stuyvesant Fish, was won round to patronizing the Castle House for the Teaching of Correct Dancing, whose rules of good taste were sufficiently strict to make the new dances acceptable. While the English were adopting a more flowing ballroom style, the Castles invented a step—the Castle walk—which was a strutting movement performed on the balls of the feet, with the knees kept straight. This odd combination of new and old could be used for most of the animal dances,

LEFT: *Irene Castle in classical pose.*

RIGHT: *Style and polish: the Castles.*

and white Americans for a while danced nothing else.

This was also the year in which Scott Joplin completed his ragtime opera *Treemonisha*, the work with which he intended to lift ragtime to the status of high art. Its failure—no one would put it on—finally finished him, and he died in Manhattan State Hospital, ill and more than half-mad, on April Fools' Day, 1917. By then ragtime was being challenged by jazz; but from 1911 until after World War I, Europe went "ragtime crazy"—some years behind the United States, a trend that has not yet been reversed.

The Castle walk.

The Fox Trot

Perhaps this started as just another animal dance, but the consensus of expert opinion derives its name from a music hall performer called Harry Fox, who executed a trotting dance to ragtime in the Ziegfeld Follies of 1914. Stage dancing, as opposed to ballet, was still an important influence on social dance—the polka was a notable example from the previous century—and Fox's trot quickly caught on. It was, in its original version, a febrile dance, which you might say was in tune with the times, although most times appear feverish if you examine them closely enough. Certainly it was extremely jerky: one movement quoted by the English dance master Victor Silvester is, "Walk four slow steps (2 bars), then take a run of seven quick steps, bringing the right foot to the back of the left on the eighth beat." The walk was added

in order not to exhaust dancers with the trotting perfected by the indefatigable Mr. Fox; and in the year of its invention in the United States, a New York teacher came to demonstrate the dance to members of the Imperial Society of Teachers of Dancing in London. It was introduced to the English public by an American music hall artist, Elsie Janis, who performed it in *The Passing Show of 1915*. Tamed by the teachers, it soon took its place in the ballroom (it required a fair amount of space, unless you did it in a trotting procession around the room) where it proved a perfect dance for ragtime music.

Dancing teachers disapproved of the high jinks that tended to accompany the fox trot—"hops, kicks, and capers" as Silvester somewhat disparagingly calls them—and the dance became, in England at least, an altogether smoother affair than its American original. Figures such as the butterfly, the twinkle, and the chassé made their appearance, and these laid the foundation of the English fox trot, or saunter, which had all its jerks ironed out. Though many English ballrooms closed upon the outbreak of war, they were soon reopened owing to public demand, and when they became crowded with American soldiers after 1917, the fox trot enjoyed a spirited revival. It is still danced today, in its smooth version, though rarely by the young. It bears no more resemblance to the original than music now played as "ragtime" does to the dynamic but controlled performances of the early years of the

LEFT: *The fox trot stylishly performed in 1925.*

RIGHT: *Not much fun: the English fox trot.*

The fox trot performed at a New Jersey dance to the music of Rudy Vallee.

century. "It is never right to play Ragtime fast," said Scott Joplin, but his injunction was not often heeded.

The Maxixe

"We were the most powerful nation. Who could tell us any longer what was fashionable and what was fun? Isolated during the European War, we had begun combing the unknown South and West for folkways and pastimes, and there were more ready to hand." Thus wrote F. Scott Fitzgerald in *Echoes of the Jazz Age*. It is as succinct an explanation as any of the craze for Latin American dances that spilled through the United States and over into Europe. The maxixe came from Brazil, where it was a wild folk dance combining syncopation with the rhythm of the Cuban habañera and the movements of the European polka. Somewhat diluted, it became popular in Brazilian ballrooms, and from there the United States took it up, just before World War I, as part of her search for culture in her own hemisphere. It was eclipsed in popularity by the tango, but it was much danced for a short time on both sides of the Atlantic, especially as its swooping body movements were considered sensational by the young.

In the United States around 1914, the maxixe was the third most popular dance after the one-step and the hesitation waltz (as performed by the Castles), which just goes to show how wide was the range of dances in vogue at any one time. The English, true to form, cut out the more "sensational" movements and converted the dance into "a series of gentle sways and dipping motions," according to dance historian A.H. Franks. The American dance experts Troy and Margaret West Kinney professed to find in 1914 a consensus among their peers that while the maxixe was "unlikely to be remembered as of the group whose spread over the occident have represented a striking social phenomenon . . . the dances of the seventeenth-century courts are the objective toward which present-day steps are moving directly." They could not have been more wrong.

The Tango

As an example of cultural colonization, the tango is unique. According to sociologist Frances Rust, it is most probably a mixture of the tangano, a dance peculiar to the African slaves transported to Haiti and Cuba in the eighteenth century, and the habañera ("Havana dance") of nineteenth-century Cuba. This combination then got taken to Argentina by migrating blacks, to mingle with the milonga, a popular dance in the slums of Buenos Aires at the end of the nineteenth century. The tango was an erotic dance, popular with the less-than-respectable poor and ignored by anyone with pretensions to gentility. In spite of that, or perhaps because of it, tango music came to be played by small orchestras in Buenos Aires for the benefit of the nightbirds among their customers. There the music was picked up by Europeans, who made several attempts to introduce it to Paris in the early years of the twentieth century.

A French dancer and musical entrepreneur called Camille de Rhynal was, according to Victor Silvester, the man chiefly responsible for making the tango popular in Europe. The music was extraordinarily catchy, but there was no way the dance could

The tango, as seen by the magazine Punch *in 1913.*

be performed, unrefined, before a sophisticated (which is to say genteel) audience. In 1907 de Rhynal "found himself at the Imperial Country Club at Nice, and he gathered round him a few enthusiasts, including the late Grand Duchess Anastasie of Russia" (according to Mr. Silvester). After much hard work, these worthies managed to rid the tango of its "objectionable features," and made it fit for the ballroom, and from Nice it went to Paris, where the presence of genuine Argentinian tango orchestras—specially imported by beady-eyed musical agents—ensured that the dance was a hit.

The tango arrived in England in 1912, as a result of demand from those who had seen it performed in the fashionable casino ballrooms of Deauville and Dinard. George Grossmith made it a desirable society accomplishment by dancing it on stage with Phyllis Dare in a show called *The Sunshine Girl*. In its "European" form it crossed to North America, and came full circle when it was danced in its new "acceptable" manner by the bourgeoisie of Argentina.

The dance took such a hold that *thés tango*, or "tango teas," suddenly became all the rage, in both London and Paris. It was around this time that people began to follow the Viennese custom of dancing in restaurants between courses, which opened up a lot more places for dancers, as well as offering more employment to dance bands. But the tango teas catered for those who could not sit still in the late afternoon and early evening—the same group, presumably, for whose benefit the cocktail was invented. In public places you could tango between the tea tables to the accompaniment of a small string orchestra (who would also perform the occasional waltz and made a stab at ragtime); in private houses, if you were ultrafashionable, you would actually have an Argentinian piano player to impress your guests, or, failing that, a gramophone.

A tea dance at the Ocean Hotel, Brighton, Sussex.

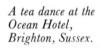

Although tamed by Europeans, the tango before World War I

was far from being a standardized affair. It boasted as many steps
as there were days of the year, with French names as well as
Spanish, and until the Castles codified the dance for the United
States market in 1914 (a service performed for the English by Miss
Gladys Beattie Crozier, who devoted some forty thousand words
to the subject), no two teachers taught it alike. Nor had the efforts
of de Rhynal and the Grand Duchess Anastasie overcome all
opposition to the dance. It came under heavy attack for the in-
delicacy of its movements, and rumors that it was banned at the
English royal court were only scotched when Queen Mary
actually asked for a demonstration at a ball given in honor of the
Grand Duke Michael in 1914, and was apparently delighted with
the results.

The outbreak of war dampened enthusiasm for the tango, but in
the 1920s it enjoyed a second wind as "the new French tango," in
which the beat was not as marked as in the prewar version, but
where the steps were more "exotic." It was this model that
Valentino made famous, and he had many would-be imitators

*Valentino embarking
on the tango in* The
Four Horsemen of
the Apocalypse.

*The London dance
experts Marguerite
and Frank Gill
demonstrate a tango
step, 1914.*

bumping into tables at the revived tango teas. The modern tango bears very little resemblance to the ballroom original (which, of course, in its turn bears little resemblance to the *true* original). It is now a staccato dance, not the sensual affair that Valentino made of it, and it is performed at an unvarying thirty-three bars a minute, following the standards laid down by the Committee of the Imperial Society of Teachers of Dancing, who met in London in the 1920s to bring order, as they saw it, out of chaos.

Sequence Dances

Before the introduction, after World War I, of proper dance halls in England, with sprung floors, a good orchestra, and little or no exclusivity as to who could come in, there were "sequence" teachers who organized "assemblies" either in their own "academies" or in the local town hall. As Victor Silvester puts it, "In a sequence dance the various movements have to be made in a set order. As a result the same step is being executed by all the couples in the room simultaneously. Sequence dances have generally been invented or arranged by teachers." Examples were the military two-step, the maxina, and the veleta, which survives today. The veleta was the invention of a Mr. Arthur Morris, who in 1900 entered it for the annual competition for new dances held by the British Association of Teachers of Dancing. Although the dance did not even get into the final round, it was picked out by Mr. Day of the music publishers Francis, Day, and Hunter, who—after a bit of polishing—published it. Played to the music of a waltz, in the same formation as that used for a barn dance, the veleta is a combination of waltz steps and chassés (a side step ending with the feet closed). It is a rare example of a dance that has lasted several years without ever reaching the program of a "society" dance. In the United States it became popular as the veleta waltz.

The Jazz Band

The most convincing explanation of the origin of the word "jazz" is given by Tony Palmer, who sees it as a corruption of the word "jezebel," when "jazz belles" was a slang term for prostitute. Certainly there was a time when "jazz" meant simply sexual intercourse; the link between the music and the brothel is a close one. So with ragtime, but there is a crucial difference between the two. Ragtime is written music, whereas jazz is (or was) largely improvised. Advancing my own definition, I would say that ragtime offered a new rhythm, while jazz offered a whole set of new musical voices.

The brothel link is easily explained. In the early years of the century the brothel was the most likely place to offer employment to itinerant musicians. Jazz (or jass or jasz; the current spelling was first authenticated by *The New York Times* on February 2, 1917) was, like ragtime, first and foremost music to move to—which, after all, was what brothels were for. But it was not only indoor music. Drawing on the same sources as ragtime, it took in a wider

The London jazz band, the Savoy Hotel Orpheans.

range of instrumentation, adding the banjo to the military band combination of clarinet, cornet, tuba, trombone, and drums. Jazz relied heavily on syncopation, but it was not the *melodic* syncopation that distinguished ragtime (though that was included), but the setting of bass against treble, a sort of harmonic competitiveness that gave birth to an entirely new musical form. Jazz absorbed the classical influences of the French Creoles whose center was New Orleans, and merged it with the songs and rhythms of black folk culture. It required enormous discipline and musical understanding, in the playing if not the appreciation, yet few of its performers had formal musical training. The Original Dixieland Jazz Band, the first to popularize the name jazz, consisted of a quintet of white musicians, none of whom knew how to score music. Their leader, "Nick" La Rocca, was a cornetist who learned to play purely by trial and error; he never learned to read music, and his band used no written scores. They learned new numbers by having the tunes played over by one of their number who could read music.

La Rocca's band was the first to leave New Orleans and achieve success elsewhere. Arriving in New York in 1913, the band was engaged to play at Reisenweber's Café (which had no less than seven dance floors), and "jazzed up" the animal dances then in vogue with enormous success. Though they did not invent the new form, and continued to rely heavily on ragtime—one of their first hits was "Tiger Rag," which they took from an old quadrille tune—they popularized the new name, and "jazz" began to replace "ragtime" on the sheets of the music publishers.

The Original Dixieland Jazz Band was booked to appear in London in the spring of 1919. The show was *Joy Bells*, and starred George Robey, "the Prime Minister of Mirth." After hearing the band perform, he threatened to leave unless they were fired. The promoter arranged for them to appear instead at various nightclubs, where their one-steps provided a welcome change for

British postwar youth. In the autumn they appeared in the newly opened Hammersmith Palais de Danse, as mighty a monument to the renewed mania for dancing as the Roseland Ballroom was in New York (which had opened on New Year's Eve, 1919). The crush at the Hammersmith Palais made it necessary for the wind players to point their instruments at the ceiling in order to be heard (according to dance band historian Brian Rust), and thus jazz bands built up ways of playing as eccentric as the new music. The huge ballrooms were, in the 1920s at least, primarily the haunts of young people (newly described as "teenagers") seeking release in fast music and steps. The waltz very nearly died, since even debutantes at society affairs insisted on the fox trot, the tango, and the newer dances. To the oft-repeated disgust of the elderly, the jazz age had come to stay.

As dance music, jazz was associated with the young primarily because the steps employed to its tunes, though simple enough, were hardly suited to the precarious dignity of middle age. But an important development secured the new music a place in millions of households, and that was the growth of radio. Popular broadcasting on a large scale began in the United States in 1920, when the advertising possibilities of the medium were recognized. It says something for the status of dance music that in the same year a dance band—Paul Specht's orchestra—was the first to broadcast, from WWJ Detroit. Of course the music had to appeal to the nebulous tastes of a mass audience, which meant that a sweetening of tone and style took place. Those who thought of themselves as jazz "buffs" demanded music that was unadulterated by commercialism: hence the divorce between "pure" jazz and that meant for dancing. But with dance bands broadcasting regularly on both sides of the Atlantic, there was no danger of the new music dying through inattention.

If the career of Scott Joplin mirrors the rise and (temporary) eclipse of ragtime, that of Paul Whiteman is an outstanding example of what happened to jazz dance and dance bands generally. Whiteman was born in Denver, Colorado, in March 1890, of a musical family. By the age of seventeen he was principal viola player in the Denver Symphony Orchestra. Although he continued his orchestral career, he found himself surrounded by the new jazz sound, which led him to try and play it for himself. Sometimes it worked, more often it did not. This led him to conclude that what worked should be written down and scored, so that mistakes would not occur. Partly because of his classical training, and partly, no doubt, because he lacked the peculiar type of musicianship required to trust in the improvisations of his fellow players, Whiteman did much to formalize jazz. This is not to accuse him of stifling the form: anybody who could employ talents like the cornetist Bix Beiderbecke, the saxophonist Jimmy Dorsey, the trombonist Jack Teagarden, not to mention the vocalist Bing Crosby, deserves a niche in the jazz valhalla. It is also fair to say that when his orchestra got to be over twenty-five in number, a fair degree of musical organization was a necessity. Yet

London gets New York's latest steps by telephone: a demonstration in the Royal Opera House, Covent Garden in 1927.

the jazz Whiteman played was very different from the free-floating, never-the-same-twice music that poured out of the pioneers. Whiteman amplified the form, but did little to enhance it; he lacked the original genius of a Duke Ellington or a Count Basie; he was a white man who was (according to some) exploiting black music by making it palatable to the white majority.

This last was a common phenomenon. The musical establishment was dominated by whites, who were in business for profit; blacks were still segregated, publicly if not officially, nearly a century after emancipation. Tony Palmer reports that until the late 1940s black performers in the smart New York Rainbow Room were all required to use the service elevator, while Lionel Hampton found that he was only able to play in the best hotels and ballrooms when he became part of Benny Goodman's first quartet. (Goodman refused to accept bookings for segregated audiences.) Whiteman became part of the musical establishment, and gave pleasure to millions who had no interest in the politics of segregation or exploitation. That does not, however, cause the facts to vanish.

Whiteman's first record with his full orchestra was an arrangement of two popular tunes, "The Japanese Sandman" and "Whispering." It went on sale in 1920 and within five years had sold more than $1\frac{1}{4}$ million copies in the United States alone. From then on recording companies wanted little but the Whiteman approach: popular tunes played with a sweet sound, a swingy precision, and featuring star soloists who stuck to the arrangements prepared for them. Whiteman had a nose for what would sell, and he was always abreast, if not ahead, of the times. In 1920

he started "jazzing the classics," with a one-step version of Ponchielli's "Dance of the Hours"; when the opening of Tutankhamen's tomb proved a sensation (in 1923), he dressed one of his bands in pseudo-Egyptian clothes; in 1924, at New York's Aeolian Hall, he introduced that legendary blend of jazz and classical music, Gershwin's "Rhapsody in Blue"; and the following year he recorded "I Miss My Swiss/My Swiss Miss Misses Me" as a novelty record complete with yodeling chorus. He negotiated a Hollywood film about himself and the orchestra, which came out as *King of Jazz*, and though the Depression forced him to cut the number of his players from thirty-four to twenty, he still kept his audience—partly by introducing female vocalists—through the era of swing and bop, by lending his commercial style and class to whatever was popular. After World War II, Whiteman stopped conducting to concentrate on guest appearances on television and radio. Had he not died in December 1967, he would doubtless have enjoyed the nostalgia for his type of music that distinguishes the late 1970s. Commercial it may have been, but it certainly kept people dancing.

The Charleston

The name comes from Charleston, South Carolina, where the dance was "discovered" being performed by black dockworkers. It appeared to be another burlesque dance, and it first hit the general public through the medium of the Ziegfeld Follies in October 1923, where it cashed in on the sentiment in favor of black culture that had scarcely abated since the ragtime era. According to Frances Rust, it next became part of a touring show

Paul Whiteman's band in action.

ABOVE: *The dangers of overindulgence: the Charleston knee.*
TOP: *An intimate night club Charleston contest.*

called *Runnin' Wild*, featuring black actors, whose success gave dance teachers the idea of getting in on the act. By toning down the side-kicking steps that only trained dancers could perform properly, and mixing in the steps of the two-step and fox trot, the teachers managed to make the Charleston acceptable to everyone. It had speed, exuberance, and an unforgettable rhythm. Soon Tin Pan Alley was turning out Charlestons for the dance bands to record.

In July 1925, the *Dancing Times* arranged a special tea dance for teachers to learn the new dance, and by the end of the year England was as Charleston-mad as the United States. It was naturally regarded in many quarters as vulgar, degenerate, and—in the words of the *Daily Mail*—"reminiscent only of negro orgies." It was also regarded as a danger to public health, because of the strain imposed by the dance on ankles, heart, knees, and other parts. Nevertheless, the Prince of Wales performed the dance with distinction; young people blocked traffic by dancing in the street; and dance halls posted notices reading P.C.Q. (Please Charleston Quietly), so great was the danger—to other dancers—of over-exuberant kicking.

Everybody did the Charleston, as shown by the vain attempts to discourage the dance in places as varied as the Hammersmith Palais and the smart hotels, where modern dancing to a small but skilled band had become a fashionable feature. It provided one of the most enduring images of the 1920s, if only because it was easy

to film. Its longevity is somewhat out of proportion to its importance, since it was not in vogue for long. The twenties, after all,
began—in the United States at least—with the May Day riots of
1919, when (in the words of Fitzgerald) "the police rode down the
demobilized country boys gaping at the orators in Madison
Square." They ended in the Great Crash of 1929. It was a decade
that included prohibition and Al Capone (who liked to relax to
the jazz of the speak-easies, and who enriched those who pleased
him with lavish tips); Kahlil Gibran and John Dos Passos; the
"Negro nationalism" (apartheid in reverse) of Marcus Garvey
and the fundamentalism of William Jennings Bryan. It was also an
age of boom (not to mention bust), of the domination of national
life by the big cities, of cynicism and self-indulgence after the
ravages of war.

"It was characteristic of the Jazz Age that it had no interest in
politics at all," said F. Scott Fitzgerald, performing a sort of verbal
equivalent of the Charleston; a modern historian, Paul A. Carter,
describes man in the 1920s as being "trapped between an Old
Society which cramped his style and a Big Society that seemed to
have no room for style at all." Whatever else they had, the
flappers and their consorts had no sense of doom, of being on the
edge of an abyss. It was an age of pleasure, for those that could
afford it, and more could than ever before. Walt Disney had an
immense hit with a cartoon character called Oswald the Rabbit,

ABOVE: *Everybody
Charlestons: Joan
Crawford . . . and
Arthur Murray in
mid-flight.*

*Getting down to it:
flapper and friend.*

Bee Jackson, world Charleston champion.

OPPOSITE: *Black bottom endurance contest at the Roseland Ballroom, New York, 1927.*

A poster advertising the Varsity drag.

before Mickey Mouse became the first animated creature to have synchronized sound. And in 1925 a pupil of Vernon Castle called Arthur Murray formulated and standardized six basic ballroom steps for the new generation.

The twenties was also an emancipated age, which showed in dances and fashions that the older generation could only think of as "abandoned." So short did skirts become that the "strippers" who had appeared around 1917 had to bare their breasts to stay ahead. On the dance floor, the "closed couple" dance that had shocked the nineteenth century gave way to dances where the constant presence of a partner was unimportant. "Cutting in"— changing partners in mid-dance—was all the rage, offering a new freedom of choice to women equal to that enjoyed by men. The Charleston was just one of the many dances that could give pleasure to the individual performer, without relying totally on somebody else. Its basic step was employed in many short-lived dances, such as the Varsity drag, that was introduced by Zelma O'Neal in the 1927 show *Good Times*.

The Black Bottom and the Shimmy

Both these dances had strong African- and Caribbean-style hip movements, and both first appeared on the stage. The black bottom was summed up by Curt Sachs, in almost approving tones, as "a lively mixture of side-turns, stamps, skating-glides, skips and leaps." The shimmy involved a turning-in of knees and toes, followed by a wiggle of the backside, which naturally excited hostile comment. It was not only the movements that caused agitation, it was the "wild" jazz rhythms that were an essential accompaniment. The two dances owed something to the fox trot and the animal dances of the previous decade; and both enjoyed a short and violent life—which is what the young were warned would await them if they persisted in such immoral behavior.

Dance Marathons

This mainly American phenomenon, which lasted from 1923 until 1933, when it was declared illegal, deserves a special section to itself. It was a spectator sport exploited, often grossly, by show biz entrepreneurs, who saw that there was a killing to be made in getting people to watch dancers gyrating until, quite literally, they dropped. The prizes were not enormous, but then by no means all the contestants were victims of the Depression, for whom a few dollars meant salvation.

It started with a nine-and-one-half-hour consecutive dance in England, but this record was quickly broken by a New York hostess, Alma Cummings, who wore out six partners in a twenty-seven-hour marathon held in the Audubon Ballroom in 1923. Endurance tests were another feature of the 1920s, a way in which the individual could rise above the crowd. Dance marathons added music and sex appeal, plus the tension of rooting for your particular hero and heroine, whose history and ambitions were

The black bottom demonstrated in Atlantic City by Deana Hunt, before an admiring audience in 1926.

LEFT: *Side turn during the black bottom.* RIGHT: *The shimmy, as performed by Gilda Gray.*

endlessly recited by a fast-talking master of ceremonies. Anyone could do it, but most preferred to watch. A marathon staged in New York's Roseland Ballroom to find the world champions was raided by the police after three days, but the proprietor simply transferred the remaining couples, still dancing away, into a removal van and from there onto a sixty-foot sloop which promptly sailed out three miles, beyond police jurisdiction. This particular session ended when the contestants became too seasick to continue, but marathons rapidly assumed the dimensions of a full-blown craze.

Contestants who stood a fair chance of winning were often sponsored by local businesses, whose wares they would advertise on their clothes. Some contestants had their teeth extracted during sessions; some got married, still dancing; some started to go crazy; and in 1932 a young man dropped dead after forty-eight days and nights of nonstop movement. Successful dancers turned professional and arrived for marathons all over the country. The rules—every organized sport has rules—were many and strict. Two minutes in each hour were allowed for toilet needs, and ten minutes every hour for a rest (but not a sleep). You were not allowed to wear shorts or slacks, or to smoke or spit. A shower every

twelve hours was compulsory, and you received eight hot meals a day. The worst part was when there were only a few couples left, and the band speeded up the music. The longest marathon, according to *The Guinness Book of Records*, lasted twenty-four weeks and five days before being stopped by the authorities in Pittsburgh. The rest allowance was progressively cut to ten, seven, six, five and in the final weeks to three minutes an hour. The thousand-dollar prize was equivalent to twenty-four cents per hour. This may have been more humane than the gladiatorial contests staged by the Romans—and of course no one was *forced* to enter—but not much more.

In 1928 the mighty Manhattan Casino in New York staged a multiracial marathon that made a hero out of George "Shorty" Snowden, champion dancer of Harlem's Savoy Ballroom. Shorty had "Number 7" stitched on his shirt, and he soon became the favorite of columnists like Walter Winchell and Ed Sullivan. At some point Shorty decided to "fling his partner out and improvise a few solo steps of his own. In the midst of the monotony of the marathon, the effect was electric, and even the musicians came to life. Shorty had started something." (Marshall and Jean Stearns, *Jazz Dance.**) When a Fox Movietone News interviewer asked Shorty what he was doing, he replied, without stopping, "the lindy." Another craze was born.

The Lindy, or Jitterbug

The Great Crash hit record companies no less than other industries: sales dropped from one hundred million in 1927 to six million in 1931. With the death of the jazz age—or suicide, as some saw it—the very word "jazz" came to have an old-fashioned ring. The music industry began looking for a new sound, something that combined popular tunes with jazz rhythms, and which was different from the "sweet" strict-tempo music favored by the older generation. The answer was swing, where the melodies were broken up by improvisations, and the complex rhythms of the expert jazz player were brought to bear on a tune designed for dancing. If that sounds no different from the procedures of the older jazz band, you have to listen to the sound of Benny Goodman, the "King of Swing," and compare it with that of Paul Whiteman, the "King of Jazz." Perhaps a new name was needed to wash out the taste of the immediate past. (Boogie-woogie was another title for swing music played on the piano. The name came from boogie, a pejorative term for a black performer, with woogie added to make up the rhyme.) The new sound was less ornate than its jazzy predecessors, less restrained, more artistic, more individualistic. The beat was new, and the effect of Goodman's swing band ripping out the tunes to the electric drumming of Gene Krupa was to bring kids out of their seats to dance in the aisles. Whatever else it was, swing was not subdued. And its new rhythms called forth new dances.

* Macmillan Publishing Co., Inc. Copyright © 1968 by Jean Stearns and Estate of Marshall Stearns.

OPPOSITE: *Asleep on the job: a couple well past their thousandth hour in a dance marathon.*

The hop had been around long before Charles Lindbergh grabbed the imagination of the entire world by flying the Atlantic single-handed. Some say that the lindy hop was named in his honor when one of a number of ecstatic dancers leaped across the floor saying, "Look! I'm flying just like Lindbergh!" Others say that the dance, with its improvised steps, was just lent Lindbergh's name by dancers oppressed by machine-induced uniformity. Within a decade, however, the new form was rechristened the jitterbug—and by then Lindbergh himself had denounced the United States, as being "immoral" and "disorderly." Nevertheless, the name lindy still stuck to the dance.

For those ten years, according to Marshall and Jean Stearns, the lindy, or jitterbug, remained the sole possession of small groups of amateur dancers in some big cities. It burst upon the general public in 1936, as a dance performed to swing music. The young who jitterbugged to Benny Goodman were thrilled by the opportunity to throw each other around the floor while keeping to the beat. For the jitterbug hustled in what looked like two major dance innovations. One was the "breakaway," or solo part, usually for the male. Although universal in African dancing, this had not been seen in Western dance since the seventeenth century, and over the last hundred years had been completely ousted by the "closed" position of the waltz and other round dances. The other innovation was the "air steps" in which the dancers simply took off from the floor. This had not appeared in the West since *la volta* of Queen Elizabeth I's time, and there were many jitterbuggers who regarded the air steps as mere exhibitionism, preferring to display their skill while staying on the ground. Neither of these "innovations" was entirely new, but to a generation who showed no interest in or reverence for the past, they seemed revolutionary.

The jitterbug was more of a style than a dance: a violent, even frenzied athleticism was often employed that made it hazardous for performers and their fellow dancers alike. The name seemed to sum up the movements of its fans, and it became current at the same time as "hepcat," a term used to describe a swing addict. (The most plausible derivation of "hep" is that it comes from the U.S. Army, where "hep" is used for "left" in drilling—so to be hep is to be in step. Later, of course, "hep" became "hip." But that is to anticipate.) Jitterbugging was sexual, exhibitionistic, cathartic, and risky. It could be performed on the spot, or the partners could whirl each other around to take up the entire floor; it was more than a young person's dance, it was a dance for *attractive* young people, for lithe beings who enjoyed flaunting their bodies. Naturally it was frowned on because of this, and was even barred from many dance halls, ostensibly because of the physical dangers involved.

Jitterbugging, which was given a new lease of life in England during World War II, largely through the efforts of American GIs, was another example of progress toward sexual emancipation. It was a dance that belied the idea that the twenties represented a lost golden age, that the young of the thirties should pay penance

OPPOSITE, ABOVE: *The lindy at the Savoy ballroom, Harlem.*

OPPOSITE, BELOW: *That uncontrollable urge: Goodman fans invade the stage.*

ABOVE: *The breakaway step in the jitterbug.*

ABOVE, RIGHT: *Swinging to Benny Goodman: a version of the lindy called the shag.*

RIGHT: *Earnest young swingers concentrate on getting it right.*

OPPOSITE, ABOVE: *Jitterbuggers at the New York World's Fair, 1939.*

OPPOSITE, BELOW: *Dancing in the aisles on board the first Long Island Railroad "Swing Train" to the New York World's Fair.*

How to do it with polish: demonstration dancers at Harrods, the London department store, 1922.

for the sins of their fathers. In its wildness, and especially in the freedom it offered to the individual rather than the couple, it anticipated jive and the rock dances of the fifties and sixties. But "Shorty" Snowden, who claimed to have invented the "breakaway"—and who was made to give up dancing by his doctor in 1938 because his feet had been pounded shapeless—was scathing about the lindy's descendants. "Lindy Hopping today seems to be mostly acrobatic tricks," he said. "The kids don't stop to learn the fundamentals first—they just start throwing each other around. To be done right, the lindy is mostly footwork, and now there's no real footwork any more. And they can't do it fast, they have to dance half-time." (From an interview with George "Shorty" Snowden, New York, 1959; quoted in *Jazz Dance*.) All revolutionaries mistrust the purity of those who come after them.

The English Style and the Quickstep

The "processional" dance, where couples proceeded around the floor in a smooth and regulated manner, following the tradition of centuries, was far from dead. On the contrary, there were many groups who rivaled the swing bands in popularity by providing sweet music for the waltz and the fox trot: Guy Lombardo's was but one of them. What was happening in the British ballroom, perhaps out of self-defense, perhaps to fight off the "anarchy" of the young, was a new standardization of steps. A ballroom branch of the Imperial Society of Teachers of Dancing was formed in 1924, which had, in the words of Victor Silvester, "as great an influence on ballroom dancing as did the founding of the Acadé-

mie Royale by Louis XIV of France on ballet." It established the English style that is still paramount in ballroom dancing the world over.

Jack Buchanan in action, 1922.

The various conferences of dance teachers during the 1920s prescribed speeds and steps for the waltz and the fox trot, while the ballroom branch laid down standards of performance that had to be attained by candidates wishing to join their ranks. Dance competitions for British, and then for world, championships made the English style the model for all good ballroom dancers. The details of performance were as minutely practiced and scrutinized as in ballet.

But the English style was by no means stiff and artificial. On the contrary, the aim was to get as much natural smoothness as possible into the movements. There was little of the posturing that had marked the ballroom dances of previous eras. A good dancer was a person of elegance and stylistic, if not sexual, appeal—someone like Jack Buchanan, perhaps, and of course Fred Astaire. Too much flashiness was as taboo as a whiff of sensuality. Valentino was one thing, his "greasy dago" imitators quite another.

The division thus established between ballroom dancers and those who preferred less formal, more individual, styles was one of attitude, not age. Ballroom dancers preferred the certainties of prescribed forms; the knowledge that there was a rigidly established right and wrong way of doing things was a great source of security. And there was their attitude to the role of the sexes. In the more frenetic dances of the 1920s and 1930s, culminating in jitterbugging, the relationship between the couple dancing was, or could be, a casual one. Changing partners frequently during a single dance was common, and individual display was encouraged on both sides. In ballroom dancing, by contrast, there was no getting away from the fact that it was the man who led. However good a dancer a woman might be, on the ballroom floor she could only perform as well as the man would allow her to. For many couples, young and old, the knowledge that such a relationship was fixed and unchangeable must also have offered a degree of comfort. I am sure it is one of the factors that has given ballroom dancing a new appeal today, to those looking for the old certainties which some find outdated and worse.

At any rate there is no denying that in the 1930s, and indeed in our own time, ballroom dancing regained popularity. For many, the appeal lay in the dancing competitions that became increasingly common all over North America and Europe. For most it was a soothing pastime that required a certain degree of skill, a chance to glide about to the sugary sounds of Glenn Miller, and banish the hepcats and their uncouth music from the mind.

An example of the new standardization was the quickstep, the name adopted for the quick fox trot, as the fox trot proper got slower and slower. It answered the need for a dance that could be performed at a fair speed but with the smooth "walking" movements, largely on the flat of the feet, that marked the English style. The requirement that feet be turned outward, the artificial position derived from the ballet in the seventeenth century, was dropped altogether. The rise and fall required in the quickstep was (and is) performed on the ball of the foot rather than the tip of the toes, and the knees were alternately flexed and straightened. As it was a dance that required a fair amount of space, it was difficult to perform it in the tiny nightclubs frequented by the smart set. The English style needed a ballroom, and an uncluttered one at that, to do itself justice.

The Lambeth walk, 1939.

Novelty Dances

There was a middle ground, at least in the English-speaking world, between the jitterbuggers and the ballroom dancers. In the 1930s this was filled by novelty dances, usually processional affairs that required certain actions to be performed in a "follow-the-leader" fashion. In New York in 1935 there appeared the big apple, a circle dance for couples who obeyed the orders of a caller and performed figures such as the lindy, the shag, and trucking. As a party dance this was brought to England by dance teachers. Its name apparently came from the Big Apple Club in Columbia, South Carolina. It offered

the pleasures of the old communal round dance at a time when *The big apple, as a* nightclubs were becoming increasingly crowded. Other novelties *round dance.* were the Lambeth walk, which started in 1937 as a musical number featuring Lupino Lane singing a cockney song about the people of Lambeth, and which was popular in England and the United States right through the war; the hokey-pokey, another cockney number (known in England as the hokey-cokey) where you "put your right foot in; put your right foot out; put your right foot in, and shake it all about"; the palais glide, which could have been danced with equanimity by the most decorous Victorian; and the boomps-a-daisy, whose chief feature was a vigorous bumping of the partners' hips.

But the most enduring of these dances was the Cuban conga, where participants snaked their way around the floor, the house, and even the town, to a strong Latin American rhythm, performing the while a one-two-three-kick step. Snake dances were popular with the most primitive people—they were a way of marking out tribal territory—while to all Freudians the snake is a potent sexual symbol. There was not much that was sexy in holding onto the back of the person in front of you, and being held in your turn, but there was a certain pleasure in "conquering" territory by dancing through it. More important, the conga (the name comes from the Congo) was evidence of the popularity of the smooth Latin American sound, best exemplified by Xavier Cugat

A dance that sank without trace: the the meebie-jeebies.

and his Waldorf-Astoria Orchestra, and in England by Edmundo Ros.

The Rumba

Latin American music had inspired such dances as the maxixe and, of course, the tango. The beguine was immortalized by Cole Porter ("Begin the Beguine," 1935), though it is doubtful if any self-respecting South American would recognize a native dance in those swooping strains; the Spanish bolero was briefly rescued from the concert platform where Ravel had left it; the *guajira* and the *danzon* flitted across the floor for a short season, while the *paso doble*, which is still seen in dancing competitions, was a Spanish one-step that was usually confused with the fox trot. But the most famous of the Latin American dances to gain popularity in North America and Europe was without doubt the rumba, a flamboyant Cuban dance that reached the United States in the late 1920s.

The European powers who colonized South America and the Caribbean—Spain, Portugal, France, and England—all imported slaves from Africa to eke out the back-breaking work of the local peons. The rumba combined African and Caribbean rhythms in a dance which in its original form was definitely erotic.

To an insistent and arousing beat the woman performed sinuous movements of hip, trunk and shoulders, while the man did his best to respond. But for the dance to be effective as a work of excitement and release, the performer had virtually to grow up with its extraordinary rhythms, and to be singularly uninhibited. Not all Cubans possessed this last quality, and for their benefit there emerged a refined version of the rumba named the *son*. The true rumba was considered low in its native country; the *son* was slower and more sentimental, with movements that were mere coquetry as opposed to the promise of the real thing. Naturally it was the *son*, speeded up and peddled as the rumba, which was exported elsewhere.

The name rumba itself came to be applied indiscriminately to many Latin American dances. In England the "Caribbean sound" did not catch on until after World War II. The rumba was first standardized by the British dance teachers in 1946, when it was taught on the United States pattern, with couples dancing in a square or "rumba box" rather than moving around the whole floor. But although Caribbean music continued to be popular right through the 1950s, with steel bands and the jazzy syncopation that produced the calypso, the rumba soon became a dance chiefly for those interested in ballroom competitions.

ABOVE, LEFT: *A serious matter: the* paso doble *performed by the champion dancer Miss Barbara Miles, 1926.*

ABOVE, RIGHT: *The rumba as performed by George Raft and Carole Lombard.*

197

The Samba

The samba is a Brazilian name for the dances originally performed by African slaves, and in Brazil itself there are a number of local sambas or batuques, each with their own variations. These are group dances, owing something to the maxixe and the African *lundu*. When it went north to the United States—it was introduced at the 1939 New York World's Fair—the samba became a couple dance, and in that form came to Europe before the outbreak of World War II, popularized in the movies of Carmen Miranda. It did not catch on in Europe, however, until after the war was over. Its reputation in the early 1950s, in England at any rate, was greatly helped by the fact Princess Margaret became adept at performing it. The characteristic samba movement, as practiced outside its native country, where it is a popular dance at carnival time, is a bouncing or dropping action, obtained by bending and straightening the knees while the weight is transferred from the ball to the flat of the foot. A jazzed-up version of the samba was the bossa nova, which was briefly popular in the early 1960s.

The samba re-created by Brazilian dancers for the benefit of a British television audience.

The Mambo

The mambo was born in Cuba, the child of jazz and Latin American music that itself owed so much to Africa. A black Cuban bandleader named Pérez Prado is credited with starting what became the big dance craze of the mid-1950s, in Havana in 1943. He took the rhythm of the dances performed by the sugar-cane cutters, and syncopated it. According to *Newsweek* the word "mambo" came from the Nañigo dialect spoken in Cuba, and has no "real" meaning. The mambo contained one peculiar feature, a

OPPOSITE: *Cover for the rumba, New York.*

The mambo at a weekly contest held in Harlem's Savoy Ballroom, 1953.

dance equivalent of its jagged rhythm: there was a beat in every bar on which the dancer took no step, but rested. The actual steps were embellished with kicks and body wiggles, the more sinuous the better. Although it was simple, dance teachers did excellent business teaching it, especially when it developed three separate rhythms: the single, double, and triple mambo—an echo of the lindy, which had also acquired three such distinct rhythms.

The Cha-cha

Based on the rhythm of the triple mambo, the cha-cha was a Latin American dance whose name, according to one authority, came from the hissing sound made by the heelless slippers worn by Cuban women. Consisting of two slow steps followed—or preceded—by three quick ones (the "cha-cha-cha" uttered by dancers and musicians alike), the dance was considered by one contemporary critic to be "a curious combination of sexy come-on and staid standoffishness. The couples make only occasional and fleeting contact. For the most part, each works intently on his own . . . with barely a glance at what his mate is up to. . . . " (Arthur Knight, "Dance in the Movies," in *Dance* Magazine, December, 1956.) Nevertheless, the dance has been extraordinarily popular with old and young alike, from the mid-1950s to today. The old enjoyed it because it could be performed with rumba

figures substituted for the sexy wiggles favored by the young. And teenagers enjoyed it because it was another of those dances that allowed for individual display.

The Merengue

This was a dance popular in the United States in the mid-1950s, performed to samba music or similar Latin rhythms with a strong beat. It supposedly came from the Dominican Republic, where it was said to have been first performed by a crippled general whose fellow guests respectfully imitated his every move as he dragged his lame right leg across the floor. This "limp" step was retained and smoothed over; the dance became quite lively, with a step on every beat, plenty of knee action, and that wiggle from side to side that seemed essential to all Latin dances. Variations included a turn under an arch made by the man's arm—a sedate, nightclub version of the jitterbug that was still alive and kicking.

Jive

By the middle 1950s dance bands had mostly disappeared: their place had been taken by jukeboxes which played the latest tunes at the drop of a nickel. The young jived to these tunes, jive being the latest name for the lindy (with all its three rhythms) and the jitterbug—dances for the individual which could be improvised.

The old jitterbuggers considered jive tame, but the newest generation of dancers scaled everything down. Television, the ultimate in passive entertainment, saw to that: life was reduced to a twelve-inch space. As ballroom and "old-time" dancing became a pursuit of the middle-aged, with nostalgia misting the polish of their shoes, the young appeared to be rejecting the rhythms and styles that had sustained the music business for half a century. The executives of music publishers, record companies, film studios, and radio and television networks cast around in desperation for a way of tapping the purses of a market rich but unsatisfied. And then they found a prematurely middle-aged, stout, baby-faced gentleman called **Bill Haley**.

OPPOSITE: *The new jazz age: jive in a London club.*

ABOVE: *The delicate touch of 1950s jive.*

203

DISCO TIME

Rock 'n' roll

HERE IS WHERE it gets personal. Though the 1950s sometimes seem as distant as the 1920s, and often more so, at least I lived through them. My detachment as a historian is therefore colored by actual experience. You have been warned.

"The professors have taken the cha out of our cha-chas," bemoans Martinez, the Latin American bandleader ousted in popularity by Bill Haley and His Comets in that seminal film of 1956, *Rock around the Clock*. But the professors were not the only ones to blame. Youth as a consumer class had gradually begun to assert its strength in the mass market. First the sales of cheap sheets of music, then of cheap records, and finally of cheap radios had shown that the young were, all by themselves, a legitimate target for the purveyors of mass entertainment. Being singled out for special treatment gave the young that same confidence in themselves that other minority groups fostered. And in the best traditions of the class struggle, they asserted their independence from those whose supremacy had until now been unchallenged: the smart set, the upper stratum who still favored the smooth rhythms of Latin American dancing, and the teachers who were considered their lackeys.

Of course, the young were as mixed a bunch as their elders. When rock 'n' roll hit Britain, I took less notice than when skirts had risen above the knee earlier in the decade. I went to see *Rock around the Clock* out of curiosity, and was both disappointed and relieved when there was no rioting in the aisles. It was aimed at people of my age group, and since everyone at school talked about it with approval, and everyone at home with disapproval, I felt both a small sense of affinity—age solidarity, perhaps—and a sense of self-protectiveness: I did not want to be treated as part of a herd. Elvis Presley was just a figure of fun. But then so was Victor Silvester.

Nevertheless, to carry any weight with my contemporaries, especially those of the opposite sex, I had to be at least aware of the new music and to be able to move to its beat. Perversely, it seemed to me, the movements had to appear both spontaneous and yet follow certain prescribed, though ever-changing, patterns (which usually eluded me). I could never have attempted the style demonstrated by Lisa Johns and her brother in *Rock around the Clock*, however different it was from the ballroom formalities which my mother had long tried, and failed, to instill into me. But the secret appeal of rock 'n' roll was that it seemed a democratic

movement, a from-the-bottom-up phenomenon, that forced its way to the top. I think that was why so many of us instinctively liked it, even if we neither wholly understood nor wholly embraced it. One could not be a traitor to one's class, could one?—even though that class had been created by commercial pressure, and not through the more usual common suffering.

Two things, then, separated the young of the rock 'n' roll era from the young of all other ages. The first was their consciousness of their separateness from the rest of society—a class not cut off from power and influence, but on the contrary pampered as only growing markets are. The second was the endless need for novelty, or rather for constantly renewed signs of this separateness. This can be blamed on, or explained by, the mass media, which made news travel at the speed of light. The courtiers of the seventeenth century, the bucks of the eighteenth, the dandies of the nineteenth, could be confident that in the time it took for their latest fad to catch on in the rest of the country, they would acquire something new and so preserve their distance from the common herd. But for the hep (later to become hip) generation of the mid-twentieth century there was no such relaxed interval. A new record was in a million shops and jukeboxes simultaneously, the whole world over. New sounds were broadcast coast to coast, new dances

ABOVE, LEFT: *The wild ones: rocking in Newcastle, 1955.*

ABOVE, RIGHT: *Rocking with Lionel Hampton, who started his career with the Benny Goodman quartet.*

appeared on the new television screens, embracing audiences so huge that nothing could be secret any more. The only hope for the new generation was to use their superior reserves of energy to keep moving fast, to dizzy the rest of the world with their perpetual motion. Of course, that has always been the hope of every new generation, but until the age of simultaneous mass exposure it was easier to change your codes and keep them secret. Now, however, there was this peculiar symbiosis: the young, anxious to preserve their mystique, both feeding on and being fed by the mass-cult creators who needed to know their secrets (so as to be able to exploit them), and to create them (ditto). The result was a pace of change fast enough to make the head ache.

It is impossible to deal with each dance of the fifties and sixties separately. For one thing, they changed at a bewildering rate. For another, their provenance remains largely a mystery. And for a third, the dances were on the scene for such a short time they left few of the traces which allow a historian to do his job. They are not even antique enough for nostalgia. Not quite yet.

The rock 'n' roll generation, like every generation of young people throughout history, thought everything they did was new. But just as, in the earlier sections of this book, I have sought for the connections between one dance style and another, and have found in them a link which is well-nigh unbroken, so now, in dealing with my own time, I find that what I had thought of as a revolution

was nothing of the sort. Indeed, perhaps the only thing about the new music that could be called truly new was its shattering volume. That was due to the invention of the electric amplifier; decibels or no decibels, the beat remained essentially that of the black dance rhythms that had steadily evolved since the 1880s.

Rocking 'em in the mid 1950s.

THE DANCES

Rock Dances

The origin of the term rock 'n' roll is, naturally, disputed. The disc jockey Alan Freed claimed to have popularized it when he introduced a radio show in Cleveland, Ohio, called "Moon Dogs Rock and Roll Party." Freed—who also figured as Bill Haley's champion in *Rock around the Clock*—considered that the older term for the type of music he was featuring in his program had racial overtones. That term was "rhythm and blues" (R and B), which in turn had been known as "race" (i.e., black) music before the growing market for its sounds made the record industry label it more respectfully. In the same way "hillbilly" music was transformed into "country and western" (C and W).

Rock 'n' roll may have come simply from the words that occurred so frequently in R and B songs—e.g., "You got to rock with me, Henry, all night long; roll with me Henry, I don't mean maybe." The sexual connotations were obvious—and this was another factor in the new music. One sure way of emphasizing the differences between the generations is to shock the old with talk of sex. There was much exaggeration by pundits about the "rebellion" of this new class of person called teenagers, but a rebellion implies more than a different way of dancing. You might say, with equal justification, that following the small groups who played rock 'n' roll was a rebellion against the corporate image of big bands, a revolt against the sheer size and commercialization of popular music. But rock 'n' roll was not a political movement. It was a sound—loud, and with an insistent beat; a style—body movements that were the antithesis of the smooth motions of the ballroom; and a language—often incomprehensible (another way of keeping it secret from the grown-ups), but undeniably sexy. Adult protests got the "rock" of "Rock with me, Henry" changed to "Dance with me, Henry," but that was incidental, a small proof that the young were succeeding in asserting their separateness. The fact was that kids often danced to rock 'n' roll in a "bump and grind" manner that their parents had forgotten. And when Elvis Presley came along with that extraordinary grinding of his hips and pelvis, the effect was nothing short of sensational.

OPPOSITE: *The pelvis as king: Elvis Presley.*

ABOVE: *The athletic nabob of sob, Johnnie Ray.*

ABOVE, RIGHT: *Group dancing: a lunchtime rock session in London, 1957.*

RIGHT: *The Madison, as performed in New York.*

Bill Haley started with a combination of C and W, Dixieland, and old-style R and B, where the band played in all sorts of weird positions to create a sense of visual excitement, from blowing on their backs to lying on top of their instruments. Elvis sang what he called "country rock," which the professionals identified as a vigorous and original mixture of R and B, and C and W. More simply, he was a white boy singing black music. And as the roots of the music lay in the rhythms and style that black musicians had been playing for years, so too the dances owed their origin largely to the black community. This fact alone was enough to upset the parents of the white kids. There were some who believed that it was a plot by the National Association for the Advancement of Colored People to subvert the morals of white youth.

But if we can trace the rock dances to their African and Caribbean sources—as Marshall and Jean Stearns have done in their book *Jazz Dance*—this does not mean that they are purely derivative. Elvis's gyrations may have been "a relatively tame version of the 'snake hips' of the negro folk, popularised in Harlem by dancer Earl Tucker during the twenties" (Stearns), and the snake hips itself may have been a wholly African dance, but Elvis did not go around boning up on the folk culture of the Ashanti. He was a poor white from Mississippi, a member of a church where music and prayer were indistinguishable, an admirer of R and B, C and W, crooners like Johnnie Ray ("the nabob of sob"), and blues singers like Bo Diddley—who was also no slouch when it came to wild leg movements. The Africa that had given birth to jazz was all around. Elvis clothed it all in a white skin—and added sex appeal.

Yet the dances were not particularly sexy. Elvis was, to millions of adolescents who writhed and screamed and wet themselves in excitement. Elvis was the first authentic rock 'n' roll superstar, the first singer to arouse the same kind of hysteria that had greeted Valentino. Sinatra was the first crooner to whip crowds into the frenzy that had once been the exclusive reserve of Hollywood stars; Johnnie Ray was the first to cause riots among hitherto docile adolescents. But Elvis was the one who really got 'em going and, like Valentino, his secret ingredient was simply sex. The more fuss that was made about this aspect of his persona—like Ed Sullivan having the television cameras shoot him from the waist up—the more his wiggle burned holes in the brains of the teenies. Music and sex, body and beat: could there by anything more exclusively, excitingly, exhilaratingly *young*?

But Elvis's sexuality was his alone. On stage or screen he set off a million fantasies, but he remained untouchable, inviolate. He was an idol, and you do not try to imitate idols—you propitiate them. The dances performed to his music, to rock 'n' roll in general, were not sexual pantomimes (Elvis always denied he was being lewd.) Pantomimes, yes, as the animal dances of the 1920s were imitations of the beasts they were named after. But not sublimations of the sexual act: that would have offended against the code of the king himself. The only act that mattered was his.

What set rock 'n' roll dance apart was that its style was a ming-
ling rather than a coupling; the dancers were loyal to their group
rather than to a partner. Obviously this had much to do with their
awareness of themselves as a class, but it was also something to do
with dancing conditions. Where people were packed tightly in
halls, arenas, or cafés, there was not much room to show off. Often
all that you could do was to make the right movements to show you
were part of the crowd. Your identity was that of the gang—which
is the very antithesis of coupled sexuality.

The move toward dancing without a partner reached back a
long way. There was of course the jitterbug, or lindy, the direct
ancestor of the intricate dances performed by Lisa Johns in *Rock
around the Clock*, where perfect timing was as necessary as superb
footwork. There was the Madison, a sort of halfway house between
jitterbug and jive, a group dance performed in a line, requiring
special music of its own that was neither rock nor ballroom. But

then there came a whole wave of rock dances that needed only a rock beat, not a special tune. What mattered in these dances was the little differences in movements that set them apart from each other. They were gang dances. Instead of needing performance *in* a group, they could be danced by individuals forming *part* of a group. The couple dance gave way to a collection of individuals who formed the gang.

Though given new labels—the jet, the locomotion, the choo-choo, the freeze, and lots of others—the movements were not entirely novel. As the Stearnses point out, the mashed potato was strongly reminiscent of the Charleston, the fly contained bits of the old eagle rock, the chicken turned out to be a parody of the lindy. The camel walk lived on in the stroll, and the slow drag came through in the fish. The influence of the Charleston showed up again in the bop, a dance popular in the United States in the mid-1950s, which spawned all sorts of variations, such as the scooter, the flea hop, the twister (five years before the twist proper), and the rock-and-around. The bop was not connected to the difficult jazz form known as bebop, pioneered by Charlie Parker. It started on the West Coast, no one knows how, and gained popularity alongside rock music that emphasized the "big beat." If you bought Ray Coniff's record, "Dance the Bop," you received a book of instruction in the dance by a Mr. Art Silva. He pointed out that the "big beat" actually comes on the upbeat of the music, overshadowing the traditionally stronger downbeat, which is the one on which dancers usually stepped out. The bop offered a dance emphasizing the upbeat, by means of a sort of marching in place. Mr. Silva considered it to be "the first distinct and significant American jazz dance to make an appearance in the last twenty years—and the only one to rival seriously the now classic jitterbug (or Swing, Lindy, Rock and Roll, or any of the various names this family of dances goes by)." He believed that the bop's "inherent vitality" gave it "an excellent chance for a place on the American dance scene for some time to come." Unfortunately, he was wrong.

The Twist

This was the dance that gave its name to an era. It was popularized by Chubby Checker, a onetime chicken plucker from Philadelphia, who in 1960 appeared on "American Bandstand," a television show aimed at adolescent pop fans. By the time the dance had caught on in the upper stratum of society—who flocked to a small and hitherto unknown New York nightspot called The Peppermint Lounge, to be photographed and written up by the press—the kids who had followed Checker's lead were on to something else. The twist was an easy dance, involving the sort of pelvic gyrations many critics called obscene (though Checker, like Elvis, denied it). Maybe the smart set adopted it because it took them five or six years to accept the movements which Elvis had pioneered. Certainly the dance received undue attention because society took it to its bosom and thus prolonged its natural life. The twist became the biggest commercial operation since the launch-

Alone in a crowd: the television show "American Bandstand."

ing of Presley: everything from spaghetti to shirts, frankfurters to ties, was given a registered "twist" trademark, and Checker became a millionaire through the franchised use of his name. It was hailed variously as a revolution in dance and a betrayal of all that dance stood for, "a valid manifestation of the Age of Anxiety" (*Saturday Review*), and a "replica of some ancient tribal puberty rite" (*Time*). For something so simple, it caused an amazing furore.

The movements of the dance consisted of the sort of mime that featured in most of the twist's contemporaries: you pretended you were toweling yourself after a bath while stubbing out a cigarette with your foot. Checker took the dance title from a song written by Hank Ballard in 1958. The kids found it fun and continued to dance it as long as their parents condemned it as lewd. Perhaps because of its very simplicity, some of the less inhibited, or more inebriated, patrons of The Peppermint Lounge happened to be giving the dance a whirl when gossip columnist "Cholly Knickerbocker" (Igor Cassini) was present. He wrote in *The New York Journal American* of the smart set slumming it, and from then on you could scarcely get into the Peppermint Lounge, unless you were titled, incredibly famous, or extraordinarily rich. Even Garbo turned up to be deafened, crushed, sweated over, jostled—and photographed, as she watched her peers attempt the twist. The Arthur Murrays arrived "to learn and not to teach." According to *The New Yorker* spy, Mrs. Murray considered the dance a nice exotic thing, good for reducing weight, and not at all vulgar. Mr. Murray thought it was not a dance at all—"no steps, pure swivel." Nevertheless, he was shortly advertising "six easy lessons for $25." And while on the subject of instructors, let me quote Mr. Seymour Kleinman (*Social Dancing*) who instructs the reader "on count one, exhale, collapse the chest and round the shoulders, on count two, inhale and straighten the shoulders"—as if the dance were a gymnastic exercise.

The twist was not the first dance for the individual rather than for the couple: as we have seen, that had been common since the beginning of rock'n'roll. But it was the first dance of the rock era to cross the generation gap, to be practiced by those long out of their teens whose attitude to the rest of rock dancing was one of indulgent ridicule. We can see now, with all the benefits of hindsight, that the twist scarcely deserved to be singled out from its very similar contemporaries. That it was is a tribute to the power of commercialization, which was responsible for the promotion of so many faddish dances, some of them linked directly to a product (like the mule and the drink that bore its name). None of these, however, rivaled the twist in popularity. By no stretch of the imagination could it be called a revolution in dance, but it was certainly a phenomenon of the mass-cult age—and one that was good for the hips.

Twisting at Roseland, New York City.

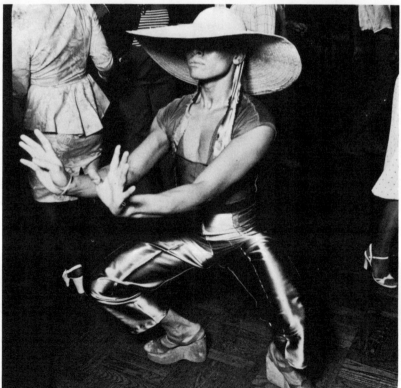

The frug, as practiced by the New York smart set.

Soul sister.

Mimic Dances

In the wake of the twist came scores of hip-swiveling dances that
involved some sort of pantomime. In performing the shake you
made your body shimmy, to do the hitchhike you just jerked your
arms, to dance the jerk you snapped your body. The monkey was
similar to the jerk, only faster; for the pony you brought your
knees up in a sort of trotting movement. In the swim you could
choose between breaststroke and crawl; in the skate you tried to
look as if you were flapping along while remaining more or less in
place. If there was nothing actually to imitate—that is, when
dances descended to the evolutionary level of the bug and the
clam—the lack of stylistic invention masked itself in odd names,
such as the boogaloo (in which the feet either tapped or brushed
across each other), the funky broadway (the same, with knee
bends), the watusi (wiggle, kick, clap), the hully-gully, the mashed
potato, the slop, the filly dog, and the frug, which involved nothing
more than shifting the weight from one foot to the other in time
with the music. In names, and often in style, these dances were
echoes of the short-lived fads of the 1920s: the aptly named fanny
bump, funky butt, squat, itch, grind and so on. The names were
sexier in the twenties than in the sixties, and so, often, were the
dances: the outrage of adult white society was nothing new. But
such inventiveness as there was soon ran out, and the dances
became as repetitive as the beat. The young who really wanted to
move had to look elsewhere for something different.

*New York night club
rockers.*

The hip culture on
Fire Island.

Soul Music

Black power was not just a political movement. It led many young whites to explore and admire black culture and submit to its influence. This was especially so in the case of black music. The Liverpool beat as played by the Beatles, which in 1962 gave pop music the kick it had long been seeking, owed much to the black rhythm and blues that the Beatles had heard in their youth. Paul McCartney even preferred to hear American black groups sing his songs, "'cos they do it better."

Reggae came from Jamaica and was popular for a while in England in the early seventies and in the United States in the middle of the decade. It had a distinct "missed" beat that made it hard for any but the best dancer to follow, and the sinuous hip movements, for example in the blue beat, were difficult even for a generation reared on the twist. It was a distinctive sound from a distinctive culture. Unfortunately, it lost both these distinctions when it became commercialized for the benefit of the white majority. Even the *reggae* dances, such as the ride-a-bike, became simplified to the point of banality.

But "soul" music—a direct descendant of the old jazz blues crossed with the rhythm and blues of the 1950s—had few distinct dances to it. By the time it became popular in the late 1960s, dance steps had almost totally given way to rhythmic movement. Dance itself was only part of a larger life-style that attempted to be all-embracing.

Lashing out in a New York night spot.

Woodstock and After

The pop culture of the late 1960s had wider ambitions than any of its predecessors. It was an offshoot, or outcrop, of the alternative society that thrived around 1968. It was, in the broadest sense, political. To rebel against everything represented by "the system" was not something that you just did in your off-duty moments. While it had been, dance was a central expression of that rebellion. Now rebellion showed in clothes, language, work, leisure, political and, above all, sexual attitudes. The rebel was instantly recognizable by her or his style. Dance was just a part of the general movement.

There were a lot of songs about revolution, about war against

Disco dancing: the bump.

society. If the revolt was not implicit in the words—such as the Rolling Stones' "Street Fighting Man"—it showed in the performance—for example in the cathartic and erotic aggression of Jimi Hendrix. Such music was almost impossible to *dance* to, but you could certainly move. Paradoxically, the more violent the message blasting out of the speakers, the more mesmerized the dancers became, the slower they moved. Possibly they were just too stoned. The noise was a drug all by itself.

And there was sex. The braver spirits of the alternative society believed in trying everything; the more timid majority tried to let it all hang out. Pop was their anthem: that meant you used it to move to, whether in or out of bed. In public, of course, sex was simulated—usually. But there was a sexuality about the sound and the movement that accompanied it that was no longer content to be merely implicit. As the older generation became more sexually tolerant, the younger had to go that much further to stay ahead. The vogue phrase "Let's get it all together," had literal as well as figurative connotations.

The apotheosis of the alternative society was the pop festival at Woodstock, New York, in May 1969. Among the thousands of fans gathered to hear, live, a galactic array of superstars, there was, quite genuinely, peace and love and an overwhelming sense of community, the contemplative ecstasy of a gathering that felt self-sufficient and able to tackle anything. The dancing was that of a generation that wanted to touch everything and each other, submerging their separateness in one mighty communing. After that, everything was an anticlimax.

The system did not break down as predicted, the Woodstock generation did not conquer the world, and the young of the late sixties became the parents of the seventies. Rebellion became once more a leisure activity; dancing as something approaching an art form revived. Discotheques—any place where records could be played with space to move—replaced café jukeboxes in popularity, in the tradition of the gramophone dances of the 1920s and 1930s. The discotheque provided an easy and instant form of the pop concert—with none of the hysteria associated with live perform- ance. Some, like New York's Le Jardin, became as fashionable (and as difficult to get into) as The Peppermint Lounge had once been. But what the discotheque provided was the opportunity for everyone to be a star. To be outrageous, extravagant, gorgeous, and bizarre was within the reach of every dance fan. It was a rebellion of peacocks against doves and ravens—strictly for appearances.

But dance has always gone backward as well as forward. The communal dances of Woodstock harked back to the earliest forms of dance, the round and the chain. Dance in the 1970s was moving back toward partner formations that an older generation had never forsaken. Not that you saw the fox trot in a discotheque, but the hustle and its variations began in what was called the "social dance position," that is, facing your partner and actually holding each other. The dance involved a step-tap-step-tap movement that the Castles might have popularized. The exhibitionism and the bisexuality of the hip generation, however, ensured that the present reflected the past through its own peculiar prism. Nothing changes, nothing stays the same—or, to put it in dance terms, there is no standing still.

FOLK DANCE

WHOLE LIBRARIES HAVE been written on the folk dances of the world—those long-lived dances of the people that have survived the vagaries of fashion. Their origins, development, and continued popularity have been studied by, among others, historians, anthropologists, sociologists, dance teachers, and critics. More important, they have been, and are, danced by enthusiasts who have not only kept alive the old traditions, but also have persuaded growing numbers of their appeal. The result is that, far from being a museum piece, folk dancing has a living dynamic of its own.

The themes common to folk dances of the entire world are those of death and resurrection, fertility, love and war. The circle dance that is the oldest form known to us survives today in many traditional dances, as does the function of dance to celebrate, initiate, or mourn. The dances of those countries I have chosen to deal with—in the main, those that are performed by ethnic groups in the United States—reflect these themes through the prism of their own traditions. Even so, it will be seen that folk dance styles and figures are remarkably similar throughout the Western world.

There is one curiosity in folk dance, which is that many of the so-called "traditional" dances are the inventions of the last 150 years. As the peasants became factory workers, many of their traditions died along with their superstitions and their way of life. A large number of folk dances performed today were heavily influenced by such popular numbers as the waltz and the polka. This is not to criticize: on the contrary, a tradition kept alive artificially and rigorously guarded against any contact with contemporary influences deserves to die. But there are not that many dances to be seen which enjoy a long and unbroken history (notable exceptions are the fertility dances such as the morris). When amateurs gather to enjoy a session of folk dancing—as opposed to professionals who are specially trained—they are usually dancing figures which are essentially modern.

This is especially so in the case of the folk dances of Israel. The movements of the hora, an ancient round dance for mixed couples that allows for exuberant displays of leaps and jumps, are common to many European nations, including Greece, Rumania, and Yugoslavia. The Israelis have made the hora the basis of many dances, of which perhaps the most famous is the couple dance *Hava Nagila* ("come let us be merry"). They have also invented

OPPOSITE: *Circle dance performed by Yugoslav women.*

Hungarian women
perform the bottle
dance.

dances to commemorate special events—such as the *vayiven uziyahu*, originally a dance for men only, composed in 1955 to commemorate the eighth anniversary of independence. Israeli choreographers have incorporated the figures of Middle Eastern dances they share with their neighbors, as well as those of their European immigrants. The dances of the Yemenite Jews, with their drumming, singing, and clapping, have also been an important influence.

In biblical times, dancing was a sacred duty. After the Diaspora, the Jews of Poland were once led to dance in synagogue, so exalted were they at the promise of deliverance. Dance used to form an important part of the wedding celebrations among the Jews of Germany and Morocco. Although certain orthodox Israeli Jews, such as the Bokharans, dance in the streets to celebrate the acquisition of a new Torah (the handwritten scroll containing the first five books of the Bible), few of the sacred dances survive in modern Israel, where the folk tradition is, reasonably enough, only as old as the state itself. The same is true of the United States, Italy, and Germany, whose nationalist aspirations have gained political shape more recently than the rest of western Europe. Folk dance has, of course, nothing to do with party politics, but it cannot escape being a part of that culture which politics also reflects.

OPPOSITE, ABOVE:
*Yemenite Jews dance
a hora.*

OPPOSITE, BELOW:
*Yugoslavs dancing
around the musician.*

THE UNITED STATES
Country dancing
The large-scale emigration from Europe to the United States that took place in the seventeenth and eighteenth centuries brought waves of English, Irish, Scottish, and German settlers, who

naturally imported their own cultural traditions as part of their baggage. Since country dancing was in its heyday in Europe at that time, it formed the basis of American folk dancing, though, of course, this did not prevent the penetration of fashionable dances like the waltz, the quadrille, the cotillion, and the polka. But country dancing rapidly developed a form that was purely American. This was especially so in New England, the Yankee heartland of the new nation, where the dances were variously labeled "contry" or "contra." This last was from the "contrary," or opposing, lines in which the dancers were marshaled, or it could have been a corruption of the French *contredanse*. French dancing masters were especially popular in the latter half of the nineteenth century, especially after France helped to subsidize the War of Independence.

The contras—as I shall call them for simplicity's sake—are almost exclusively danced in the longways progressive formation, which is to say the "top couple" in the line leads off the dance and moves down one place after performing the figure. Their place is then taken by the second couple, and so on until everyone has reached the top. Many of the dances have names denoting Scotch or Irish ancestry—for example, "Pea Straw" (otherwise known as "Pease Strae"), "Bonny Lass of Aberdeen," or "Money Musk" (originally "Sir Archibald Grant of Moniemusk Reel"). The use, too, of hornpipe, reel, and jig tunes danced to a fiddler's music shows a strong Celtic influence at work. But new dances were being invented all the time, and were named after specifically American events, such as "Hull's Victory," commemorating the defeat of the British warship *Guerrière* by Isaac Hull's frigate *Constitution* during the War of 1812.

Another form of American country dance which mingled with the contras to form the basis of the modern square dance was the Appalachian mountain dance. This comes from the mountains that stretch across Kentucky, North Carolina, West Virginia, and Tennessee—an isolated area largely settled by Irish and German

The reel performed in New England.

people who developed their own dances separately from the more

fluid traditions of the eastern seaboard. In 1916 Cecil Sharp studied the Kentucky Running Set, which is one of the mountain dance's main figures, and came to the conclusion it was one of the earliest forms of the English country dance, predating the collections of John Playford (which were immensely popular in the United States). He found that the running set shared the speed, step, and rhythm of the very ancient sword dance; but more likely it is of Celtic origin, as its rhythms and fiddle accompaniment testify. The running set is performed in as large a circle as the space can accommodate. After an introductory figure—without the courtesy movements of bowing and curtsying that mark the quadrilles and square dances—the leading couple moves around the circle dancing a figure with each couple in turn. The rest of the couples follow suit, and the dance ends with what Lloyd Shaw called "a sort of chain stitch of continuous and furious dancing." Since there are many figures, the leading dancer selects the one to

be danced and calls out directions to the other dancers. This habit of "calling"—frowned upon but not unknown in Britain, especially in the morris dance—was what gave American square dancing its unique quality.

A descendant of the Appalachian Mountain dance which has become popular throughout the United States is clogging, or dancing with strips of metal attached to the shoes. Taken from the exhibition step-dancing in clogs practiced by English and Irish folk dancers (wooden clogs are still used in the north of England), American clogging differs from tap dancing in that its rhythm is usually even, and its steps more limited than the infinite variety of tap. Clogging has recently become sufficiently standardized for it to be the subject of competitions, although for many it continues to be a spontaneous and exuberant addition to the circle or square dance.

Square Dancing

The contra dances were relatively simple compared to the French "squares" or contredanses, such as the quadrille, which overwhelmed the United States in the early part of the nineteenth century. According to the square dance historian, S. Foster Damon, it was the War of 1812 that ensured the popularity of the dance in the United States. The contras, which were still considered "British" in origin, were dropped in favor of the French form—chiefly quadrilles and cotillions—partly in a fit of patriotism, partly because of the need for novelty. Except, that is, in New England, where contras continued to be danced without interruption, as they are today.

New England contra dance. The participants are obeying the call "Down the center, four in line."

OPPOSITE, ABOVE:
Clogging team in a square dance in North Carolina.

OPPOSITE, BELOW:
Modern cloggers show off their footwork.

OPPOSITE: *The seal
of royal approval:
Princess Elizabeth (as
she then was) and
Prince Philip square
dancing in Ottowa,
1951.*

Perhaps "calling" was invented because of the complicated sequences of figures demanded by the French squares (cards giving directions for the quadrille were available in the United States as they were in Britain). Or perhaps calling was related to the "lilting," or wordless chanting, to a dance practiced by the Irish when there was no musical instrument available. Certainly some American dancers were forced to rely on vocal accompaniment alone, since a fiddle or banjo would have made the occasion "profane" and risked religious denunciation. In any event, what happened was that the fiddler or orchestra leader started to tell the dancers what to do next. The performers were expected to know the figures, but the "caller" made it unnecessary for them to remember their order. The caller was thus able to "create" the dance by juggling the order of the figures.

In the second quarter of the nineteenth century, when fashionable eastern ladies took to the crinoline, and thus found their freedom of movement severely hampered, the pioneers trekking west took with them the old-fashioned dances and so maintained them undiluted by eastern languor. Combining simplified versions of the French squares with the flexible running set, they invented the western square dance, and provided it with a running call to keep everyone on their toes. Even today these origins show: the calls of promenade, honors, allemande, and grand chain demand steps exactly like those of the old quadrilles (which, like their European ancestors, were originally danced in five sections, though these were later condensed to three).

The dance was the most popular way of attracting together settlers from scattered homesteads, and the reveling might go on for an entire week. As more settlers arrived, they added their own ethnic strains to the square dance, so that it developed endless local

*A Californian miners'
ball of the late
nineteenth century.*

variations. But it was always a fluid, makeshift, and often boisterous affair, held in barns, kitchens, or any convenient space. If there were no white women available, Indian squaws were pressed into service—their grace in dancing the cotillion impressed a Swiss painter visiting Fort Union in 1857—and if there were no squaws, men simply sewed patches on their trousers and took the ladies' places.

In the 1860s, the term "country dance" became unfashionable, except among dancing masters and New Englanders. The square dance ruled supreme as the dance of the people, and it was around this time that, according to S. Foster Damon, "some Yankee invented 'swinging,' which revolutionized square dancing in the north east." Swinging was a way of combining the whirls of the waltz, which was still frowned upon by church leaders, with the figures of the square dance. It became the basis of all northeastern square dancing.

The "singing call"—more closely related to lilting—became common in the 1870s, by which time the fast rhythmic patter and quirky expressions of the good caller sounded odd only to the novice. The natural development of the spoken call caused the singing call to become an essential part of the square dance, taking precedence even over the all-important fiddler. A skilled caller needed skilled dancers to work on, since the novice would scarcely be able to work out what the calls meant without a thorough knowledge of the steps. But the rhymes, pleasantries, and inventive wit of the singing caller gave square dancing the character of all-around popular entertainment that it has never lost.

A round dance during the 1955 "family week" held by the Country Dance and Song Society of America.

Round Dances

These were originally those partner dances criticized by the church: the waltz, polka, schottishe, and *varsovienne*. As square dancing developed, waltzes and polkas (much to the moralists' distress) were woven into the end of each figure, to add variety and a whirl of movement. Gradually, American round dancing combined the rhythms of the waltz and other ballroom favorites, such as the two-step, tango, or even cha-cha, with the steps of the square dance, adding a leader who "cued" the movements as the dancers performed them. Interest in round dancing grew alongside that in square dancing from the 1940s on. Some of its routines are complicated and very carefully choreographed, but round dances are often used as "mixers" (choreographed so that there is a continual exchange of partners) or "icebreakers," which get everyone into position for the square dance without searching for a place in the set.

The Modern Revival

American folk dance, as Mr. Damon puts it, is both a survival (in the country) and a revival (in the city). Around the same time as Cecil Sharp was "rediscovering" the English morris dance, Dr. Luther H. Gulich, the newly appointed athletic director of schools in Greater New York, decided that folk dancing was more beneficial than simple gymnastics, and put a hundred thousand boys to work learning European folk dances. A few years later girls were allowed to do the same. There were two drawbacks to this educational project. One was that it ignored the native dances of the United States in favor of European imports. The other was that it was an artificial revival, imposed from the top down instead of growing from the bottom up.

Community pageants, which included folk dancing by native immigrants as well as square dancing, were popular before World War I, and in 1916 the American Folk Dance Society was formed. In 1918 there appeared *Twenty-eight Contra Dances, Largely from New England States*, the first American book to work out the steps of the old dances with the avowed intention of getting more people to perform them. Its author was Dr. Elizabeth Burchenal, a pioneer in the field of dance in education.

In the early 1930s Henry Ford decided to give formal expression to his preference for folk tunes over jitterbug and jazz. He funded an historical project for the revival of square dance at Dearborn, Michigan, which was presided over first by a caller and fiddler called Mellie Dunham, and then by Benjamin Lovett, who insisted that no one could join his group until they had perfected the "proper" style—the same demand as was made by the dancing masters of the previous century. But square dancing survived without the help of scholars. Barn dances were still popular in small communities, and they excluded neither square dances nor the modern steps from an evening's program. Also in the 1930s, Lloyd Shaw, who had started off teaching European folk dances in Colorado, began collecting the old cowboy dances. His pupils put

Square dance exhibition in Sun City, Arizona.

on a widely successful show of these in 1938. The next year Shaw published his first book on the subject, and a national folk festival was held in Washington, D.C.

In 1939 at the New York World's Fair the square dancing, directed by Ed Durlacher, was a smash hit. The Rainbow Room at Rockefeller Center began to hold weekly square dance nights. Since the 1940s both square and folk dancing have risen steadily in popularity. Through folk dance the various nationalities that make up the United States have maintained their own dance traditions; through square dancing they have merged them. Their success can be measured by the number of books, records, magazines, and societies dedicated to the art. But more than that, it can be seen in the number of dancers who enjoy themselves performing figures that effortlessly bridge the gap between past and present.

CANADA

Folk dancing in Canada owes its origins to the earliest settlers of the territory, the Eskimos and Indians, whose traditional dances of war, fertility, celebration, and death were performed to the beat of a drum and the rhythm of a chanter. In many cases these dances have been supplanted by the music and style of later settlers. (The Eskimos on the northern tip of Labrador performed dances brought over by the first Scottish whalers.) The Scotch brought their reels and sword dances, the French their contredanses, which developed into the Canadian square dance just as they did south of the border. Callers were considered necessary only where there were strangers present.

European dances were as popular in Canada as in the United States, and so were the traditional dances of German, English,

Irish, French, Slavic, and Negro immigrants. In New Brunswick the custom of "dancing down" the northern lights was a celebration of the appearance of this phenomenon; the lights were supposed to be the souls of those who were neither in heaven nor hell. In Saskatchewan the men invited to the customary wedding dance "paid" for dances with the new bride by pinning money bills onto her gown. If no instruments were available, what the Irish call "lilting" was known in Canada as cheek music, chin music, mouth music, or jigging. But the French Canadian fiddler established a special place for himself, especially following the migration of French Canadians to New England to work as lumberjacks and, later, textile workers. According to Ralph Page —a caller who has done much to keep alive the New England contra dances—more and more French Canadian fiddle tunes are used both in squares and contras. Canada may not have yet exported a dance, but it has certainly seen a brisk trade in folk musicians.

MEXICO

Mexican tradition was deeply affected by the years of Spanish occupation, but her folk dances, Indian as well as Spanish, share the themes of European culture. For instance, *los huapango*, "the dance of the platform," was a wooing dance performed on the platform at which (like the Irish) the Mexicans used to meet weekly for a celebration. The occasion was used to sell produce and men would also arrive, often straight from the fields, to choose a bride. The dancers were accompanied by violin and bango (a large guitar), or a *jarana* (a sort of ukulele), or simply by the men singing. If two men were rivals for the same girl, they would compete in improvised songs—an old Spanish tradition as well as an Indian one—aimed at the loved one, who would dance on regardless. Much drink was taken by the men, and sometimes the contest ended in an actual fight with knives.

Los huapango began with the men standing silently in front of their chosen partner and removing their hats as a declaration of intent. They would then move into place, with the girls following. If a man watching wished to dance with a girl already on the platform, all he had to do was to get up and put his hat on her partner's head—a girl's appeal was measured by the number of men who danced with her. They were also opportunities for the men to show their skill, for example, by dancing with full bottles on their heads.

Another courtship dance is *el jarabe*—*jarabe* meaning "sweet"— in which the tempo quickens as the wooing intensifies. Perhaps, like the Spanish saraband, this got out of control, since in 1802 *el jarabe* was banned, and anyone dancing it was to be publicly punished and then jailed for two years. Spectators, too, could be jailed for two months, although by 1862 this ban had been relaxed and the dance became widely popular. There are two styles, one the Spanish courtship dance, the other an Indian version which opened a wedding feast, where the bride's parents danced with

Los huapango *performed by children in Santa Barbara.*

plates of food in their hands, others following with different dishes. The Indian *jarabe* forms the climax of *las sembradoras*, "the dance of the sowers," performed in February after harvesting, which begins with men—holding hoes or shovels—and women (with baskets of corn and food which is thrown to the audience) dancing around their richly decorated cattle, following the directions shouted out by a dance leader and accompanied by a man on horseback cracking a long whip.

Also involving a caller is *los matlanchines*, a complicated dance for any number of couples who follow the commands of a *matlanchia*, or "leader." It begins, exceptionally, with two diagonal lines of dancers facing the leader, but after these lines have crossed the dancers arrange themselves into circles around the leader. From there the dance becomes a series of interweaving figures in which men and women pass alternately through an arch made by the others. It ends with a circle of women inside a circle of men, each moving in opposite directions.

Mexico has several dances based on the Spanish *moresque*. *Los moros*, the dance of the Moors, is a dance for four men, one of whom is known as Santiago or St. James, and who carries an ebony cane with a silver head decorated with ribbons. The

OPPOSITE, ABOVE: *A Spanish wooing dance involving "fights" with sticks, knives, and machetes, from Venezuela.*

OPPOSITE, BELOW: El jarabe *at a ranch dance.*

dancers wear a sort of ornamented turban made of reeds and silk,
but instead of having blackened faces, as in the *moresque*, they are
disguised by a triangular silk handkerchief attached to their
turbans, which hides all of their faces except their eyes. In place of
bells they sport spurs, but there is no doubt that this costume is
based on that of the Moorish Arabs. The steps are marked by the
jingling of the spurs and the dancers exchange positions in line and
circular formations, as in the English morris. In certain places the
dance begins in the church porch—an echo of *los seises*, the
moresque danced in Seville Cathedral—but it then continues
around every house, with gifts being offered to the performers, and
ends up in the house of the community's leading personage, who
offers hospitality to all, and a special gift to the Santiago figure.

There is also *los negritos*, the Negroes' dance mostly performed by
the natives of the ancient town of Tzintzuntzan, on the shores of
Lake Patzcuaro. Again this begins in the church porch and
proceeds around the houses of the dancers and musicians, but
though performed on religious occasions it is a native dance
apparently based on the ceremony followed when the Negroes
paid the equivalent of their taxes. Thirteen dancers take part,
wearing shirts, trousers, and necklaces similar to those of *los moros*,
though hoods are worn instead of turbans, and the only face
disguised is that of the dance master, known as Señor Amo, who
has a wooden mask and who rides on a white mule. The dance is
performed in two files, like the *moresque*.

One further dance that begins in the church is *los Apaches*, again
for men only, in which half of the sixteen dancers paint their faces
red and half white (on top of which rouge is added). Wigs of black

hair are worn, topped by crowns of beads and feathers. The dancers also carry bells and ribbons on their stockings. One additional dancer dresses as a devil and wears a huge black mask with protruding teeth, on top of which is a pair of deer's antlers. Two small boys represent monkeys and have innumerable small bells attached to their costumes. As in the morris, the devil and the monkeys (who are the Mexican equivalent of the European fool figures) perform exaggerated steps a little apart from the files of Apaches.

There is an Apache woman's dance (*danza de la mujer Apaches*), but this is a wooing dance in which one of a circle of "squaws" goes and taps the shoulder of one of a circle of "braves" and performs a simple dance with him and another squaw, to the accompaniment of chanting and the beat of tom-toms.

Finally, there is the maypole dance *los Inditos*, "dance of the little Indians," in which men and women begin dancing in lines, and move to circle around the maypole and weave its ribbons into a pattern. Instead of the European Queen of the May, the dance is presided over by a Saint Señor de Chalma, who receives tributes in the form of flowers, beads, eggs, and even blankets. Thus in Mexico there have survived some of the oldest folk traditions of which only faint traces remain in Spain and the rest of Europe.

ENGLAND
The Morris Dance

The English morris dance is unique both in the length and the manner of its survival. Undoubtedly its origins are deep in the soil of the pre-Christian era, since it is primarily a dance of regeneration, that theme which is the basis of most religions. But the English morris is not a single dance: it consists of a number of local

An intricate dance for women, from Trinidad.

ABOVE, LEFT:
Thomas Hardy pointed out that the difference between genuine traditionalists and enthusiastic revivalists showed in the glum faces of the former. The Hemmings brothers, 1923.

ABOVE, RIGHT:
Morris men with unicorn in front of the Houses of Parliament, 1955.

variations around a common theme. In the early part of the twentieth century Cecil Sharp discovered what he thought of as the last embers of a once roaring tradition, in the Cotswold morris dance. By preserving these, by enlarging his researches, and by spreading the word, Sharp encouraged the revival of morris dancing as a living tradition rather than a museum piece. Now new figures are often added to the traditional ones, just as new tunes replace the old, which were frequently taken from the popular songs of the day. But the habitual wariness of the researcher into folk dance has to be redoubled when it comes to the morris, for not only are there innumerable "traditions" to deal with but, as those traditions have been evolved by the performers themselves, they are jealously guarded against misinterpretation by mere observers. Morris dancing is also something of an exclusive art, confined (until very recently) not only to men, but often to the men of certain families and their connections. Nevertheless, there are growing numbers of people seeking admission to a morris "side," and certainly the dances are performed to increasingly appreciative audiences.

The connection between the morris and the Spanish *moresque* is a tenuous one. There are striking similarities: both frequently employ two files of dancers—six is the usual number in England, twelve in Spain; the dancers have bells and ribbons on their clothing; and they execute similar formations, weaving and intertwining around one another. Perhaps the two dances also have in

*Morris hobby horse,
from Somerset, 1925.*

common that mimic war element of Christian against Muslim, "us" against "them." (The English no less than the Spanish were influenced by Arab culture, as a result of the Crusades to "liberate" Jerusalem. But war dances, of course, go back to long before the Crusades, and represent the battle between good and evil, life and death, spring and winter.)

Most likely, the term morris simply comes from the word "Moorish," and was applied to the dance because of the common habit of blacking the face of some or all of the dancers. Such disguise was important in all primitive dance, when an ordinary member of the community had to appear extraordinary. Arbeau noted it, when describing the French *moresque*, which was danced by a single black-faced youth with bells on his legs. The tune he gives for this was printed in England as a morris dance in 1550 and is still in use. Up to Elizabethan times, the double-file morris was danced in churches at Pentecost, just as it was on the Feast of Corpus Christi in Seville and Toledo. So we seem to have a fusing of the two types of *moresque*—the solo dance with "Moorish" black face, and the ritual dance for six or more participants.

The dance historian Curt Sachs believed that the English six-man dance is older than the Spanish, and that it refers back to the fertility rites of a pagan past. The *moresque* too has pagan origins, like most religious rituals, but in the English morris these are more remarkable. It was a leaping, stamping dance for men only; it was traditionally performed at sowing time (though today the morris

The Abbots Bromley Horn Dancers.

is danced all year); in many of the innumerable local variations of the dance there appears an imitation horse, or bull, or unicorn— all of them fertility symbols. The Padstow hobby horse, from Cornwall, which is paraded on May Day, is a huge grotesque that would do credit to an African or Polynesian tribal dance. In Staffordshire, in the Abbots Bromley horn dance, the performers actually carry reindeer horns, which are kept in the church when not in use. Everywhere the dancers make gestures with their arms that are unmistakably phallic—and there is also the fact that the morris was once part of the May dances, performed in the presence of that most ancient regenerative totem, the maypole. There is even the presence of that ageless character from primitive lore, the man dressed as a woman, often known as the "Betty."

The English embellished their morris with heroic characters of the time. The ancient vegetation sprite, Jack-in-the-Green, which can be seen on early church stone carvings, became Robin Hood. The pagan characters that once figured in the old folk plays were made respectable in the persons of contemporary legend. The Robin Hood characters have mostly disappeared now, but there is one character essential to most morris dances—the fool. He has to be one of the side's best dancers, since one of his functions is to strike with a bladder tied to a stick anyone who gets out of step. He wears a slightly different costume from the rest, and may make up his face like a clown; sometimes he doubles as a squire or leader of the side, who manages the club and maintains its standards. The squire generally came from one of the oldest families in the community, and was usually a working man; one of his functions

was to teach the steps of the figures to those admitted to the side before Cecil Sharp and his followers arrived to write everything down. Today the squire acts more like the captain of a sports team; as well as prescribing the figures to be danced during the performance—and calling them out—he may also introduce new figures to celebrate special occasions, such as the Silver Jubilee of Queen Elizabeth II.

The fool's chief function in the morris is to act as a bridge between dancers and spectators. The more he plays about the better. As a character he must be descended from the fool or jester who started as a sort of troubadour playing and reciting *gestes*, or legendary romances. These *gestes* soon took on a different meaning, that of a witty story or joke, and a "gestour" came to mean a clownish wit, kept by many rich people to amuse them through the long winter evenings. Traditionally the English fool's dress consisted of parti-colored hose and tunic—a popular fashion for courtiers of the time of Richard II—topped with a hat with bells. Bells, apart from their obvious use in awakening people's attention, and in helping a dancer to maintain a rhythm, have all sorts of sacred associations. They were once supposed to have power over evil spirits, to dispel storms, avert pestilence, and, above all, to frighten off evil spirits. There are reminders of these superstitions in the modern custom of naming, anointing, and consecrating new bells. Perhaps, then, the bells that figure in the morris dance, the bells that were also a prominent part of the costume of the fool, had a similar superstitious purpose, that of warding off evil spirits.

Morris dancers in jesters' costume, from the early fourteenth century.

The morris is essentially a step dance with highly developed foot, hand, and body movements; its figures are few in number and comparatively simple in character. It is important to stress that there is no common basic step; while many villages share *similar* steps and themes, each of these is interpreted differently. Each figure has a name, such as the gyp, the hey, a hands-around, a back-to-back (the dos-à-dos of the square dance), or the galley, a leg-twisting caper possibly descended from the galliard. The dancers follow the order prescribed by the squire, who calls out the figures. They are dressed in ritual costume, with bright-colored ribbons, rosettes, flowers, and greenery, in addition to the pad of bells they wear on their legs. They usually carry sticks, handkerchiefs, or twists of cotton. The old accompaniment to the morris was the pipe and tabor, which in Oxfordshire were known as the "wittle and dub." These instruments were augmented by fiddle and concertina, while today melodeons or accordions are employed. In the Bampton morris, a cake is carried around on a sword and distributed to the spectators, while a bagman (or treasurer) collects donations. Some Cotswold variations include jigs for a single dancer—perhaps a reminder of the solo *moresque*—which is an opportunity for one man to exhibit his skill and the others to have a drink.

Clog dances for one or two dancers, long a favorite in northern England, are sometimes seen in the south in intervals of the morris proper.

The morris almost died out when the Industrial Revolution forced agricultural workers off the land. Now, however, it flourishes as never before, a link with the primitive and pagan past that nearly two thousand years of progress has failed to bury.

The Sword Dance

Though associated with the morris, the sword dance was most likely introduced to England by the Danes around the sixth century A.D. Certainly it is known throughout Europe and among all primitive peoples. The English version was another pagan dance, enacting a saga of death and resurrection featuring the fool and his assistants, disguised with black faces, who formed a "secret society." Originally the sword dance was part of a folk play that was performed in midwinter, although now it is only a dance executed in Yorkshire, Northumberland, and Durham (counties which maintained the Danish presence long after Alfred the Great had vanquished the Danes in battle). As Douglas Kennedy describes it, the fool's "'act' is to suffer death in order that the community shall survive. His 'sons' (the members of the secret society) have to kill the head of the house, their 'father.' While he acts this sacrifice he visits the underworld, taking with him all the accumulated evils, burdens and difficulties of the past year. When his task is done he returns, a revived leader, to resume his earthly responsibilities, fortified for a new year." The death of the "father" and his rebirth figures in classical no less than Christian myths, and the sword dance play also acquired characters from legend as well as from the early morality plays. As a dance, it now consists of elaborate and complex figures, executed in ring formation by five, six, or more men, each holding a wooden or metal sword in his right hand and clasping the tip of the sword of his left-hand neighbor. The swords are either long and blunt or short and flexible ("rappers") and have handles at both ends. Athletic leaps, turns, and somersaults are performed without breaking the ring. The dance ends with the weaving of the swords into a tight knot (known also as a lock or glass), which is then placed around the neck of the fool to symbolize his execution. In the folk play, the fool then returned to life and competed with his eldest "son" for possession of the lady (a man-woman figure), whom the fool won. These mimic elements of the dance have now been lost or have dwindled to mere fragments. Nevertheless, the dance, which like the morris has several local variations on the main theme, has effortlessly preserved its ancient lineage. In the old sword dance play, a man with a broom or sword came on, to "make room" and clear away evil influences. This ancient superstition lives on in today's civic processions where a mace or ceremonial sword is carried in front of the chief personage.

May Dances

These were originally fertility dances performed on the first day in May around the maypole, a tree emblem symbolizing regeneration. The maypole was decked with greenery in the hope that the dancers' crops would be encouraged to flourish in imitation, and the performers circled the totem as their ancestors had done, in order to absorb and enhance its power. To this end ribbons were attached to the pole, through which its magical influence was to be transmitted to the dancers. The ribbons were twisted into intricate patterns by the interweaving of the performers, a motif found in Alsace, Provence, Germany, Italy, Spain, India, and Central America. May dances were not confined to northern Europe. They were performed by Basques, Hindus, in the Celebes, and in northern Mexico. So powerful was the fertile magic of the may-

A sixteenth-century maypole in the Strand, in London.

pole that in Bohemia only virgins were allowed to dance around it.

In England maypoles were erected on every village green until condemned by the Puritans as a sign of idolatry. They were sometimes so huge that twenty oxen were needed to haul them into place, and they were "covered with flowers and hearbes and bounde with strings of different colours and often two or three hundred men, women and children follow it with great devotion, and when it is raised and they have feasted they begin to leape and daunce about it as the Heathen did at the dedication of their Idolles," according to a seventeenth-century description. A lord and a lady of the May were elected by each community, and these led the dancing, accompanied by capering characters from popular lore such as members of Robin Hood's band of outlaws. A hobby horse and perhaps a dragon would often feature in the ceremonies. In the United States in 1628 a maypole was erected in Mary Mount (now Quincy, Massachusetts) which was eighty feet high with a pair of buck's horns nailed to the top, and "sundry rimes and verses affixed." Those responsible for its erection set about "drinking and dancing aboute it many days togeather, inviting the Indian women for their consorts, dancing and frisking togeather like so many fairies or furies rather." But their pleasure was short-lived: the "idoll maypole" was cut down by the Puritan theocrats, and the merrymakers received a stern lecture. But in England the restoration of Charles II saw the May dances restored to favor. In 1661 a pole 130 feet high was erected in the Strand, and was afterward used by Sir Isaac Newton as a mount

ABOVE: *Children of
the London slums
improvise a maypole
dance, 1892.*

*Kent schoolchildren
dutifully perform at
the end of the May
Day festivities in
1949.*

Midsummer eve dance in Sweden, where traditional costumes mingle with modern ones.

for his telescope. London milkmaids, a traditionally coquettish section of the community, would in Pepys's time borrow silver plate and pile it, adorned with flowers, on their heads (where they usually carried their pails), and thus encumbered dance along accompanied by a fiddler. Nor was the Puritan ban all that effective in the United States: Judge Samuel Sewall noted that in May 1687, the people of Charleston had cut down a maypole "and now a bigger is set up and a garland upon it." The next day he told how Father Walker had "overheard some discourse about the maypole, and told what manner it was in England to dance about it with music; and that 'twas to be feared such practices would be here."

The May dances, which were of course rounds, gave way to the country dances, some of which—for example, Sellenger's Round and the Circassian Circle—used the old figures, but without the maypole. By the nineteenth century, May dancing had died out as a regular community activity, in both England and the United States. It was ousted by the newer dances that gave all the pleasure of intricate sets of figures without the business of setting up and decorating a maypole. The May dances survive in England today solely because they are taught, shorn of their pagan trappings, to schoolchildren. There are, however, May (or rather midsummer) pole dances to be seen in Sweden, Finland, and other parts of northern Europe.

WALES

Until the nineteenth century, on May Day or at midsummer the men of Welsh villages went out dancing in a serpentine procession, equipped with specially prepared branches of the "summer birch" tree and with white handkerchiefs. They performed dances in columns of six, as do the English morris men, and they were accompanied by a fool and a man-woman figure known as the Kate, or *Cadi*, who collected donations and supervised the figures.

Reels for three or four dancers with different figures enjoy a long

Traditional dancing at the Llangollen International Eisteddfod, Wales.

history in Wales, as do jigs and clog dances to the music of the harp, and perhaps the hornpipe, or *pib-gorn*. There was also the squatting dance known as the Toby or Kibby dance, and one performed over a broom handle or two clay pipes laid on a sheepskin. But the dissenting movement, which in the eighteenth century converted much of Wales to a puritanical religious attitude, was responsible for the decline of mixed dancing. Folk dance, however, was preserved by enthusiasts and has now been revived, though perhaps more as a curiosity than as a living and unbroken tradition.

SCOTLAND

The Scots early evolved their own dances, quite different in style and rhythm from those of England. The fifteenth-century Scottish ballad called "The Colkelbie Sow" mentions twenty native dances unknown farther south. Even when the fashionable French dances reached their shores, the Scots continued to develop variants of their own which were special enough to be adopted elsewhere. Arbeau, the sixteenth-century expert on French dance, described the *branle d'Écosse*, or Scotch *branle*, as being fashionable around 1560, and it continued to be performed well into the nineteenth century, by four dancers in a row who shouted to accompany the music.

When Mary Queen of Scots took possession of the Scottish throne in 1561, she naturally imported with her the dances she had learned in her long years at the French court. But even her many accomplishments did not win favor for French fashions. John Knox (who had been a prisoner on the French galleys) inveighed against her and all she stood for, and his denunciations of all things popish were soon spread by zealots to include "wanton and lascivious dance." Nevertheless, the traditional folk dances of Scotland—the reel, the fling, the strathspey—survived and flourished. There was morris dancing, certainly in the fifteenth century, which required peculiar skill, in that the dancer produced a tune from bells attached to his costume. Dance formed the chief part of any celebration, from weddings to funeral wakes, at least until the nineteenth century.

The Scotch reel is a gliding and springing dance performed largely on the points of the toes by two (a foursome), three (a sixsome), or four couples (an eightsome). That it is of northern origin cannot be doubted, as it is a Norwegian folk dance as well as a Scottish one. Like all folk dances, it has acquired innumerable different tunes and figures. The chief instrument used to accompany the dance, the bagpipes, is by no means confined to Scotland: it is to be found from Ireland to central Asia, and was probably of Middle Eastern origin, being popular in courtly France under the name *cornemuse* or *musette*, in Germany as the *dudelsack*, in Spain as the *flaviol*, and in Italy as the *piva*. But the reel was also performed without instruments to a simple vocal refrain. So bewitching were the rhythms and figures of the reel that superstitious Scots detected

The reel of Tulloch on its native heath.

250

in it the hand of the devil, who was said to turn up in person, in human form, or disguised as an animal. But despite church disfavor—which certainly repressed the spread of fashionable social dances—the reel never faltered in popularity.

The strathspey gets its name from the valley (*strath*) of the river Spey, one of the swiftest flowing in Scotland. It is closely related to the reel (in four-four time as opposed to the reel's two-four time), and though its music is slower, its performance calls for a good deal of energy since the dance is full of rapid movements. Mrs. Grove records, as an example of the instinctive manner in which the Scots perform the dance, the story of a man who "played the fiddle, played bass on the bagpipe, smoked, spoke Gaelic and explained it by means of question and answer, all the while he was dancing a strathspey!"

The Highland fling was originally a step performed to the music of the strathspey, though it was soon transformed into a dance by itself. The name comes simply from the "kick" which is characteristic of the step: the Highlander will dance on each leg in turn, while "flinging" the other one in front of and behind him.

The sword dance, which bears no resemblance to the English sword dances, is one for specialists, involving as it does intricate footwork among the sharp points of two swords laid crosswise on the ground. Such dances date back to Greece and Rome, and were known from Germany to the Far East (where even more dexterity was required as the sword was swung in the air). It was danced in Scotland at least from the seventeenth century on, when

it possibly formed part of the Scottish morris dance, but it developed into an exhibition of skill by young soldiers, the descendant of ancient war dances.

The hornpipe was originally a country dance like the jig, both well known to seventeenth-century Scots. There was a Highland hornpipe which became fashionable in the eighteenth century. As a dance it bore no relation to the sailor's hornpipe, which was a stage invention supposedly taken from the mimic dance invented by seamen, and which became popular in the nineteenth century.

IRELAND

Though sources on Irish dancing are scanty, her people were renowned for their skill and the pleasure they took in the pastime, even under Elizabeth I who tried so hard to reduce the country to uniformity with England in everything from religion to social customs. It is a tribute to the independence of the Irish spirit that an Elizabethan critic described them as "using no arts of slow Measures of lofty Galliards, but only Country dances of which they have some pleasant to behold such as Bulrudery and The Whip of Dunboyne, and they dance commonly about the fire in the midst of a room holding withes in their hands and by certain strains drawing one another into the fire." (Fynes Moryson, quoted in *Dances of Ireland* by T. and G. O'Rafferty).

Homage to trees and fire, common to most northern peoples, was still practiced in Ireland in the eighteenth century, when May Day was celebrated in some parts of the country with a circular, serpentine dance around a tree or bonfire. This custom was probably connected with a *rinnce fada*, or fading, the long dance that was one of the country's oldest. It was performed by dancers connected by white handkerchiefs, the first rank proceeding three abreast and the rest following in pairs. When the tempo of the music quickened, the couples passed in succession under the handkerchiefs of the three in front, then turned about and performed a variety of figures, including entrechats, or leaps during which the positions of the feet were altered, before coming together and resuming their original places. The dance, which was often used to conclude balls, was accompanied by the bagpipes, the Irish harp, or the Jew's harp. It is similar to the *faddy*, or furry dance, performed at Helston in Cornwall—a county with strong Celtic connections—and it has been revived as a longways dance for modern folk enthusiasts.

The dance that endured longest in Ireland was undoubtedly the jig. Etymologists doubt that this word is derived from the Provençal *gigue*, a sort of fiddle, or even from the old French *giguer*, "to

The Helston Furry dance, which resembles the Irish fading dance.

gambol or sport"; the origin of the term is unknown. But the jig itself was once common to the whole of Great Britain, and was danced at court until the accession of George I of Hanover. Lawyers were apparently particularly addicted to the dance, as there are jigs named after all of London's Inns of Court; there was even one named after Oliver Cromwell, "Old Noll's Jig," who was no killjoy as long as dancing was not "profane." In England the jig became a stage dance commonly used to end a play—"Kemp's Jigge" was named after the Shakespearean actor who also morris-danced his way from London to Norwich. But in Ireland the dance was popular with all classes of society until well into the eighteenth century. Jig tunes for bagpipes, harp, or fiddle were the basis of most Irish dances, not to mention their military music. The rhythm was based on groups of three beats dividing into "single" or "double" jigs, depending on the number of beats to the bar. The steps were similar to the hopping figures of the Scotch reel, though certain dances called for the floor to be rhythmically struck with the foot.

Jigs were also performed in wooden clogs, and the Irish clog dances were among the most rapid and complex known.

The jig today is a step dance performed as part of the *ceilidhe*, or organized folk dance. *Ceilidhes* include round, long, and square dances, and feature jigs, reels, and hornpipes (which some maintain come from the Irish instrument, the *cornphiopa*). The old custom of performing jigs at a funeral wake, alternating with dirges and plentiful helpings of whiskey, has lapsed. But until World War II many Irish villages boasted at their crossroads a dance platform, usually made of concrete, where dancing would take place every Sunday afternoon after church. While the older generation were in the pub or teashop, the young—with the girls strictly chaperoned—would dance jigs and reels, their hands held behind their backs, the boys keeping their bodies virtually immobile above the hips. If there was neither fluter nor fiddler, the dancers would be perfectly content with a "lilter," who would keep a wordless stream of rhythmic accompaniment going for as much as four hours at a time.

GERMANY

Many Germans considered dancing sufficiently important for it to mark the ceremonial consummation of marriage at wedding celebrations. May dances survived in Bavaria until the twentieth century, where a living tree was decorated with ribbons. Trees were important in other dances also: the Pentecostal tree (a fir or a birch) was made into a dancing pole, around which young villagers used to "buy" their partners for the year at an "auction"; while in Silesia on Christmas night, men and women danced around their fruit trees with ropes. Fire, too, featured in these ancient rituals: at midsummer people danced around fires swinging burning brooms or leaped across them in elaborate tests of skills, whose successful conclusion was supposed to bring fertility and good fortune. Until recently the festival known as the *Kirmes*

used to take place regularly on the saint's day of the community church. A harvest celebration with pagan origins, it lasted three days and ended with the villagers, decorated with gold paper, proceeding to the fields behind a pole adorned with ribbons and handkerchiefs. A sheep was chosen, adorned with red ribbon, brought back to the village, and killed in the midst of a *Reigen*, or "ring of dancing people," the most ancient dance of all.

That the European peoples share a common dancing tradition is given further proof by the existence of the sword dance of Uberlingen on Lake Constance, which was performed regularly until 1939. This featured the king, the fool (*Hänsele*), bedecked with ribbons, bells, and foxtails, and four sword dancers who wove a knot with their weapons under which the fool crept. The king concluded the dance by waving a flag over the dancers and making everything all right.

Most German dances of today are not more than 150 years old. In the north they are of the contredanse type, sometimes overlaid with immemorial figures like the chain and the wheel. In central Germany there are sung couple dances dating from the days of the waltz and the polka. An example is the *Schwälmer*, a round dance from the Schwälm region, in which the women perform waltz

A harvest celebration, painted by Leopold Robert.

255

A Tyrolean dance with bells to celebrate the end of winter.

A Salzburg Schuhplattler.

steps with their hands on their hips while the man clicks his heels and claps in time to the music. The *Schwarzwälder Bauertanz*, a peasant dance from the Black Forest, is a step dance in which first the women and then the men act as if they were indifferent to each other, and which ends in a series of bows and curtsies. From the Hanover region there is a typical German version of the French quadrille, the *Kegel-Quadrille*. From Bavaria and the Tyrol, there is the wild wooing dance known as the *Schuhplattler*. In this the man claps, slaps his thighs, clicks his tongue, hisses, and leaps in the air to attract a girl's attention, not to mention jumping around her and even turning somersaults to work off his frustration. He also yells along with the music, in the noisy and exuberant tradition of the oldest German folk dances.

Finally, there is the *Ländler*, from the mountains of Austria. Still a speciality of Bavarian and Austrian folk dancing, it is a direct descendant of the medieval *Drehtanz*, or "turning dance." To a moderate tempo, the partners spin in opposite directions holding hands high above their heads; the girl is spun by the man on his upraised hand while he stamps out a rhythm; they glide under each other's arms or dance past each other back to back; or they turn holding each other tightly. As one critical spectator noted, "the faces are pressed together, even if the sweat is running down both of them." Sometimes the man lets go of his partner's hand and claps to the music, when he might be joined by the rest of the men, clapping in a circle while the girls parade around outside it. Dancing in couples is resumed when the boys get bored.

Musicians passed *Ländler* tunes from one generation to another, guarding them possessively. Not that these would have made much sense to an outsider: the written music was extremely cryptic, most of the basic themes being played from memory and the rest being improvised.

That the dance was one of wooing cannot be doubted: apart from the close hold the partners had on each other, and the kissing which was an integral part of most German dances, the boys incited each other to greater fervor with their clapping and stamping. Such behavior attracted attention from critics inside and outside the country, yet the turning dance, with all its indecorousness, remained an important part of German culture, especially in the south. The *Weller* employed the same principles, and that was a forerunner of the shocking *Walzer*.

SPAIN

Trees and fire play a large part in the ritual dances of Spain. In the eastern Pyrenees, at both Easter and midsummer, men danced through their villages carrying tree trunks on their shoulders that were lit at both ends. Sword and stick dances, as well as maypole dances (often with an enormous artichoke or pomegranate—both fertility symbols—suspended from the pole or roof), were common all over Spain at least until World War II. The Ball de Cascabels (bell dance) from Catalonia featured dancers with bells on their legs and carrying sticks, led by a chief devil with a whip who gave the orders. Mock battles between Moors and Christians took place all over the country toward the end of April; and there were in addition processional dances featuring giants and dwarfs. The traditional *moresques*, or dances by files of men often disguised in masks and wigs, which share a common origin with the morris, are seen more often in former Spanish colonies such as Mexico than in the mother country.

There are many Spanish provincial dances, but of those performed nationally perhaps the most important are the jota, the fandango, and the bolero. The jota is claimed by the Aragonese to be their own invention, a derivation of the Andalusian fandango brought to their province by an exiled Moorish poet, Aben Jot. Whatever the case, it is a couple dance in three-four time, performed to the accompaniment of castanets. As with many Spanish dances, the man performs the steps first in an exhibition of rapid hops, springs, and athletic footwork; and the woman then follows him. The knees are frequently flexed and straightened, a movement requiring much agility. The jota also features a singer, during whose verses, which often have topical references, the performers rest. It was once performed at wakes, and there were those who credited it with everything to arousing the dead to making the spectators fall in love.

Granada gypsies in their cave.

The fandango is extremely ancient—the very word means "go and dance"—and may well be the prototype of all Spanish

258

Early nineteenth-century Spanish dancing.

Couple dance for women, performed by natives of Madrid.

Spanish dancers parade through the streets during a folk festival in London, 1935.

dances. It is again a couple dance, in six-eight tempo, accompanied by castanets and a singer. It begins slowly and works up gradually to a climax of intense and furious dancing. Mrs. Grove quotes a traveler in 1700, the Chevalier Bourgoing, who related the story of the consistory court of Rome waxing indignant that so godless a dance as the fandango should be allowed in pious Spain. They were about to issue a condemnation when one judge remarked that it was unfair to censure what one did not know. The court therefore sent for two well-known fandango dancers to perform before it. They danced so effectively that everyone joined in, and the idea of condemnation was laid aside.

The bolero was introduced to Spain from Provence, and the name is supposed to come from *volar,* "to fly," because an expert had danced it so lightly he appeared to take to the air. Performed to voice or guitar and castanet accompaniment, the dance allows more opportunity than some of its peers for the woman to show her skill. It was an ancestor of the seguidillas, a dance for mixed couples or two women only, accompanied by a song, castanets, and in some regions the characteristic drumming of the heels, known as *taconeado.*

The *flamenco* is from Andalucía, and probably originated with the Spanish occupation of Flanders, since Spanish soldiers quartered there were known as *flamencos.* Possibly the dance was an expression of joy at returning home with pay and without injury. Today the term is used more to describe an improvised style, of flamboyant stamping and fiery display, than a particular

dance. There are many regional variations, such as the malagueña (from Málaga) or the granadina (from Granada).

All these dances were originally courtship dances. Casanova
himself described a fandango he saw in Madrid in 1767, in which
the dancers "make a thousand gestures so lascivious that nothing
can compare with them. This dance is an expression of love from
beginning to end, from the sigh of desire to the ecstasy of enjoy-
ment. It seemed to me impossible that after such a dance a girl
could refuse anything to her partner." The dances were princi-
pally evolved to allow the male to exhibit his prowess and prove
himself irresistible, though the woman too had opportunity to
show her quality. No other European country boasts so many
dances in which sexual rivalry is so passionately expressed.

ABOVE, LEFT:
*Flamenco dancers
urged to greater
efforts.*

ABOVE, RIGHT: *A
Spanish dance of love.*

ITALY

There is a sword dance of Ischia in which half the dancers (who
number from sixteen to twenty) are designated women by the
wearing of a blue doublet and a pink sash. The "men" wear a scarlet doublet and a blue sash, and the dance is accompanied by a
flute and a drum equipped with little bells. In Piedmont two
characters from the commedia dell'arte appear in a sword dance:
Harlequin (the fool), who is tried, condemned, raised on a lock
made of the swords, and "killed," and another sort of fool,
Brighella, who is dressed all in white. Moors also feature among
the characters of this dance, which includes a maypole figure; all
the elements of European fertility dances are present. There are

The tarantella, as performed in Naples in the early nineteenth century.

also sword dances in which the participants "fight"—in Corsica it is Moors against Christians, but on the Adriatic island of Lagosta, which for centuries was in Italian hands, the *moresca* features Moors fighting Turks for the possession of the desirable slave.

As Italy did not become a unified country until 1870, there are no modern national dances, and no survivals from the days of ancient Rome. The saltarello is still performed as a courting dance, and its Campanian version features a mime in which the man pursues the woman who feigns reluctance before giving in. Elsewhere it remains a *bassa danza*, as it was in the fifteenth century, performed either as a couple dance or by a ring of dancers who link their arms around each other's shoulders and bend forward so that their heads are almost touching. In Romagna it is danced by two or three couples, the men joining hands and gradually working themselves into a circle, the women exhibiting their poise by dancing with a full glass of water balanced on their heads. This form of saltarello has a violin accompaniment and a sung interlude with topical and satirical verses, as in the Spanish jota.

The tarantella was originally from Taranto in Apulia, and its constant movements and rapid turning were supposed to be effective in working the poison of the tarantula spider's bite out of the system. Some even believed that the spider itself would dance to the fast and catchy rhythms of the tarantella, which has since become a courting dance, to the accompaniment of hand clapping and the ever-accelerating rattle of the tambourine.

Curt Sachs maintained that the oldest European couple dances feature a miming theme of courtship alternating with a more straightforward partner dance. The bergamasca (a sixteenth-century dance from Bergamo) began with a circular procession, after which the music changed and the couples waltzed together, before returning to the procession. The trescone, a dance of similar age, used to be performed at weddings, with four couples forming a ring or square. Again it began with a stamping procession, the men passing in front of the women and demonstrating their prowess before pairing off into a couple dance. The monferrina, now seen mainly in Piedmont, is performed by several couples who begin by promenading and miming a teasing courtship. When the music changes they join hands and perform complicated cross steps. Lastly, there is the furlana from north-eastern Italy, which probably originated in Venice. In six-eight time, this is a wild courtship dance for one or two couples, similar to the tarantella. The dancers approach and withdraw, skip and turn around each other, holding hands or handkerchiefs, and end by waltzing around the room at an ever-increasing tempo. "No national dance is more violent," said Casanova, who performed one in 1775, and who had a certain claim to expertise in such matters.

The tarantella as a courtship dance.

GREECE

OPPOSITE: *Easter
dance performed by
girls of marriageable
age in Megara,
Greece. Bachelors are
invited only as
spectators.*

Unlike Italy, the Greeks boast several dances that have survived from classical antiquity to modern times. There are the death-and-resurrection dances of the carnival season preceding Lent, some of which feature the hobby horse, the man-woman figure, and (on the island of Skyros) a character laden with sheep bells which clash as he jumps. Even more ancient are the circle dances performed by men only, with the women looking on. A descendant of these is the *kalamatianos*, known all over the country, in which the group is led by a dancer who sings, waves a handkerchief, and periodically detaches himself from the chain to perform complicated jumps and turns. Women now participate in the dance, though leaving the leaps to the men. There was a song which was once accomplished by a lyre, but which has given way to a guitar, mandolin, clarinet, or drum. When the leader is worn out he gives his handkerchief to another dancer, who performs in his turn.

Other dances for men only, also circular in form, derive from the nineteenth-century guerrillas (the klephts) against the occupying Turks. The *tsamikos* gives an opportunity for a man to display his athletic skill: to cries of "Oppa!" each performer will try to outdo his rival in high jumps and gymnastic effects. In modern times women have begun taking part in this chain dance, their smooth steps contrasting with the men's turns and leaps.

The *sousta*, now a courting dance performed mainly in Crete, claims descent from Pyrrhus, the son of Achilles. The demigod himself was supposed to have danced it around the pyre of his friend Patrocles. As a dance to prepare the performers for battle, it became a Spartan military exercise, taught to small children in the seventh century B.C., and was extolled by Plato. In the fourth century A.D., women began to perform this pyrrhic dance, which is when it became a couple dance with love rather than war as its theme.

As in the rest of Europe, all these dances alternate slow and fast passages, mimic dance and couple dance. Greece was the cradle of European dance, the crucible where the ancient Eastern culture melted into that of the nascent West. The traditions of a past shared by all Europe live on there in uninterrupted splendor.

GLOSSARY OF DANCE

Allemande, early spellings also almain and almayne, meaning "German dance," a round dance popular from the sixteenth century. The only German court dance to achieve popularity outside that country until the waltz. The allemande survives as a figure in modern square dance.

Animal Dances, mimic dances performed to ragtime, popular in the first two decades of the twentieth century. Examples are the bunny hug, grizzly bear, and turkey trot.

Apaches, Los, Mexican *moresque* for men only, featuring disguised dancers and a masked devil figure topped with antlers.

Appalachian Mountain Dance, country dance of Celtic origin from the mountains that stretch from Kentucky to North Carolina. Its principal set is the Kentucky Running Set, and it mingled with the contras to form the basis of the square dance.

Bacchic Dances, frenzied dances dedicated to the god of wine, called Bacchus by the Romans and Dionysos by the ancient Greeks. See *Dionysia.*

Bal Champêtre, rustic French ball held in the open air.

Bal Masqué, ball in fancy dress or masks.

Bal Paré, formal dress ball.

Ballo, term applied by the fifteenth-century Italian dancing masters to mimic dances performed by the highborn. In time these dances were taken over by professionals and led to the development of ballet as a separate act from social dance.

Barn Dance, a nineteenth-century American couple dance in 4/4 time, taking its name from the rural custom of dancing to celebrate the completion of a new barn. Known also as the *pas de quatre* and the military schottische, the steps involved walking, hopping, sliding, turning, and footstamping, which shocked many who believed all dancing should be decorous.

Basse Danse, fourteenth-century court dance originating in France. The name meant that the feet were to be kept low, as opposed to the *haute danse,* which applied to dances with hops and jumps. Led by the highest ranking couple, the dancers proceeded around the hall in pairs, performing simple steps in an agreed order. In France too much exhibitionism by the man was frowned upon, but the Italians encouraged invention in their *bassa danza.* The dance often formed part of a suite which included other types of dance as well.

Batuque, Brazilian name for local variants of the samba.

Beguine, originally a French West Indian dance in bolero rhythm, this was immortalized by Cole Porter in "Begin the Beguine," 1935.

Bergamasca, a sixteenth-century dance from the Italian town of Bergamo—and known in England, as Shakespeare has Bottom dance a "bergomask" toward the end of *A Midsummer Night's Dream.* In the nineteenth century it became a folk dance in which the couples alternated between waltzing and progressing in a circle.

Big Apple, a party dance that appeared around 1935 in New York, taking its name from the Big Apple Club of Columbia, South Carolina. Couples arranged themselves in a large circle and performed figures according to the instructions of a caller.

Black Bottom, a dance employing strong African- and Caribbean-style hip movements, which first appeared on Broadway in 1926, and which scandalized older dancers on both sides of the Atlantic because of its gliding, skipping, leaping, and stamping—not to mention its flaunting of the backside.

Blue Beat, Jamaican rhythm and blues dance introduced to England around 1959. Also known as the *ska,* the dance involved strenuous hip movements to a rapid and hypnotic rhythm that emphasized the offbeat.

Bolero, Spanish dance in 3/4 time that came from Provence in the Middle Ages, but which by the nineteenth century had developed into an exhibitionistic folk dance to a throbbing rhythm from vocal or guitar and castanet accompaniment.

Bonny Lass of Aberdeen, late eighteenth-century American country dance, of Scottish origin, performed in the longways progressive formation.

Boogaloo, solo dance of the 1960s in which the feet either tapped or brushed across each other.

Boomps-a-daisy, novelty dance featuring a vigorous bumping of the partners' hips.

Bop, American solo dance popular in the mid-1950s, consisting of a sort of marching in place to music that emphasized the upbeat. Variations were the scooter, the flea hop, the twister, and the rock and around.

Bossa Nova, a combination of American jazz rhythms with those of the Brazilian samba, popular as a dance in the United States in the early 1960s.

Boston, a way of walking, as opposed to turning, to waltz music that became popular in the early 1900s. Also known as the hesitation waltz, it involved a rocking "hesitation" movement on the second and third beats that developed into the Boston dip, where the man leaned right over the woman. It took up a lot of space on the floor, and gave way to the one-step around 1914.

Bourrée, a sixteenth-century French folk dance from the Auvergne, originally performed by peasants in clogs. The women held their skirts off the ground and performed skipping steps opposite their partners. Because of this indecorousness the dance was only performed by professionals as part of the French court ballet, where it often formed part of a suite along with the gavotte and rigaudon.

Branle, one of the earliest court dances, dating from before the twelfth century, and the first to require instrumental music as an accompaniment. The name comes from the old French, *branler*, "to sway." The dance was performed by a chain of dancers swaying first to left, then to right. It was the first dance to contain alternating rhythms, quick and slow, and formed the basis of much French court and folk dance, as well as lending itself to countless local variations.

Bug, solo dance to the rock music of the 1960s.

Bunny Hug, animal dance involving a close embrace between the partners that got it banned from many American dance halls. The ban was defeated by the girls wearing "bumpers" to keep their men at a proper distance.

Buzzard Lope, animal dance in which the principal movement was a grinding of the hips.

Cakewalk, a prancing or strutting dance, originally performed by American Negroes in competition for a cake. It became popular with white America around 1880, and spread to England shortly afterward where it was especially popular in the North.

Camel Walk, an animal dance to ragtime.

Canaries, a fifteenth-century couple dance from the Spanish Canary Islands. Originally danced around a corpse, it became a courtship dance containing pantomime wooing between the partners. By the second half of the sixteenth century it had disappeared from the court dances.

Cancan, a boisterous French dance performed by professionals who in nineteenth-century Paris delighted in showing their legs and underwear, maintaining a tradition going back at least to the sixteenth century. During the *triori* from southern Brittany, the women lifted their skirts and kicked their legs up, in an erotic fertility dance.

Carmagnole, a circle dance popular during the French Revolution, when it was performed around the tree of liberty.

Carol, a song-dance of prehistoric origins. By the Middle Ages it had two distinct forms, the farandole or line dance and the *branle*. Danced by all classes in circles or lines, the carol became the root of all court dances from the twelfth century, when the performers would sing their own musical accompaniment.

Cha-cha, a Cuban dance derived from the mambo, possibly named after the noise made by the slippers of Caribbean women: it consisted of two slow and three quick steps, to an insistent Latin American sound in 2/4 or 4/4 time. First popular in the middle 1950s, it is still around today.

Chaconne, originally a wild Spanish folk dance of around the sixteenth century, this was incorporated into the French court ballet, when it was performed by two lines of dancers. It was also danced in this form at the conclusion of French balls in the seventeenth century.

Charleston, from Charleston, South Carolina, where black dock workers danced to amuse themselves. Transported to New York, it became a hit in the Ziegfeld Follies of 1923, and its side-kicking steps were soon adopted by the flappers and their partners. It had a short life, but came to symbolize the gaiety of the twenties.

Chicken, solo dance of the 1950s, a parody of the lindy.

Cinq pas, sixteenth-century court dance with five steps (hence the name) in which four hops are called for.

Clam, solo dance of the 1960s involving a swiveling of the hips.

Conga, a Cuban dance in which performers formed a long chain by holding onto the waist of the person in front, and snaked their way around the floor, house, or even town, performing a one-two-three-kick step to the music of a Latin American band. First popular in England and the United States in the 1930s, it survives today.

Contra, American form of country dance perfected in the late seventeenth century. Sets of couples faced each other, usually in a square pattern, and exchanged positions using complicated figures and steps. The name also refers to the fact that the dancers performed counter to, or opposite, each other, instead of facing the top personage present, which was the usual form of court dances.

Cotillion, more usually cotillon in Europe, a French contredanse, taking its name from the French word *cotillon*, meaning "petticoat," and reimported to England as a square dance for four couples in the early eighteenth century. By the middle of the century it had reached the United States, where it enjoyed long popularity both as a dance and a game with forfeits. It is one of the oldest direct ancestors of the square dance.

Country dances, group dances that date from the earliest times, but which were formalized in the sixteenth and seventeenth centuries, and performed by courtiers as well as the working people who originated them. To the music of popular tunes of the day, the country dances were performed by two or more couples facing each other in squares or, later, lines. Each dance involved the partners changing position, in relation to each other and the other couples in their set, often employing complex steps and floor patterns. In the eighteenth century, the design of the assembly rooms in which society danced ensured that the square gave way to the line pattern, or "longways progressive," as each couple worked its way up to the top of the line of facing dancers. Leading directly to the modern square dance, country dance enjoys uninterrupted popularity today.

Courante or Coranto, a late Renaissance development of the farandole, this became one of the most popular court dances in the late sixteenth century, when it featured a promenade by all the couples taking part. The pantomime of wooing that the dance had originally contained was dropped; in the seventeenth century the tempo of the dance changed from 3/4 to 6/4, and it became a stately affair for couples known as the slow courante, at which Louis XIV excelled.

Crab, jerky ragtime dance popular in the early twentieth century.

Csárdás, Hungarian folk dance with a slow section followed by a fast one, deriving its name from the Hungarian for "inn," and tracing its ancestry back to the Middle Ages.

Danse Macabre, a dance of death in which one dancer impersonates a skeleton, reminding the living of their mortality. Popular, especially in Germany, after the plague known as the Black Death hit Europe in the fourteenth century.

Danzon, a Latin American dance briefly popular in the 1930s.

Dionysia, ancient Greek ecstatic dances dedicated to the god of wine, Dionysus (whom the Romans called Bacchus), and which included women known as maenads who were in a state of sacred frenzy. The Greeks divided their Dionysia into four, all of them public holidays. In the last of these the sacred frenzy led to orgiastic excesses that finally got the festivals banned.

Eagle Rock, animal dance to ragtime, popular in the early twentieth century.

Écossaise, a French contredanse of the early nineteenth century, inspired by Scottish lore (the name means "Scottish dance"), but bearing little resemblance to the reel or strathspey. Often danced to the bagpipes, it was performed in two lines; it disappeared around 1833.

Estampie, the earliest formal couple dance, invented in the French courts around the twelfth century. It was a sedate, gliding dance led off by the highest ranking couple. Although its name was connected with the Frankish stamping dance, the *stampon,* it had become slow and subdued by the time it reached the courts, where it was the first dance with a focus—aimed at the top personage present.

Fading, ancient Irish long dance also known as the *rinnce fada,* and performed by dancers connected by white handkerchiefs, in pairs behind a leading threesome. The couples passed under the handkerchiefs of the trio, then turned and performed a variety of figures before resuming their original places. Accompanied by the bagpipes, Irish harp or Jew's harp, it was similar to the *faddy* or furry dance performed at Helston in Cornwall.

Fandango, a Spanish couple dance in 6/8 time, so ancient it is perhaps the prototype of all Spanish folk dances. The word means "go and dance," and from a stately beginning the performers work up to an intense and furious climax.

Fanny Bump, ragtime dance of the early twentieth century, especially popular in Harlem and characterized by the collision of the partners' backsides.

Farandole, a carol or song-dance in which the dancers held hands in a line or chain. Well known to the ancient Greeks, the dance survived until ousted by the couple dances of the Middle Ages, to which it bequeathed the idea of moving around the dance floor in a set pattern.

Filly Dog, solo rock dance of the early 1960s.

Fish, rock couple dance of the late 1950s, reminiscent of the ragtime dance the slow drag.

Fish Tail, ragtime animal dance popular in the early twentieth century, and involving an erotic grinding of the hips.

Flamenco, Andalusian folk dance probably dating from the Spanish occupation of Flanders in the seventeenth century, since Spanish soldiers quartered there were called *flamencos*. A wild dance of joy and passion, it has come to mean an unbridled style of dancing with heel-drumming (*taconeado*) and castanet accompaniment. There are many regional variations including the malagueña (from Malaga) and the granadina (from Granada).

Fly, rock couple dance of the late 1950s, owing something to the ragtime dance the eagle rock.

Fox Trot, ragtime dance best credited to Harry Fox, a music hall entertainer who performed a fast trotting dance that electrified the Ziegfeld Follies of 1914. Tamed by dancing teachers, it became a popular ballroom dance to ragtime, while the English smoothed out its jerks and rechristened it the saunter.

Frohntanz, meaning "compulsory dance," German folk dance from Langenberg, said to date from the Middle Ages, when the villagers were so busy cavorting around their lime trees they ignored the demand of their prince for a change of horses. As a result, they were ordered to dance every year, at Pentecost, until a beer barrel placed under the tree was empty.

Frug, solo rock dance of the early 1960s, involving little more than shifting the weight from one foot to another.

Funky Butt, ragtime dance of the early twentieth century, popularized by American blacks and involving a grinding of hips and backside.

Funky Broadway, solo rock dance of the early 1960s, in which the feet were tapped together in combination with a bending of the knees.

Furlana, medieval Italian dance in 6/8 time, probably originating in Venice, where it was a wild courtship dance for one or two couples. In the ragtime era, Pope Pius X suggested that Catholics dance it in preference to the turkey trot, of which he strongly disapproved, but it never gained general popularity.

Galliard, sixteenth-century court dance deriving its rhythm—which is that of the tune "God Save the Queen" and "America"—from the *branle* and pavane. The dance allowed for florid exhibitionism in the steps, particularly those of the man; such was the agility required in the leaps and crossings of the feet that Queen Elizabeth I used to perform several galliards before breakfast, for exercise.

Galop, a rapid dance in 2/4 time, introduced in the middle of the nineteenth century, and originally used to conclude a quadrille. The couples, in the waltz position, moved in straight lines, zigzagging up and down the floor with a gliding step.

Gavotte, seventeenth-century French contredanse taken from the peasants of Gap (who were known as Gavots), in the Dauphiné. Originally a wooing dance, when it reached the court the kisses exchanged in the original were replaced by posies, and from being a lively folk dance the gavotte became rather stately.

Gigue, French for jig, a lively dance that in the seventeenth century became an exhibition dance and a member of the orchestral suite.

Granadina, see *Flamenco*.

Grind, ragtime dance of the early twentieth century whose sinuous hip movements were especially popular with American blacks.

Grizzly Bear, ragtime dance involving a swooping and swaying walk that culminated in a hug between the partners.

Guajira, Latin American dance briefly popular in the United States in the early 1930s.

Habañera, nineteenth-century Cuban dance (the name means "from havana"), whose rhythm contributed both to the maxixe and the tango.

Haute Danse see *Basse Danse*.

Hey, also spelled hay, heye, etc., fifteenth-century dance descended from the ancient farandole, whose name came from the French word for a hedge or hurdle made of interwoven sticks. The dance involved the interweaving of each performer around the others in turn, and it still figures in modern square dance.

Hava Nagila, "come let us be merry," Israeli couple dance taken from an old hora melody.

Highland Fling, originally a kick-step in which the Scottish dancer "flings" one leg forward and backward while dancing on the other leg. This developed into a dance involving jumps and turns as well as the special kick-step.

Hitchhike, solo rock dance of the early 1960s in which the arms were jerked to and fro in imitation of the hitchhiker's gesture.

Hokey-Pokey, (in England, Hokey-Cokey) novelty group dance of the 1930s, originally a cockney song which instructed the audience to "put your right foot in; put your right foot out; put your right foot in, and shake it all about."

Hora, ancient round dance for mixed couples, common to many European nations, and which the Israelis have made the basis of several folk dances.

Hornpipe, lively dance from the fifteenth century, originally performed to the accompaniment of a wind instrument with a horn mouth piece. The dance became a popular stage act in the nineteenth century, and was associated with sailors' merrymaking.

Horse Trot, jerky animal dance to ragtime, popular in the early 1900s.

Huapango, Los, Mexican courtship dance performed on the community dance platform.

Hull's Victory, American contra dance, to commemorate the defeat of the British warship *Guerrière* by Isaac Hull's frigate *Constitution* during the War of 1812.

Hully-Gully, solo rock dance of the early 1960s.

Hustle, rock couple dance of the 1970s invented in discotheques in the United States, with regional variations (The New York hustle, The Los Angeles hustle, etc.), all beginning with dancers holding or facing one another, in contrast to the solo dances of the 1960s.

Inditos, Los, Mexican maypole dance presided over by a figure known as Saint Señor de Chalma.

Itch, ragtime dance of the early twentieth century, popular with American blacks.

Jarabe, El, Mexican wooing dance also performed at Indian weddings.

Jerk, solo rock dance of the early 1960s, involving a snap of the body in time to the beat.

Jig, solo country dance, mainly associated with Ireland but known throughout Europe from the seventeenth century. In France and Germany it became part of the musical suite, and in England it became a stage dance to end a play. But in Ireland it was popular with all classes until at least the eighteenth century, as a step dance performed to the bagpipes, harp or fiddle.

Jitterbug, another name for the lindy, a product of the swing music of the 1930s, in which athletic couples moved energetically, alone and together, to a rapid beat. There were two types of basic step, those in which the feet stayed on the ground, and the "air steps" in which the dancer left the floor entirely.

Jive, a tamed version of the jitterbug that came into fashion in the 1950s, where the steps could be improvised without a partner.

Jota, Spanish folk dance for couples, in 3/4 time, performed with castanets, and said to have been brought to Aragon by an exiled Moorish poet, Aben Jot.

Kalamatianos, Greek folk dance, originally for men only, though now women also take part. The dancers are led by a singer who waves a handkerchief and performs complicated leaps and twists until exhausted, when another dancer takes his place.

Kangaroo Dip, ragtime animal dance of the early twentieth century.

Knees up Mother Brown, English novelty group dance, dating from the 1930s, in which a sort of rhythmic running in place is performed to a rapidly sung chorus of "Knees up Mother Brown." This gave rise to the English expression "knees up," meaning a boisterous dance.

Lambeth Walk, novelty dance dating from 1937.

Lancers, derived from the quadrille in 1817 and named for the regiment then stationed at Fontainebleau. It was a rapid couple dance involving military-style salutes and a progress and retreat across the floor, and it ended with a grand march and a waltz. It was popular throughout the nineteenth century.

Ländler, Germanic folk dance from the Ländl region of Austria, in which the partners spin in opposite directions while holding hands or stamping and clapping to keep the rhythm going. An ancient wooing dance, the tunes were passed from one generation of musicians to another.

Langaus, a form of Viennese waltzing of the early nineteenth century, in which couples attempted to outlast each other in circling the dance hall at dizzying speed.

Lindy Hop, or Lindy, first appeared as a jazz dance in the late 1920s, and was apparently named to commemorate Lindbergh's solo flight across the Atlantic (1927). It reappeared in the swing era of the 1930s, when it was also known as the jitterbug, and featured improvised steps for solo or couple dance.

Longways Dance, country dance performed in a line pattern.

Lundu, group folk dance from Africa, whose influence on Caribbean dancing gave rise to the samba.

Madison, 1950s dance midway between jive and the rock dances, in which couples danced in a line.

Malagueña, see *Flamenco*.

Mambo, Cuban dance popular in the United States and Europe in the mid-1950s, a combination of Latin American and jazz rhythms. There was one beat in each bar on which the dancer took no step, but the other steps were embellished with kicks and body wiggles.

Mashed Potato, solo rock dance of the late 1950s, reminiscent of the Charleston.

Matlanchines, Los, Mexican weaving dance performed by circles of men and women obeying the commands of a *matlanchia* or "leader."

Maxina, English sequence dance of the early twentieth century, in which every couple performs the same step simultaneously.

Maxixe, Brazilian folk dance combining the rhythms of the habañera and the movements of the polka that became an immensely popular ballroom dance in Europe and the United States around 1914.

May Dances, fertility dances performed around a tree or similar totem, e.g., a maypole, to celebrate the arrival of spring, common to most early cultures and the folk dance tradition of most Western countries.

Mazurka, originally a Polish round dance of the people, this was probably introduced to English ballrooms by the duke of Devonshire, who brought it back from a mission to Russia in 1826. It was performed by four or eight couples, and the second beat was often marked by a heel tap. It found more favor as a theatrical dance.

Measure, Elizabethan English version of the *basse danse*, a slow and stately court dance.

Merengue, couple dance supposedly from the Dominican Republic, performed to Latin American music, with a "limp" step in which the right foot is brought up the left; popular in the United States in the 1950s.

Milonga, Argentinian dance popular in the poorer quarters of Buenos Aires in the late nineteenth century, which mingled with the habañera to become part of the tango.

Minuet, French court dance of the late eighteenth century, the name coming either from *pas menu*, "small step," or the *branle à mener de Poitou*, *mener* meaning "to lead," referring to the man leading the lady. A couple dance in 3/4 time, with variations, it was more of a ritual than a dance.

Money Musk, American contra dance of Scottish origin, whose original name was "Sir Archibald Grant of Moniemusk Reel."

Monferrina, Italian folk dance from Piedmont, performed by several couples who mime courtship.

Monkey, solo rock dance of the early 1960s, involving rapid body snaps, supposed to resemble the movements of the monkey.

Mooche, hip-grinding ragtime dance of the early twentieth century.

Moresque, mimic dance popular in the fifteenth century in European courts, involving a solo performance by a dancer blacked up to look like a Moor—a *Moresco* was a Moor, some of whom converted to Christianity. It came to mean a choral dance in double-file formation, possibly symbolizing the war between Moors and Christians.

Moros, Los, Mexican *moresque*, or dance of the Moors.

Morris Dance, English folk dance dating back to pre-Christian times, primarily a dance of regeneration, and performed by two files of dancers, usually six each in number, equipped with bells and ribbons. There is a tenuous connection with the *moresque*, but the English morris probably got its name from the "Moorish" appearance of some of the dancers, who occasionally blacked their faces. There is no prescribed step, as every morris side has its own variations on the common theme. The morris is very much alive today.

Negritos, Los, Mexican *moresque* originally performed by Negroes.
Nizzarda, Provençal couple dance from the town of Nice, related to the turning dance *la volta.*
Novelty Dances, a series of dances for groups of performers, often named after music hall songs, (e.g., the Lambeth walk, hokey-pokey, etc.), and popular in England and the United States toward the end of the 1930s.

Old-time Dancing, nineteenth-century round and square dances such as the polka and the *varsovienne,* which were revived by enthusiasts around the 1930s, in reaction to the jazz dances.
One-step, also known as the turkey trot, the most ubiquitous ragtime dance, universally popular among the young of the early twentieth century, simply requiring a single step per beat.

Pachanga, a Latin American dance from the Caribbean, popular in the United States in the 1960s.
Palais Glide, a formation novelty dance for groups, popular in the swing era of the 1930s.
Passacaglia, from the Spanish for "street song," this became a slow French court dance in 3/4 time, with gliding steps and the crossing of the feet.
Paso Doble, Spanish one-step originally popular in the 1930s.
Pavane, from Italy (the name meaning "a dance from Padua") this was a court dance of the mid-sixteenth century, stately and simple, and performed in 2/2 time in which a man might show off his legs in strutting steps.
Pea Straw, American contra dance from Scotland, whose original name was "Pease Strae."
Piva, once an Italian peasant dance performed to the *piva,* or bagpipes, this became a court dance, the last of the *bassa danza* suite, performed fast in 4/4 time.
Polka, from Bohemia, the name is connected to the Czech word *půlka,* meaning "half"; a half-step is much used in the dance. The catchy rhythm in 2/4 time made the dance widely popular in Europe and the United States after its performance on the Paris stage in 1844.
Polka-Mazurka, neither a polka nor a mazurka, since it was in 3/4 time, and stressed the third beat instead of the second of the mazurka. Requiring much flexing of the knees and gliding steps, it was fashionable in Vienna and Budapest in the mid-nineteenth century.
Polonaise, Polish dance briefly popular in the mid-nineteenth century. In the seventeenth century it was a stately court dance, and became part of the instrumental suite; it retained its processional and courtly form despite the liveliness of its rhythm.
Pony, solo rock dance of the early 1960s, in which the knees were brought up to imitate trotting.

Quadernaria, second dance of the Italian *bassa danza* suite, in 4/4 time, from which it got its name.
Quadrille, square dance for four couples, taking its name from the Italian *quadriglia,* a troop of horseman who formed a square, and popular throughout the first half of the nineteenth century. Under Napoleon it became a contredanse, and it was brought to England in 1816; from there, it rapidly became popular in the United States, where it contributed to the growth of the modern square dance. Though the music always had five sections, later reduced to three, the dance developed an infinite variety of figures.
Quickstep, English version of the quick fox trot, adopted as a name in 1929, and performed smoothly with gliding steps and turns.

Ragtime Dances, dances performed to the syncopated music of ragtime that was popular from the end of the nineteenth century.
Redowa, Bohemian folk dance in 3/4 time taken from the *redjovak,* which had much in common with the waltz, but which featured an advance down the room in which one partner had to go backward. It was popular, especially in the United States, from the mid-nineteenth century.
Reels, Scotch, gliding and springing dances in 2/4 time, for two, three, or four couples, with innumerable figures and tunes.
Reigen, German round dance of prehistoric origin.
Ride-a-Bike, solo dance of the early 1970s to *reggae,* Jamaican blues music, influenced by early jazz and the rhythm and blues music of the 1950s.
Rigaudon, also rigadoon, originally a French folk dance of courtship, this became a court dance in the

seventeenth century, performed to a lively rhythm in 2/4 or 4/4 time.

Rock Dances, solo or occasionally couple dances, usually with improvised steps, performed to the heavy beat of rock music that became popular from the 1950s.

Round Dances, prehistoric group dances around a central object or totem; in the nineteenth century these became country dances in a round or circular formation (as opposed to the square), in which the couples exchanged positions. The term is also used for the nineteenth-century couple dances such as the waltz or polka, which feature a constant turning of the partners.

Rumba, from Cuba, originally an erotic dance combining African and Caribbean rhythms, it reached the United States in the late 1920s in a tamed version in 2/4 or 4/4 time that remained popular for a generation.

Saint Vitus's Dance, frenzied dance (*chorea*) in which large numbers of the victims of a dancing madness or mania that erupted all over Europe in the middle of the fourteenth century, probably caused by the poisonous fungus ergot, danced to the shrine of Saint Vitus, whose holy water was supposed to cure the affliction.

Saltarello, third part of the Italian *bassa danza* suite, a lively dance which included the striking of one leg against the other and a series of small hops which gave the dance its name (from the Latin for leaping).

Samba, Brazilian couple dance in 2/4 or 4/4 time whose name came from the dances performed by African slaves, it was introduced in a modified ballroom version at the New York World's Fair in 1939, and became popular in Europe after World War II.

Saraband, sixteenth-century dance from Spain, where it was considered so indecent it was banned. Once a sexual pantomime, it was sufficiently tamed by the French court to become Cardinal Richelieu's favorite dance in the seventeenth century, and later was to figure in the instrumental suite, in 3/4 time.

Saunter, smooth English form of the fox trot.

Schottische, German round dance to the music of the polka, with waltzlike turns alternating with hopping gliding steps, popular in England and the United States in the mid-nineteenth century. The military schottische was a barn dance.

Schuhplattler, wild wooing dance from Bavaria and the Tyrol, in which the man performs a variety of noisy antics to attract the woman's attention.

Schwälmer, German round dance from the Schwälm, in which the women perform waltz steps while the men click their heels and clap.

Schwarzwälder Bauertanz, German folk dance deriving its name from the Black Forest, involving a pantomime of wooing, indifference and amorousness.

Scotch Reel, See *Reels.*

Seguidillas, Spanish couple dance derived from the bolero.

Seises, Los, "the sixes," Spanish church dance or *moresque* dating from the Middle Ages and still performed, originally by twelve though now by ten choirboys in two files, who dance various weaving and crossing figures, in the presence of the full clergy, on the Feasts of Corpus Christi and the Immaculate Conception.

Sellenger's Round, fifteenth-century English country dance in the form of a carol, whose name is a corruption of the St. Leger round, and which was danced in lines as well as circles.

Sembradoras, Las, Mexican harvest dance of thanksgiving.

Sequence Dances, dances in which the set movements are made by every couple simultaneously, popular in the early twentieth century.

Shake, dance to Jamaican rhythm and blues involving shaking movements of the hips and widely popular in the mid-1960s.

Shimmy, jazz dance of the 1920s that first appeared on the stage, and which required a turning-in of the knees and toes like the Charleston.

Siebensprung, German folk dance performed at Easter in which the man had to make seven (in German, *sieben*) different body movements.

Sir Roger de Coverley, sixteenth-century country dance whose movements survive in the Virginia reel. It was often used to conclude nineteenth-century balls, and the tune is a variation of a Scottish song called "Roger the Cavalier," which is the same as that known in Virginia as "My Aunt Margery."

Ska, See *Blue Beat.*

Skate, solo rock dance of the 1960s with fishlike flapping movements.

Slop, solo rock dance of the 1960s.

Slow Drag, ragtime couple dance popular in the early twentieth century, in which the partners would hold onto each other and grind to and fro for extended periods.

Sousta, ancient Greek courting dance, originally used by the Spartans as a military exercise, now performed mainly in Crete.

Son, refined version of the rumba.

Square Dance, American form of country dancing, drawing inspiration from the contras and quadrilles popular in the early nineteenth century, in which couples face each other in a square formation, and exchange places in relation to their partners and to the other couples, with the addition of a caller who announces the figures or floor patterns they are to perform.

Squat, ragtime couple dance popular in the early 1900s, especially among American blacks.

Strathspey, ancient Scottish dance in 4/4 time from the valley (*strath*) of the river Spey, slower than the reel but full of energetic movements.

Stroll, solo rock dance of the late 1950s, reminiscent of the ragtime dance the camel walk.

Swim, solo rock dance of the 1960s, in which the arms made swimming movements.

Sword Dances, ancient dances on the theme of death and resurrection, common to most primitive peoples and surviving in much of European folk dance. Usually danced at mid-winter, they feature a character known as the fool, who suffers mimic decapitation from the swords, woven into a lock or knot; after some complicated step dances, the fool is then resurrected.

Tango, originally an erotic dance from the Caribbean and the Argentine, the dance was tamed in France in the early twentieth century, and became a craze in England and the United States, where "tango teas" took place, offering a small space for fashionable dancers to show off their skill. There were innumerable different tango steps in 2/4 time, although the dance was standardized, at least for ballroom performers, in the 1920s.

Tarantella, Italian folk dance from Taranto in Apulia, whose constant movements and rapid turns were supposed to be effective in working the poison of the tarantula spider's bite out of the system. Now a courtship dance.

Tordion, also called *tourdion,* final section of the *basse danse* suite, a slow processional dance in 3/2 time, requiring restrained forward kicks.

Trescone, sixteenth-century Italian country dance (*tresca*), originally performed by four couples forming a square or ring, to celebrate a wedding.

Tsamikos, nineteenth-century Greek folk dance, originally performed by the klepht guerillas, in which the dancers rival one another in athletic leaps and jumps.

Turkey Trot, or one-step, a ragtime dance of extreme simplicity that included a flapping of the arms in imitation of the bird, and which was frowned upon by, among others, dancing teachers and Pope Pius X.

Two-step, dance requiring two steps per beat, first performed to John Philip Sousa's *Washington Post March* (1891), and rapidly applied to other dances of the period, until ousted by ragtime and the one-step.

Twist, solo rock dance that first appeared in 1961, performed by Chubby Checker, and which became commercially fashionable for a brief period.

Varsity Drag, dance loosely based on the Charleston, introduced in 1927 by Zelma O'Neal in the show *Good Times.*

Varsovienne, also *varsouvienne* and *varsovianna,* from the French for Warsaw, a round couple dance that arrived in western Europe in the 1850s, and as a combination of the polka and mazurka is still performed in the United States.

Veleta, a sequence dance invented in 1900 that is a combination of waltz and gliding steps.

Virginia Reel, See *Sir Roger de Coverley.*

Volta, La, sixteenth-century dance probably from northern Italy (the name means "turning dance"), which was considered immoral by many because of the close embrace of the partners and the requirement that the man lift the woman high in the air. Nevertheless, it was a favorite dance of Queen Elizabeth I.

Waltz, originally a German turning dance, this couple dance in 3/4 time conquered the rest of Europe in the early nineteenth century, though it had to contend with fierce criticism because of the close hold required and the speed with which the dancers revolved around the floor. The waltz step is employed in countless square and round dances, while the waltz itself still figures in ballroom competitions.

Watusi, rock dance of the early 1960s, whose wiggle-kick-clap movements could be performed by individuals or lines of facing dancers.

Weller, rapid German turning dance that was an ancestor of the waltz.

TEMPO TABLE

$\mathbf{2/2}$	Charleston Pavane		

$\mathbf{2/4}$	*Basse Danse* Bergamasca Black Bottom *Branle* Cha-cha Galop Habañera Hornpipe	*Los Matlanchines* Maxixe Merengue *Moresque* Morris Dance *Paso Doble* Polka Reel	Rigaudon Rumba Samba Schottische Shimmy Tango Trescone

$\mathbf{3/2}$	*Tordion*		

$\mathbf{3/4}$	Allemande *Basse danse* Bolero Bourrée Chaconne Courante Fandango	Galliard Jig Jota Mazurka Minuet Passepied Polka–Mazurka	Polonaise Redowa Saltarello Saraband Seguidillas *La Volta* Waltz

$\mathbf{4/4}$	Barn Dance Cha-cha Fox Trot Gavotte Hornpipe	Mambo Morris Dance *Piva* *Quadernaria* Rigaudon	Rock Dances Rumba Running Set Strathspey Tango

$\mathbf{6/4}$	Slow Courante		

$\mathbf{6/8}$	Fandango Farandole	Furlana Jig	Tarantella Two-step

$\mathbf{9/9}$	Jig		

$\mathbf{12/8}$	Jig		

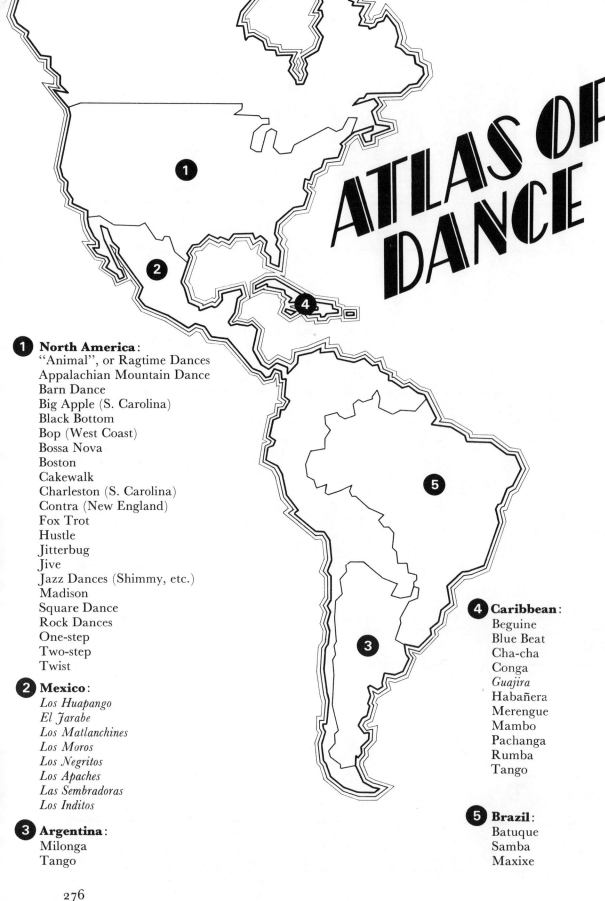

ATLAS OF DANCE

1 **North America**:
"Animal", or Ragtime Dances
Appalachian Mountain Dance
Barn Dance
Big Apple (S. Carolina)
Black Bottom
Bop (West Coast)
Bossa Nova
Boston
Cakewalk
Charleston (S. Carolina)
Contra (New England)
Fox Trot
Hustle
Jitterbug
Jive
Jazz Dances (Shimmy, etc.)
Madison
Square Dance
Rock Dances
One-step
Two-step
Twist

2 **Mexico**:
Los Huapango
El Jarabe
Los Matlanchines
Los Moros
Los Negritos
Los Apaches
Las Sembradoras
Los Inditos

3 **Argentina**:
Milonga
Tango

4 **Caribbean**:
Beguine
Blue Beat
Cha-cha
Conga
Guajira
Habañera
Merengue
Mambo
Pachanga
Rumba
Tango

5 **Brazil**:
Batuque
Samba
Maxixe

276

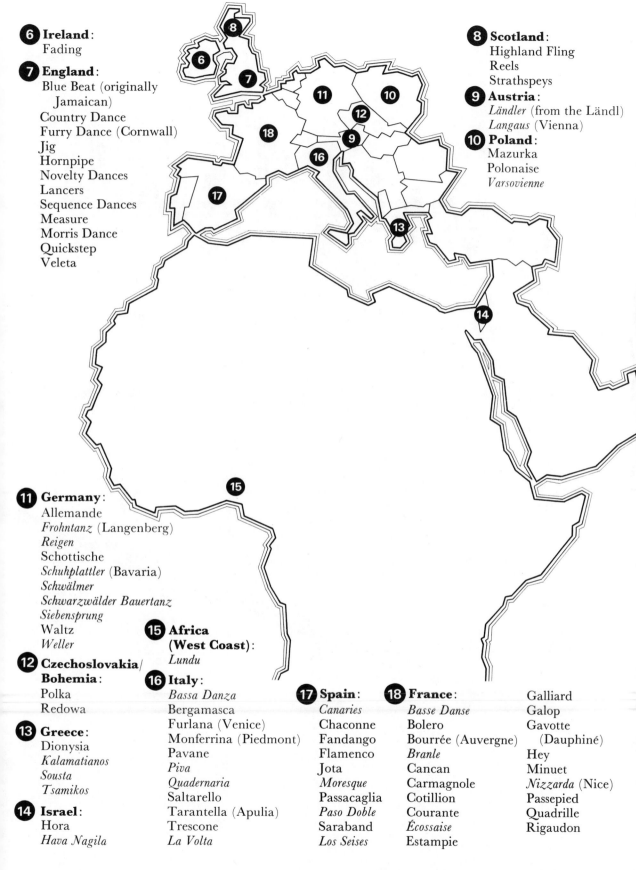

6 Ireland:
Fading

7 England:
Blue Beat (originally
   Jamaican)
Country Dance
Furry Dance (Cornwall)
Jig
Hornpipe
Novelty Dances
Lancers
Sequence Dances
Measure
Morris Dance
Quickstep
Veleta

8 Scotland:
Highland Fling
Reels
Strathspeys

9 Austria:
Ländler (from the Ländl)
Langaus (Vienna)

10 Poland:
Mazurka
Polonaise
Varsovienne

11 Germany:
Allemande
Frohntanz (Langenberg)
Reigen
Schottische
Schuhplattler (Bavaria)
Schwälmer
Schwarzwälder Bauertanz
Siebensprung
Waltz
Weller

**12 Czechoslovakia/
Bohemia**:
Polka
Redowa

13 Greece:
Dionysia
Kalamatianos
Sousta
Tsamikos

14 Israel:
Hora
Hava Nagila

**15 Africa
(West Coast)**:
Lundu

16 Italy:
Bassa Danza
Bergamasca
Furlana (Venice)
Monferrina (Piedmont)
Pavane
Piva
Quadernaria
Saltarello
Tarantella (Apulia)
Trescone
La Volta

17 Spain:
Canaries
Chaconne
Fandango
Flamenco
Jota
Moresque
Passacaglia
Paso Doble
Saraband
Los Seises

18 France:
Basse Danse
Bolero
Bourrée (Auvergne)
Branle
Cancan
Carmagnole
Cotillion
Courante
Écossaise
Estampie
Galliard
Galop
Gavotte
   (Dauphiné)
Hey
Minuet
Nizzarda (Nice)
Passepied
Quadrille
Rigaudon

TIMELINE OF DANCE

16th Century:
Allemande
Bergamasca
Bourrée
Chaconne
Cinq Pas
Country Dance
Courante
Galliard
Measure
Pavane
Saraband
Sir Roger de Coverley
Trescone
La Volta

18th Century:
Appalachian
   Mountain Dance
Contras (American
   Country Dance)
Carmagnole
Cotillion
Minuet
Passepied

Middle Ages:
12th to 14th
centuries
Basse Danse
Branle
Estampie
Danse Macabre
European Folk Dances
Furlana
May Dances
Saint Vitus's Dance
Sword Dances

Prehistoric:
Carol
Farandole
Fertility Dances
Line Dances
Medicine Dances
Round Dances
War Dances

1800–1850:
Bolero
Écossaise
Galop
Lancers
Langaus
Mazurka
Polka
Polonaise
Quadrille
Schottische
Tsamikos
Waltz

17th Century:
Contredanse
Flamenco
Gavotte
Jig
Passacaglia
Rigaudon

15th Century:
Canaries
Hey
Hornpipe
Moresque
Sellenger's Round

Classical Antiquity:
Bacchic Dances/Dionysia
Hora
Kalamatianos
Morris Dance
Sousta

278

1950–1960:
Blue Beat
Bop
Cha-cha
Chicken
Clam
Fish
Fly
Jive
Madison
Mambo
Mashed Potato
Merengue
Stroll
Twist

1930–1940:
Beguine
Big Apple
Boomps-a-Daisy
Conga
Danzon
Guajira
Hokey-Pokey
Jitterbug
Knees Up
Lambeth
Walk
Palais Glide
Paso Doble
Samba

1970–1980:
Hustle
Ride-a-Bike

1850–1900:
Barn Dance
Batuque
Cakewalk
Cancan
Habañera
Milonga
Redowa
Round Dances
Square Dance
Two-step
Varsovienne

1910–1920:
Fox Trot
Lindy Hop

1940–1950:
Jitterbug

1960–1970:
Boogaloo
Bossa Nova
Bug
Filly Dog
Frug
Funky Broadway
Hitchhike
Hully-Gully
Jerk
Monkey
Pachanga
Pony
Shake
Skate
Slop
Swim
Watusi

1920–1930:
Black Bottom
Charleston
Quickstep
Rumba
Shimmy
Varsity Drag

1900–1910:
Boston
Bunny Hug
Buzzard Lope
Camel Walk
Crab
Eagle Rock
Fanny Bump
Fish Tail
Funky Butt
Grind
Grizzly Bear
Horse Trot
Itch
Kangaroo Dip
Maxina
Maxixe
Mooche
One-step
Slow Drag
Squat
Tango
Turkey Trot
Veleta

BIBLIOGRAPHY

1 Beginnings

No student of dance can avoid indebtedness to Curt Sachs, whose *World History of the Dance* (translated by Bessie Schönberg, New York, 1937) is the most comprehensive anthropological study of dance in existence. *Dancing*, edited by Mrs. Lilly Grove (who married the anthropologist J.G. Frazer), in the Badminton Library Series (London, 1895) contains almost as full a narrative, and has endless fascinating anecdotes, though of course it has none of the analytic techniques available to the twentieth-century expert. For a good modern account, see *Social Dance: A Short History* by A.H. Franks (London, 1963). On the dances of the American Indians, I relied on the observations of Father Joseph François Lafitau, who in 1724 published *Customs of the American Indians Compared with the Customs of Primitive Times* (volume I translated by W.N. Fenton and E.L. Moore, Toronto, 1974). Rudolf Laban's analysis of dance is contained in his influential *Modern Educational Dance* (London, 1948).

2 Court and Country

In addition to the general histories cited above by Sachs, Grove, and Franks, I recommend *Dance in Society* by Frances Rust (London, 1969), which contains a fascinating sociological analysis of the historical relationship between dance and society, chiefly in England but drawing on Europe and the United States for examples. There is also the excellent short history of popular dancing by Belinda Quirey and others, called *May I Have the Pleasure?* (London, 1976). For the medieval picture, the best introduction is Sir Richard Southern's *The Making of the Middle Ages* (London, 1953). Those who want to know how to dance the ancient dances must consult Mabel Dolmetsch's *Dances of England and France: 1450 to 1600* (London, 1949) and *Dances of Spain and Italy: 1400 to 1600* (London, 1954). Though much is conjecture, Mrs. Dolmetsch's academic scrupulousness is beyond reproach. In the same category comes Melusine Wood's *Historical Dances: Twelfth to Nineteenth Century* (London, 1952), *More Historical Dances* (London, 1956), and *Advanced Historical Dances* (London, 1960). Arbeau's *Orchésographie* has been translated by C.W. Beaumont (New York, 1965). John Playford's *The Dancing Master* is still to be found in some academic reference libraries, while the latest facsimile reissue, of the 1651 edition, was published in London in 1957.

3 The Ballroom Era

Much fascinating detail about the history of dance in the United States is to be found in *America Learns to Dance* by Joseph E. Marks III (New York, 1957). See also *The Puritan and Fair Terpsichore* by Arthur C. Cole, a lively account of American dance and its critics that first appeared in *The Mississippi Valley Historical Review*, Vol. xxix, No. 1 (June, 1942); Rosetta O'Neill's essay on "The Dodworth Family and Ballroom Dancing in New York" in *Chronicles of the American Dance*, edited by Paul Magriel (New York, 1948); and S. Foster Damon's valuable "History of Square-Dancing" in the *Proceedings* of the American Antiquarian Society, April 1952. Captain Gronow's *Reminiscences and Recollections* recounts the gossip of fashionable society in England and France from 1810 to 1860; they were published in two volumes in London in 1900. For impressions of society dances, see *Memorable Balls* edited by James Laver (London, 1955). Lucile K. Czarnowski's *Dances of Early California Days* (Palo Alto, California 1950) gives a good picture of the Spanish culture of the American Southwest impinging on that of the European pioneers. Mosco Carner's *The*

Waltz (London, 1948) is exhaustive without being exhausting. P.J.S. Richardson's *The Social Dances of the Nineteenth Century* (London, 1960) is indispensable for the study of English ballroom dance. The most penetrating essay on Victorian England is G.M. Young's *Portrait of an Age* (London, 1936).

4 The Dance Band Years

The history of popular music from ragtime to the present is dealt with succinctly and entertainingly by Ian Whitcomb in *After the Ball* (New York, 1973). A more lavish, but no more penetrating, treatment is Tony Palmer's *All You Need Is Love* (London, 1976). Rudi Blesch is the ragtime biographer: his *They All Played Ragtime* (with Harriet Janis, New York, 1950) is considered to be the standard work, though Peter Gammond has produced a useful study of *Scott Joplin and the Ragtime Era* (London, 1975). Brian Rust's *The Dance Bands* (London, 1972) is based not only on painstaking research but also on personal interviews and experience. The feel of the time can be got from contemporary books, records, and magazines like *Vanity Fair* (of which a one-volume selection was published in New York in 1960). But for those who prefer digests of the material, I recommend *Twenty-five Years of American Dance*, edited by Doris Hering (New York, 1951); *The Aspirin Age*, edited by I. Leighton (New York, 1950); and Russel Nye's *The Unembarrassed Muse: The Popular Arts in America* (New York, 1970). There is a splendid short study of *The Twenties in America* by Paul A. Carter (New York, 1967). *The Story of American Vernacular Dance* is the subtitle of the pioneering *Jazz Dance* by Marshall and Jean Stearns (New York, 1968), which is a marvelous blend of social anthropology, anecdote, and insight. Those who want to know how to do modern ballroom dances can rely on Victor Silvester's *Modern Ballroom Dancing* (London, 1974), which has a useful historical introduction. More fun can be had by looking up the manuals that were popular in the past, such as *Social Dancing of To-day* by Troy and Margaret West Kinney (New York, 1914), or Irene and Vernon Castle's *Modern Dancing* (New York, 1914). Gladys Beattie Crozier produced *The Tango and How to Dance It* for the benefit of the British in 1914. Finally, the *Dictionary of Dance* by W.G. Raffe (New York, 1964) is a useful, if partisan, reference work.

5 Disco Time

For those who need to jog their memory about the music of the immediate past—and who does not?—I recommend *The Sound of the City* by Charlie Gillett (New York, 1970) and *Awopbopaloobop Alopbamboom: Pop From the Beginning* by Nik Cohn (London, 1969). Mr. Seymour Kleinman published his *Social Dancing* (Columbus, Ohio) in 1968. For the rest, the films of the 1950s and 1960s are constantly being shown on television, the records are forever being reissued, the fashions have already been back in vogue, and the commentators have never ceased to reinterpret our youth for the benefit of those who are now young. That social dancing is still the "in" thing is proved in a book published by *Rolling Stone*, that arbiter of the modern musical scene (*Dancing Madness*, edited by Abe Peck, New York, 1976). But you don't need to read anything: just get out and move.

6 Folk Dance

The United States: Pioneers in the folk dance field were Dr. Elizabeth Burchenal (*Folk Dancing and Singing Games*, New York, 1922, and see her article "Folk Dances of the United States: Regional Types and Origins," in the *International Folk Music Journal*, Vol. III, 1951); Ralph Page and Beth Tolman (*The Country Dance Book*, first published 1937, new edition, Vermont, 1976; Ralph Page also published *Heritage Dances of Early America*, Colorado, 1976); and Lloyd Shaw (*Cowboy Dances*, Idaho, first edition, 1939, revised 1950; *The Round Dance Book*, Idaho, 1948). The history of square dancing is dealt with at length by S. Foster Damon, in an article of that title appearing in the *Proceedings* of the American Antiquarian Society of April, 1952. For teachers, there is a handbook of folk, square, and social dance by Jane A. Harris, Anne Pittman, and Marlys S. Walter (*Dance a While*, Minnesota, 1950; third edition 1964). There is also the series of volumes *Folk Dances from Near and Far* published by the Folk Dance Federation of California, Inc. For those who want actually to learn how it was and is, I recommend *Twenty-four Early American Country Dances, Cotillions and Reels* by James E. Morrison of the Country Dance and Song Society (New York, 1976); *A Choice Selection of American Country Dances of the Revolutionary Era* by Kate van Winkle Keller and Ralph Sweet (New York, 1976); *Dances of Early California Days* by Lucile Czarnowski (California, 1950); *The Square Dancers Guide* by Gene Gowing (New York, n.d.); *How to Dance* by Thomas E. Parson (New York, 1947, second edition 1969); *Folk Dancing* by M.B. and C.R. Jensen (Utah, 1973); and *The Complete Book of Square Dancing and Round Dancing* by Betty Casey (New York, 1976). For Mexico I recommend *Legends and Dances of Old Mexico* by Norman Schwendener and Averil Tibbels (New York, 1933).

England: Cecil Sharp and others published 6 parts of *The Country Dance Book* between 1909 and 1922, 5 parts of *The Morris Book* between 1909 and 1913, and 3 parts of *The Sword Dances of Northern England* between 1909 and 1913. In 1924 Sharp also published, with Paul Oppé, *The Dance*, an historical survey. The best one-volume guide to the subject is *England's Dances* by Douglas Kennedy of the English Folk Dance and Song Society (London, 1949), which has a full bibliography. There is also *Dances of England and Wales* by Maud Karpeles and Lois Blake (London, 1950); and Mrs. Grove's exhaustive volume on *Dancing* in the Badminton Library series (1898).

Europe: I relied on the excellent series of small illustrated *Handbooks of European National Dances* (general editor Violet Alford) published in London under the auspices of The Royal Academy of Dancing and the Ling Physical Educational Association. These constitute a brief general guide to the subject, and include some history, some notes on costume and music, examples of the dances, and a scholarly bibliography. The English volume is one of the series; others are *Dances of Ireland* by P. and G. O'Rafferty (1953); *Dances of Scotland* by J.C. Milligan and D.G. Mclennan (1950); *Dances of Germany* by Agnes Fyfe (1951); *Dances of Spain* by Lucile Armstrong (Pt I, 1948; Pt II, 1950); *Dances of Italy* by Bianca M. Galanti (1950); *Dances of Greece* by Domini Crosfield (1948). There is also much valuable information on European dance in the oft-quoted books by Mrs. Grove and Curt Sachs. For Israel's dances, most of them modern, there is Dvora Lapson's *Dances of the Jewish People* (New York, 1954).

PICTURE ACKNOWLEDGMENTS
The author and publishers thank the following for permission to reproduce the illustrations on the pages indicated:

WARING ABBOT: 212, 215, 216 (bottom), 219. ALBERTINA: 52–53. ALDUS ARCHIVES: 22. ASHEVILLE, NORTH CAROLINA, CHAMBER OF COMMERCE: 228 (bottom). ANNE BOLT: 36, 37, 223, 225 (bottom), 237, 238, 258, 259 (bottom). BRITISH TOURIST AUTHORITY: 249, 251. BROWN BROTHERS: 120, 168 (top right), 170, 174 (top), 180 (top), 181 (top left and right), 185 (right), 188 (bottom), 195. BULLOZ: 43, 44–45, 49, 91, 100, 154–155. CULVER PICTURES: 106, 107, 197 (right). STANLEY DEVON/*The Sunday Times*: 231. FOTO MAS: 84. LISA HOFFMAN/PHOTO TRENDS: 20. ISRAELI GOVERNMENT TOURIST OFFICE: 225 (top). LINCOLN KIERSTEIN: 121. STAN LEVY: 229. MAGNUM, NEW YORK: 188 (top), 210 (bottom), 214, 216 (top); 217, 218, 220, 234. MANSELL COLLECTION: 14–15, 23, 30, 34, 64, 68, 71, 75, 78–79, 81, 82, 90, 94, 101, 102, 123, 124, 132, 134, 138, 143, 151, 156, 169 (left), 171, 176, 224, 236, 242, 250, 252, 256, 261 (right), 264. MUSÉE NATIONAL DES ARTS ET TRADITIONS POPULAIRES: 77. MUSEUM OF THE CITY OF NEW YORK: 122, 126, 144 (left), 161, 182 (bottom), 191 (bottom), 198. NEW YORK HISTORICAL SOCIETY: 117. NEW YORK PUBLIC LIBRARY: 105, 108, 116, 118, 119, 168 (bottom), 181 (bottom), 190 (bottom), 227, 230. DAVID PARAMOR: 130, 139, 140, 149, 173. PHOTO TRENDS: 209. AXEL POIGNANT: 24, 25, 248. POPPERFOTOS: 9. RADIO TIMES HULTON PICTURE LIBRARY: 12, 16–17, 26, 27, 28, 29, 31, 32, 33, 35, 38, 39, 40, 42, 47 (bottom), 48, 50, 55, 57, 60, 66, 70, 74, 87, 92, 95, 96, 98, 99, 109, 110, 111, 112, 113, 115, 129, 133, 135, 136, 137, 142, 145, 147, 148, 150, 153, 157, 158, 162, 163, 164, 165, 166, 168 (top left), 169 (right), 172, 174 (bottom), 177, 178–179, 180 (bottom), 182 (top), 185 (left), 192, 193, 194, 196, 197 (left), 199, 201, 202, 203, 205, 206, 207, 208, 210 (top left and right), 226, 239, 240, 241, 243, 244, 246, 247, 253, 255, 259 (top), 260, 261 (left), 262, 263. SCALA: 41, 46–47 (top), 59, 62–63, 65, 76. JIM SPARKS: 228 (top). SUZANNE SZASZ: 232. UNITED PRESS INTERNATIONAL: 13, 183, 184, 186, 190 (top). UNITED STATES MILITARY ACADEMY ARCHIVES: 144 (right). WIDE WORLD PHOTOS: 10, 191 (top), 200.

INDEX

Fox, Harry, 168, 169, 269
fox trot, 167, 168–70, 180, 193, 194, 269, 273, 277; *169, 170*
France, 250; ballroom dancing, 114, 124–46 *passim*; *71*; court dances, 67–74; folk dances, *32*; jongleurs, 56; masques, 96; medieval, 57, 58–60; types of dances, 30, 51, 77, 78, 84, 88, 92, 93–5, 96, 97–8, 103
Francis I, King of France, 67
Francis, Day and Hunter, 175
Franks, 80, 268
Franks, A.H., 11, 171
Freed, Alan, 207
freeze, 213
French Revolution, 113–14, 116–17, 267
Frohntanz, 61, 269
frug, 217, 269; *216*
funeral dances, 30, 40; *40*
funky broadway, 217, 269
funky butt, 167, 217, 269
furlana, 167, 263, 269, 277
furry dance, 253, 269; *253*

gagliarda, 89
gaillarde, 89
galliard, 89–90, 91, 101, 269, 277; *68, 90*
galop, 138, 152, 269, 277; *139*
Gammond, Peter, 159
Gap, 95, 269
Garbo, Greta, 215
Garvey, Marcus, 181
Gavots, 269
gavotte, 95, 267, 269, 277
The Gentleman and Lady's Book of Politeness, 125–7
George, Prince Regent, 114, 125, 142
George I, King of England, 254
George III, King of England, 108
Germany, 57, 250; *64*; ballroom dancing, 14, 123–4; "bridal round", 30–1; carnivals, 49; courtship dances, 36; craft guilds, 37–8; folk dances, 245, 251, 254–7; Jews, 224; in middle ages, 60–4; Minnesingers, 59, 60, 61; *60*; types of dances, 25, 56, 93, 103
Gershwin, George, "Rhapsody in Blue", 179
Gibran, Kahlil, 181
gigue, 101, 269
Gill, Marguerite and Frank, *174*
Gleave, Richard and Janet, *19*
gleemen, 56
"God Save the Queen", 90
Goethe, Johann Wolfgang von, 55, 123
goliards, 59
Golias, Bishop, 59
Good Times, 182, 274
Goodman, Benny, 178, 187, 189; *188, 190*
Gottschalk, Louis M., 159
Granada, 86, 261, 269; *258*
granadias, 269
granadina, 261
Grant, Ulysses S., *120*
Gray, Gilda, *185*
Greece, ancient, 32, 40, 43–50, 51, 266; *43–7, 49, 50, 264*; folk dances, 222, 251, 265, 270

Greene, General, 107
Greene, Mrs. Nathanael, 107
grind, 167, 217, 269
grizzly bear, 167, 266, 269
Gronow, Captain, 114, 124, 135
Grossmith, George, 172; *173*
Grove, Lilly, 251, 260; *Dancing*, 131–3
guajira, 196, 269
Guajira Indians, *36*
Guerrière (warship), 226, 270
Gulich, Dr. Luther H., 233
gymnopaidiai, 48

habañera, 170, 171, 269–70, 271, 277
Haiti, 171; *26*
Haley, Bill, 203, 204, 207, 211; *205*
Halle, Goodwife, 104
Hamilton, Dr. Alexander, 105
Hammersmith Palais, 177, 180
Hampton, Lionel, 178; *206*
Handel, George Frederick, 97, 147
Hanover, 257
Hapsburgs, 60
Hardy, Thomas, *240*
Harlem, 211, 269
Harley, 133
Harrods, *192*
harvest dances, *42, 55, 255*
Hastings, Battle of, 58
Hatton, Sir Christopher, 86
haute danse, 82, 266
Hava Nagila, 222, 270
Havana, 199
Helston, 253, 269; *253*
Hemmings brothers, *240*
Hendrix, Jimi, 209
Henry II, King of England, 58, 67
Henry VIII, King of England, 67, 68, 98
hesitation waltz, 131, 267
hey, 89, 270
Highland fling, 250, 251, 270
Highland Games, *251*
hitch hike, 217, 270
hokey-pokey (hokey-cokey), 195, 270, 272
Homer, *Iliad*, 43, 77
hora, 222, 270; *225*
hornpipe, 249, 252, 270, 277; *12*
horse trot, 166, 270
Horticultural Society, New York, 118
los huapango, 235, 270; *236*
Hull, Isaac, 226, 270
"*Hull's Victory*", 226, 270
hully-gully, 217, 270
Hume, David, 141
Hungary, 268; *224*
Hunt, Deana, *184*
hustle, 221, 270
hyporchemata, 46–8

Illustrated London News, 146
Imperial Country Club, Nice, 172
Imperial Society of Teachers of Dancing, London, 169, 175, 192
India, 32, 245
Indians, North American, 234; *28*
los Inditos, 239, 270
initiation dances, 31
International Council of Ballroom Dancing, 14–15
Ireland, 31, 101, 230, 250, 252–4, 268, 270

Iroquois, 27, 29, 32–5
Isabella, Queen of Spain, 85, 86
Ischia, 261
Israel, 29, 222–4, 270
Italy, 30, 250; commedia dell'arte, 68; folk dances, 245, 261–3; individual dances, 83, 86, 88; in middle ages, 64–7; *65*; tarantism, 55
itch, 167, 217, 270

Jackson, Bee, *182*
Jamaica, 218, 266, 272, 273
James I, King of England, 73
Janis, Elsie, 169
Japan, 13–14
el jarabe, 235–6, 270; *237*
Le Jardin, 221
jazz, 121, 159, 175–9, 187
Jefferson, Thomas, 107
jerk, 217, 270
Jersey, Lady, 110–11, 133, 136; *112*
Jesus Christ, 51–4
jet, 213
Jews, 43; *225*
jigs, 101, 249, 252, 253–4, 269, 270, 277; *117*
jitterbug, 187–92, 193, 201, 212, 213, 270, 271; *190, 191*
jive, 201–3, 212, 270, 271; *202, 203*
"Joan Sanderson", 100
John, St., 61
Johns, Lisa, 204, 212
Johnson, Dr., 110
Jones, Inigo, 96
jongleurs, 56, 59
Jonson, Ben, 96
Joplin, Scott, 159–62, 170, 177; 'Maple Leaf Rag', 160–1; *Treemonisha*, 168
Jot, Aben, 258, 270
jota, 87, 258, 262, 270, 277
Joy Bells, 176
Jullien, 136
"Jump Jim Crow", 157

kalamatianos, 265, 270
kangaroo dip, 166, 270
Kegel-Quadrille, 257
Kemp, William, 102, 254; *102*
"Kemp's Jigge", 102, 254
Kennedy, Douglas, 245
Kentucky Running Set, 227–9, 277
Kibby dance, 249
King of Jazz, 179
Kinney, Margaret West, 171
Kinney, Troy, 171
Kleinman, Seymour, 215
klepht guerillas, 274
Knees up Mother Brown, 270
Knight, Arthur, 200
Knox, John, 250
Korponay, Gabriel De, 144–6
Krell, William H., 159; "Mississippi Rag", 159, 160
Krupa, Gene, 187

Laban, Rudolf, 21
Labrador, 234
Lafitau, Father Joseph François, 33–5
Lagosta, 262
Lambeth walk, 195, 270–1, 272; *194*
lancers, 121, 131, 137–8, 160; *138*
Ländler, 64, 123, 257, 271